International Capital Flows and the Lucas Paradox

Muhammad Akhtaruzzaman

International Capital Flows and the Lucas Paradox

Patterns, Determinants, and Debates

Springer

Muhammad Akhtaruzzaman
Toi Ohomai Institute of Technology
Rotorua, New Zealand

ISBN 978-981-13-9068-5 ISBN 978-981-13-9069-2 (eBook)
https://doi.org/10.1007/978-981-13-9069-2

This Springer imprint is published by the registered company Springer Nature Singapore Pte Ltd.
The registered company address is: 152 Beach Road, #21-01/04 Gateway East, Singapore 189721, Singapore

For my beloved son Ishayat Zaman

Acknowledgements

First and foremost, I want to thank my supervisors, Dorian Owen, Chris Hajzler, and Nathan Berg, for their excellent advice, feedback, and mentorship. I am deeply indebted to my supervisors for their continued guidance and support throughout my Ph.D. journey at the University of Otago. I highly appreciate the time and patience my supervisors devoted to my thesis and I will always be grateful. I thank them for their advice and support to me on the job market. The book is based on my Ph.D. thesis at the University of Otago completed in 2015.

Contents

List of Figures

List of Tables

Chapter 1
Introduction

1.1 Introduction

Capital flows across borders have increased significantly and have become a key aspect of globalization. Historically, global capital flows have mainly comprised flows among advanced economies; however, flows to and from emerging and developing economies have increased substantially in recent years. Capital flows (private) to emerging markets in 2013 have reached $1.35 trillion, an all-time high level of inflows (IIF 2015). Overall, global FDI flows experienced a surge in 2015 since the global financial crisis in 2008 but developing countries experienced slight fall in the FDI inflows due to modest growth in developed economies and recent improvements in transitions economies. As a result of the growth in developed economies, 59% of global FDI flows was acquired by the developed economies in 2016 (UNCTAD 2017). The World Bank's Global Development Horizon (2013) predicts about future capital flows and forecasts a fundamental shift in global capital inflows such that the developing economies will account for 60% of global capital inflows in 2030, up from only 20% over the last four decades through the 1990s. It predicts that with improved institutional quality and with solid economic growth and supportive demographic trends for growth in developing countries, global investors are showing increasing interest in developing countries beyond the small group of emerging markets that have traditionally attracted most of the foreign investment. However, recent trend and dynamic nature of the trend of capital flows are not consistent with the predictions.

The prediction about future capital flows attracts attention from academics and policymakers. Because, capital inflows have been considered part of the development strategy in many developing countries, as foreign capital offers large potential benefits. Low levels of capital per worker (e.g., due to lack of skills, savings, or foreign exchange) have long been considered a major constraint on economic growth in developing countries and borrowing from capital-abundant countries could ease these constraints (Chenery and Strout 1966). In particular, capital inflows can augment domestic private savings, helping capital-scarce countries to achieve higher

M. Akhtaruzzaman, *International Capital Flows and the Lucas Paradox*,
https://doi.org/10.1007/978-981-13-9069-2_1

rates of capital accumulation and growth. Some types of capital inflows (e.g., foreign direct investment) facilitate the transfer of managerial and technological know-how (Borensztein et al. 1998). Portfolio investment and foreign bank lending develop domestic financial sector in developing countries by increasing liquidity of domestic stock markets, providing access to international financial markets, and improving regulatory framework. Others argue that free capital flows act as a reward for good polices and a penalty for bad policies ensuring more disciplined macroeconomic policies in developing countries (Obstfeld 1998).

Capital, if allowed to move freely, should flow from capital-abundant (i.e., rich) to capital-scarce (i.e., poor) countries based on the relative differences in the marginal product of capital (Solow 1956), leading to converging cross-country levels of per capita income. However, observed international capital flows from rich to poor countries are much lower than what is predicted by the standard theory. Observing this inconsistency in international capital flows, Robert Lucas, almost a quarter of a century ago, posed a simple question: "Why doesn't capital flow from rich to poor countries?" (Lucas 1990, p. 92). This is also known as the 'Lucas paradox' in the macro-finance literature. This question remains relevant and unresolved today, even though a substantial number of empirical studies have investigated this issue and have attempted to find a solution to this paradox.

1.2 Trends in Capital Flows: Historical Data

In Fig. 1.1, the line plots show the distribution of net capital flows (equity and debt) among different income groups: High Income (HI), Upper Middle Income (UMI), Lower Middle Income (LMI) and Lower Income (LI). *Panel a* for FDI equity, *Panel b* for portfolio equity, and *Panel c* for external debt from 1968 to 2017. In regards to equity (FDI and portfolio) flows, HI countries were the prime destinations for FDI over the last five decades and received far larger amount of FDI compared to other income groups. There is no significant change in the pattern of FDI flows to HI countries and is upward trending although a slight drop is evidenced during the period of recent global financial crisis (GFC) in 2009. The UMI country group received a significant amount of FDI, which were substantially higher than the LMI countries. LI countries received an insignificant amount of FDI inflows compared to HI and UMI countries over the last five decades. Portfolio equity flows to LI countries were also very low which might reflect the underdevelopment of financial sector in most of the LI countries. The UMI country group received a significant amount of external debt, as shown in *Panel c*, compared to that of LMI and LI countries. Overall, over the last five decades, there was no major change in terms of compositions of capital flows to different income groups of countries.

Figure 1.2 shows region-based distribution of equity flows (FDI and portfolio). FDI flows surged in the East Asia Pacific region (*Panel b*) in the early 90 s, and in Europe and Central Asia (*Panel a*) in the early 2000s. In regards to the volume, East Asia Pacific and Europe and Central Asia captured most of the equity flows compared

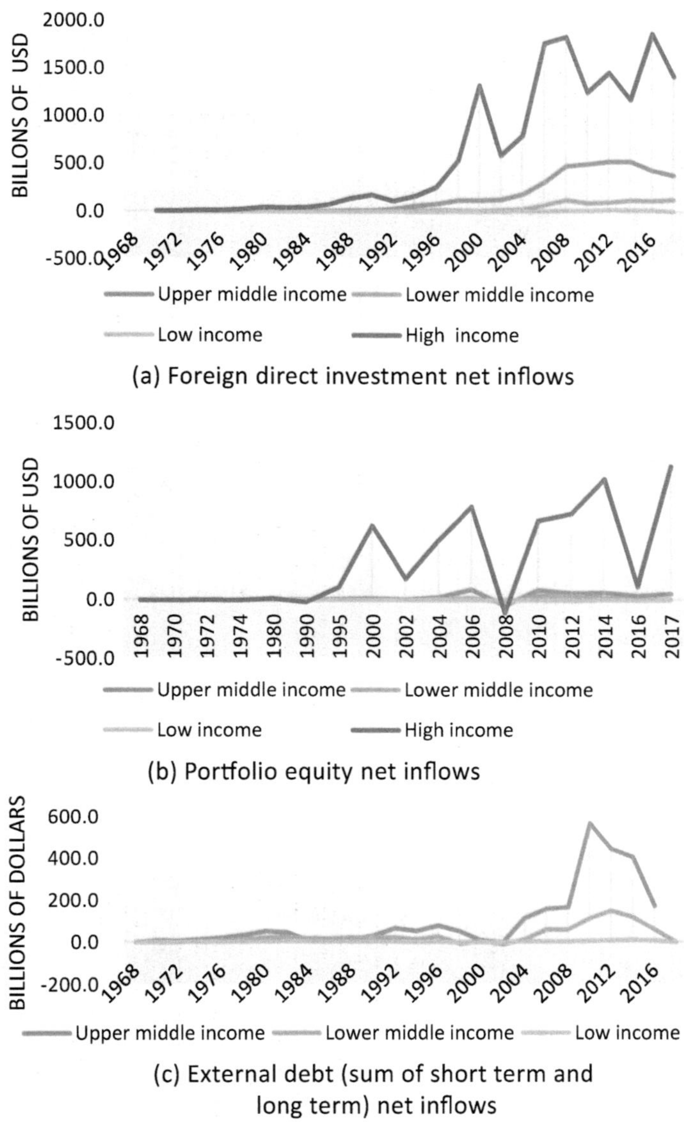

Fig. 1.1 Income-based distribution of capital flows (FDI, portfolio and debt): 1968–2017

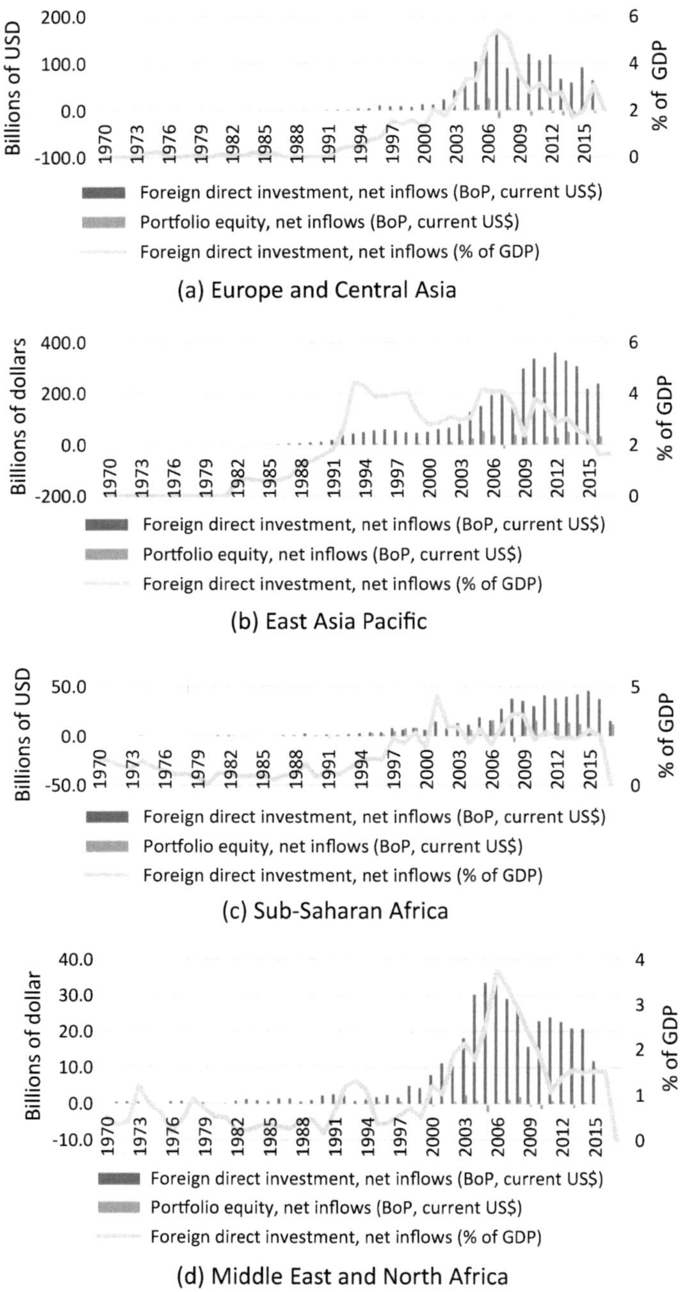

Fig. 1.2 Region-based distribution of equity flows (1968–2017)

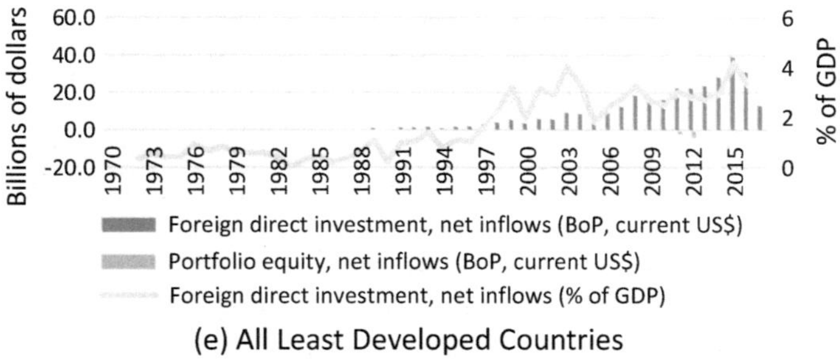

Fig. 1.2 (continued)

to other regions, such as in the least developed region (*Panel e*) or in the Sub-Saharan Africa (*Panel c*). The surge in FDI flows in the East Asia Pacific region is dominated by the emerging market economies. The collapses in the flows are evidenced in every region during the recent GFC.

This book searches for a better understanding of what actually determines cross-border capital flows and explains of the Lucas paradox. The findings of the research conducted in this book document important information for academics, policymakers and investors concerning the factors that determine international capital flows, which have substantial implications for economic growth, development, and the well-being of societies. In particular, it provides new knowledge to academics for a better understanding on the determinants of capital flows and documents guidelines for policymakers and investors to develop a coherent approach to attracting international capital and to expand mutually beneficial cross-border investments.

Chapter 2 of this book presents a simple theoretical framework, based on the standard neoclassical model, for reviewing the determinants of capital inflows. This includes a brief discussion of the neoclassical growth model prediction on international capital inflows, and the constraints that prevent international flows from rich to poor countries. An empirical specification, based on this theoretical framework, is developed for conducting empirical examination of the determinants of cross-border capital flows and to find possible answers to the Lucas paradox.

A large number of empirical studies have already investigated possible solutions to the Lucas paradox and have drawn different conclusions concerning its key determinants. The main drawback of the studies in this empirical literature is that they attempt to identify a specific factor as a 'magic bullet' solution to the paradox. One such attempt to account for the Lucas paradox is to revise the conventional approach to measurement of the marginal product of capital (MPK) and hence obtain revised measures of the differences in returns to capital. For example, Caselli and Feyrer (2007) revise the conventional MPK estimates by dividing total capital into reproducible capital (e.g., equipment, machinery) and non-reproducible capital (e.g., land and natural resources) and argue that, when properly measuring the share of income accruing to each category of capital, the average MPK of reproducible capital in poor countries is relatively low, which they suggest accounts for the Lucas paradox.

Chapter 3 examines whether such revisions of MPK help to understand the patterns of international capital flows using a simple bivariate scatter plot analysis of capital inflows and capital returns estimates. The finding of this analysis suggests that if the revised estimates of MPK are used, international capital is flowing from high-return to low-return countries, a pattern which contradicts standard theory.

This limitation of the MPK-based analysis leads us to examine the Lucas paradox in the context of the wider regression-based literature. This literature, based on the estimation of reduced form empirical models, has focused on fairly narrow channels of the determinants of capital inflows and in many cases suffers from model misspecification that consequently leads to unreliable findings on the determinants of capital inflows.

A comprehensive review is conducted on the regression-based literature to examine the relative importance of a broad set of factors that can potentially explain the Lucas paradox. Specifically, in modelling international capital flows, a variety of potential determinants are used in existing literature. Initial level of economic development is used in this literature to identify the Lucas paradox in empirical data. More specifically, by examining the statistical significance of a measure of initial economic development in all models, it is examined which factor or combination of factors can account for the Lucas paradox in the sense that inclusion of these factors in the model renders the initial level of economic development statistically insignificant (or at least non-positive) as a determinant of capital inflows.

From this perspective, the regression-based analysis of this book proceeds as follows. In Chap. 4, a cross-section analysis begins by replicating one of the most highly cited cross-sectional empirical studies. In particular, the Alfaro et al. (2008) study is replicated, which claims to provide a definitive answer to the paradox and argues that the quality of institutions determines international capital inflows and can fully explain the Lucas paradox. It is demonstrated in Chap. 4 of this book that when the empirical model specification is adjusted to better fit the data, or when data outliers are removed, the findings of Alfaro et al.'s empirical model are no longer valid in the sense that the institutional quality index can no longer solve the Lucas paradox. This finding is confirmed using an updated dataset including data for the more recent decade and shows that the institutions index does not solve the Lucas paradox and, other things equal, capital still flows to rich countries. This finding is robust in the sense that it passes a battery of robustness checks and is based on a more appropriately specified empirical model. An additional empirical test is completed in this chapter to see if the Lucas paradox is explained by a difference in a country's level of capital stock per worker. In particular, this analysis examines the effects of differences in capital stock per worker on capital inflows, when controlling for differences in overall productivity between rich and poor countries. The empirical finding suggests that the Lucas paradox is not simply an artifact of higher total factor productivity (TFP) in relatively high-income countries. In other words, capital does not flow to poor countries even if differences between rich and poor country TFP are controlled for.

Cross-sectional models do not exploit many important features of the data such as time- series variation and the dynamic nature of investment relationships.

In Chap. 5, a panel data analysis is employed to examine potential explanations for the Lucas paradox when considering these characteristics of the data. Again, the results of this analysis suggest that the institutional quality index does not solve the Lucas paradox and, indeed, institutional quality is statistically insignificant when country-specific characteristics of capital recipients are controlled for. Moreover, restrictions on capital account transactions are a relatively robust determinant, although the results do depend on the specific panel model estimator used.

Some of the panel data studies in the existing literature (e.g., Reinhardt et al. 2013) suggest that the independent effects of the determinants are not sufficient to understand the Lucas paradox and asks for an interaction effect analysis of the independent variables. Chapter 5 also examines whether a solution to the Lucas paradox hinges on interactions between the determinants (i.e., a multiplicative term of two independent determinants). Having analysed several specifications allowing such interaction effects, our findings suggest that none of the interaction effects can fully account for why capital flows to relatively rich countries. In sum, the empirical chapters in this book document the robust survival of the Lucas paradox, in a sharp contrast to the existing literature. That is, the Lucas paradox stands, as yet, unresolved.

Chapter 6 presents the findings of an empirical question of why FDI flows to many poor countries remain so small and examines how much of the lack of FDI inflows can be explained by a country's political institutions. The existing literature examining the determinants of FDI in developing countries emphasises government corruption and political regimes (i.e., democracy and autocracy). Other studies argue that property rights and the risk of expropriation (i.e., losing 100% of invested capital) in developing countries are important determinants of FDI. However, none of the studies provides a clear picture of how foreign investors value property rights and risk of expropriation relative to other political risks (e.g., lack of democracy, corruption) when deciding whether to invest in a foreign location. This chapter estimates the effects of various forms of political risk (e.g., expropriation risk, corruption, lack of democracy) and evaluates their relative importance for FDI inflows based on perceived differences in political risks of the foreign investors. The findings suggest that expropriation risk has a large negative effect on FDI and tends to trump all other forms of political risks. More specifically, expropriation risk has among the largest impacts on FDI and helps account for the low levels of FDI flows to many capital-scarce poor countries. Based on the findings of empirical chapters and on the analysis of recent developments in geopolitics, a prediction about future of the Lucas Paradox is made in Chap. 7.

References

Alfaro L, Kalemli-Ozcan S, Volosovych V (2008) Why doesn't capital flow from rich to poor countries? An empirical investigation. Rev Econ Stat 90(2):347–368

Borensztein E, De Gregorio J, Lee JW (1998) How does foreign direct investment affect economic growth? J Int Econ 45(1):115–135

Caselli F, Feyrer J (2007) The marginal product of capital. Q J Econ 122(2):535–568
Chenery HB, Strout AM (1966) Foreign assistance and economic development. Am Econ Rev 56(4):679–733
Global Development Horizon (2013) Capital flows in the third age of financial globalization. Retrieved on Nov 2018
IIF (2015) Capital flows to emerging markets, Jan 14, 2015. IIF, Washington, DC
Lucas RE (1990) Why doesn't capital flow from rich to poor countries? Am Econ Rev 80(2):92–96
Obstfeld M (1998) The global capital market: benefactor or menace? J Econ Perspect 12(4):9–30
Reinhardt D, Ricci LA, Tressel T (2013) International capital flows and development: financial openness matters. J Int Econ 91(2):235–251
Solow RM (1956) A contribution to the theory of economic growth. Q J Econ 70(1):65–94
UNCTAD (2017). World investment report. Retrieved on Nov 2018. New York and G World Bank (2018) World development indicators, online data. World Bank, Washington, DC

Chapter 2
Review of the Neoclassical Theory of Capital Flows and Related Empirical Literature

Abstract This chapter provides a brief introduction of theoretical models related to international capital flows and discusses neoclassical and new growth theory and their implications about cross-border capital flows. Notations are used to show a simple empirical specification of neoclassical model for cross border capital flows and the determinants of capital flows. This chapter systematically reviews the vast empirical literature describing and attempting to resolve the Lucas paradox of why capital doesn't flow from rich to poor countries.

2.1 Introduction

The simplest benchmark neoclassical growth model (e.g., Solow 1956) suggests that capital should flow from capital-abundant rich countries to capital-scarce poor countries as the simple result of *diminishing returns to capital.* Allocative efficiency of capital is the main focus of neoclassical growth theory and predicts a reallocation of capital from richer to poorer countries. This reallocation is doubly beneficial because capital recipients have higher marginal productivity of capital than capital lenders (assuming they share the same technology) and it speeds up global income convergence (Barro et al. 1995; Gourinchas and Jeanne 2006). Based on a similar view of the neoclassical mechanism underlying international investment flows, Chenery and Strout (1966) suggest that poor countries could borrow from rich countries to ease the constraints (e.g., lack of skills, savings, or foreign exchange) that they face in the early stages of development, which negatively affect rates of growth. This neoclassical perspective suggests a view that cross-border capital flows should generally succeed at putting scarce capital to its best use, thereby beneficially boosting investment and rates of growth (Summers 2000).

This normative neoclassical assessment of allocative efficiency has drawn a number of criticisms. In particular, the neoclassical predictions of higher marginal productivity of capital (MPK) in poor countries and the beneficial impact of higher investment and economic growth resulting from the hypothesized reallocation attract heavy criticism in the literature (Lucas 1990; Caselli and Feyrer 2007; Bhagwati 1998; Rodrik 1998; Eichengreen 2001). This literature emphasizes the role of constraints

M. Akhtaruzzaman, *International Capital Flows and the Lucas Paradox*,
https://doi.org/10.1007/978-981-13-9069-2_2

that prevent allocative efficiency from being realized by reallocation of capital from rich to poor countries. In particular, the critics argue that realizing the gains from international capital flows which reallocate countries' positions along their respective production functions is not straightforward once the many other constraints, which in turn depend on the economic and other characteristics of the recipients of capital, are considered. The constraints include poor institutional quality (i.e., poor enforcement of property rights), capital market imperfections (i.e., restrictions on cross-border capital flows), and lack of absorptive capacity of the country resulting from lack of factors complementary to capital (e.g., the stock of human capital). Specifically, these constraints cause the realized rate of return on capital to be much lower than is predicted by neoclassical growth models. Therefore, when trying to square observation with theoretical prediction questions remained unresolved as to why economic growth and development may deviate from perfect allocative efficiency.

New growth theory (NGT) abandons the neoclassical assumption of diminishing returns to capital in the aggregate. It introduces ideas such as learning by doing, spillover effects, and economies of scale, and these factors may imply that MPK is not diminishing in the aggregate capital stock.[1] This alternative strand of analytical framework may offer a richer set of predictions on the relationship between capital flows and growth than the traditional reallocation mechanisms of neoclassical model. However, the focus of this chapter is to gain a deeper understanding of barriers to international capital reallocation predicted by the neoclassical model. The following section reviews the benchmark neoclassical model, considers potential constraints that prevent conditional convergence in income per worker, and lays down a specification for an empirical investigation of this theoretical framework.

2.2 Review of the Neoclassical Model

Consider a small open economy that uses capital *(K)* and labour *(L)* to produce output *(Y)* with constant-returns-to-scale technology in time period *t*:

$$Y_t = A_t B(K_t, L_t) \tag{2.1}$$

where A_t represents total factor productivity and is assumed to be identical across countries. The per capita production function can be expressed as:

$$\frac{Y_t}{L_t} = A_t B\left(\frac{K_t}{L_t}, \frac{L_t}{L_t}\right) \tag{2.2}$$

$$y_t = A_t b(k_t) \tag{2.3}$$

[1] Romer (1986) considers 'knowledge' as an additional input to the production function and points to the fact that research and development activities create new knowledge and have positive externalities to society. The externalities referred to here imply that knowledge generated by one economic agent will tend to flow to other economic agents.

where lower case letters denote per capita values. Consider two countries, i and j where $i \neq j$, characterized by different domestic rates of return on capital. The marginal products of capital in a competitive equilibrium are equal to the returns on capital (r) in each country[2]:

$$\frac{dy_{it}}{dk_{it}} = A_t b^{'}(k_{it}) = r_{it} \tag{2.4}$$

$$\frac{dy_{jt}}{dk_{jt}} = A_t b^{'}\left(k_{jt}\right) = r_{jt} \tag{2.5}$$

The basic neoclassical growth model suggests that capital should flow from relatively capital-abundant, low-return countries to capital-scarce, high-return countries, based on diminishing returns to capital, until the rates of return are equalized. In this set-up, assuming that capital is perfectly mobile across countries, capital flows from relatively low-return to relatively high-return countries until returns to capital are equalized with the global rate of return (r*) implying that:

$$A_t b^{'}(k_{it}) = r_t^* = A_t b^{'}(k_{jt}) \tag{2.6}$$

Lucas (1990) argues that there are gross violations of the competitive equilibrium condition of Eq. 2.6. To gain a better understanding of what might plausibly account for such violations, Lucas considers a series of numerical examples employing the simple Cobb-Douglas aggregate production technology:

$$y = Ak^{\beta} \tag{2.7}$$

where β is the capital share, $0 < \beta < 1$. The corresponding marginal product of capital (MP_k) in terms of income per worker (y) is:

$$MP_k = \beta A^{1/\beta} y^{(\beta-1)/\beta} \tag{2.8}$$

Taking natural logs of both sides, this relationship can be expressed as:

$$log(MP_k) = log\beta + \left(\frac{1}{\beta}\right) \log A - \left(\frac{1-\beta}{\beta}\right) \log y \tag{2.9}$$

which suggests that, for a given A, capital should flow from low-MP_k, high-income countries to high-MP_k, low-income countries until the condition (2.6) holds. However, Lucas argues that sustained differences in income per worker (and hence also capital per worker) tend to violate this condition, and that substantial differences in TFP (A) between rich and poor countries may account for observed differences.

Specifically, Lucas compares MPK differences between India and the United States assuming that capital shares ($\beta = 0.4$) are the same for both countries.

---

[2]Returns here mean gross returns to capital inclusive of depreciation.

He uses Summers and Heston's (1988) data and finds income per worker (y) in the US is 15 times higher than that in India. For a given A identical in both countries, parameter estimates from Eq. 2.8 reveal that the MP_k in India should be 58 times higher than that of the United States. Lucas argues that if this calculation is correct, in the face of return differentials of this magnitude, we should see capital goods flow from the US and other rich countries to India and other poor countries. Lucas searches for a potential explanation for this puzzle and emphasizes the differences in labour quality between rich and poor countries drawing on Kruger's (1968) data.[3] More specifically, Lucas includes human capital per worker, h (i.e., amount of education per worker) as an additional input to the per capita production function as follows:

$$y = Ak^{\beta}h^{\gamma} \tag{2.10}$$

A higher value of γ would suggest a higher income share of human capital. The corresponding marginal product of capital (MP_k) in terms of income per worker, expressed in natural logs, is:

$$log(MP_k) = log\beta + \left(\frac{1}{\beta}\right)\log A - \left(\frac{1-\beta}{\beta}\right)\log y + \left(\frac{\gamma}{\beta}\right)logh \tag{2.11}$$

Equation 2.11 suggests that, for a given A, a higher level of human capital per worker increases the MP_k. Lucas revises the parameter estimates adjusting for human capital per worker using available data on schooling level and finds that the MP_k differential between India and the US is reduced to a factor of 5.

Lucas further examines whether any MP_k differentials remain between rich and poor countries when external benefits of human capital are factored into the MP_k estimation. More specifically, Lucas argues that there is a potential externality arising from human capital per worker (i.e., education per worker) and the externality effects of the aggregate level of education in an economy can show up in total factor productivity (A). After taking into account plausible human capital externality effects, Lucas finds the differences in MP_k between the US and India disappears. From Lucas's point of view, such differences in fundamentals (e.g., human capital stock per worker) between rich and poor countries possibly explain why capital does not flow from rich to poor countries. Lucas considers alternative explanations such as capital market imperfections or political risk; however, he rejects them as explanations for differences in capital per worker. In particular, Lucas argues that, before World War II, many of today's poor countries were colonies and subject to rich countries' laws and investors in rich countries could expect contracts to be enforced in a similar fashion in both rich and poor countries.

However, more recent literature has argued that capital market imperfections or political risk constitute a wedge between expected and ex-post returns to capital and cause violation of the competitive equilibrium condition of Eq. 2.6. In particu-

[3]Krueger's data give estimates of labour income shares based on particular factors such as age and level of education, which in turn contribute to labour productivity differences across countries.

lar, differences in institutional quality capturing differences in political risks (e.g., Alfaro et al. 2008) and differences in restrictions on cross-border capital flows (e.g., Reinhardt et al. 2013) constitute a wedge between expected and ex-post returns to capital and therefore influence the competitive equilibrium. If the political risks are very high, resulting from poor institutional quality, then the risk-adjusted returns are very low. Similarly, a higher restriction on cross-border capital flows reduces the rate of return and causes the economy to deviate away from the competitive equilibrium condition. Therefore, a competitive solution for the marginal product of capital including these additional factors can be expressed as:

$$A_t b^{'}(k_{it}, z_{it}) = r_t^* = A_t b^{'}(k_{jt}, z_{jt}) \tag{2.12}$$

where differences in fundamentals (i.e., stocks of human capital), institutional quality (i.e., political risk), and capital market imperfections (i.e., restrictions in cross-border flows) that prevent equalization of capital per worker are captured by z, where $b^{'}$ (marginal product of capital, MP_k) is assumed to be a decreasing function of k (capital stock per worker) and an increasing function of z (in terms of stronger fundamentals and lower frictions of institutions and capital markets). Equation 2.12 suggests that, in the face of a MP_k differential, the extent of reallocation of capital depends on these additional factors. In other words, the ex-post returns to capital are adjusted for fundamentals, institutional quality, and capital market imperfections that consequently determine international flows. The specific theoretical perspectives on these additional factors in influencing international capital flows are discussed below.

A higher level of favourable fundamentals raises the marginal productivity of capital (i.e., equivalent to increasing z for a country) and enhances a host country's attractiveness as a destination for others to send capital; thus more capital tends to flow to countries with stronger fundamentals (e.g., a larger stock of human capital). In contrast, in the absence of stronger fundamentals (as explained in Lucas 1990), it is possible to see that a low marginal product of capital and a low capital stock per worker can co-exist, consistent with a failure of reallocation of capital from a capital-abundant country (say, country j) to a capital-scarce country (say, country i).

Institutions affect economic activity through the incentives provided to investors, such as property rights, independent judiciary, rule of law, and protection from expropriation risk (Acemoglu et al. 2001). In particular, inclusion of an index of institutional quality in the analysis helps to explore the response of international investors to institutional change, for example, how much foreign investments increase due to a significant reduction in the risk of expropriation in a specific economy. Foreign investors are concerned about the quality of institutions of capital-recipient countries and the 'risk premium' is likely to be higher if quality institutions are lacking. In this case, inclusion of an institutional quality index is equivalent to decreasing z for a country with low quality institutions. For example, if the quality of country i's institutions responsible for contract enforcement and property rights is low, then the expected ex ante marginal product of capital will be low even if realized ex post returns to investment are sometimes high (whenever property rights are secured).

In this set-up, further foreign investment may not take place in country i despite its marginal product of capital (risk-unadjusted) being higher than in country j.

The third additional factor in Eq. 2.12 is capital market imperfections representing frictions and constraints in a country's capital account transactions. Capital flows are prevented from flowing to capital-scarce countries if the capital accounts restrictions are high and foreign investors are concerned about the convertibility restrictions. For example, if country i faces high capital account constraints (e.g., controls of cross-border capital flows) and is blocked off from world capital markets, this can be represented by a relatively low value of z for a given level of all other factors, and capital inflows may not materialize despite a higher marginal product of capital in country i.

These perspectives provide a theoretical basis for explaining the impacts of various constraints that lead to deviations from perfect equalization of capital per worker. Empirical model presented below (2.13a) incorporates these constraints factors:

$$F_i = Ag_1(k_i, z_i) \tag{2.13a}$$

where country i's capital inflow (F_i) is a function of capital stock per worker (k_i), and the additional factors (z_i) concerning fundamentals, institutions, and capital market imperfections. Following the neoclassical prediction (as described in Eq. 2.9), for a given A, an inverse relationship is observed between capital inflow F_i and k_i, suggesting that capital flows to capital-scarce, low-income (i.e., poor) countries. However, this relationship is influenced by the additional factors (z_i) that ultimately determine international capital flows. For an empirical test of the Lucas paradox, Eq. 2.13a can be expressed in terms of income per worker as follows:

$$F_i = g_2(y_i, z_i) \tag{2.13b}$$

In Eq. 2.13b, a negative and statistically significant relationship between income per worker (y_i) and capital inflows (F_i) supports the neoclassical prediction and capital flows to poor countries. A positive and statistically significant coefficient of income per worker (y_i), by contrast, constitutes empirical evidence of the Lucas paradox. If inclusion of any or all of the additional factors (z_i) discussed above can fully explain (i.e., renders insignificant or reverses) the positive and statistically significant association between F_i and y_i, then we would interpret such a finding as a solution to the Lucas paradox. Conversely, if the positive and statistically significant relationship does not disappear when these factors are included, individually or collectively, then we would interpret that finding as demonstrating that the Lucas paradox stands, as yet, unresolved. Before turning to our empirical analysis, the following section reviews the closely related empirical literature and summarizes its findings.

2.3 Review of the Empirical Literature

This section reviews the existing empirical literature and finds two main streams of analyses are used to account for the Lucas paradox: marginal product of capital (MPK)-based analysis (i.e., the studies that aim to directly measure country MPK differences) and the regression-based analysis (i.e., the studies that use reduced form regression models). The MPK-based analysis proposes alternatives to conventional MPK estimates and helps answer why relatively rich countries also have relatively high marginal products of capital. On the other hand, the regression-based analysis attempts to directly identify the determinants of capital inflows using different empirical models and estimation approaches. The remainder of this section summarizes the empirical literature broadly considering the literature under the two main streams.

The MPK-based literature begins with Lucas (1990), who finds that fundamental differences (e.g., differences in stocks of human capital) between countries potentially explain why capital does not flow from rich to poor countries. Following Lucas (1990), there are a few alternative suggestions on how conventional MPK measures can be revised in order to empirically account for the observed directions of capital flows. Caselli and Feyrer (2007) revise the MPK estimates by calculating cross-country differences in endowment of natural resources (i.e., non-renewable resources) and renewable resources (e.g., machinery and equipment). They argue that the share of renewable resources is relatively higher and therefore MPK is relatively higher in rich countries if properly measured.[4] Chirinko and Mallick (2008) find, in contrast, MPK is, on average, 100–200% higher in poor countries than in rich countries if adjustment costs are considered in the MPK estimates. Similarly, Swan (2008) argues that credit market imperfections explain the MPK differences between rich and poor countries. More recently, Lowe et al. (2012) re-estimate MPK for a large number of countries by further refining Caselli and Feyrer's reproducible capital (i.e., renewable resources), dividing it into public sector capital and private sector capital. They find the higher overall MPK (public sector MPK plus private sector MPK) in rich countries is driven by higher MPK in the public sector, whereas MPK in the private sector is almost identical between rich and poor countries. They argue that the difference in inefficiencies in the public sector between rich and poor countries, which accounts for the higher MPK in rich countries, explains the average MPK variation between rich and poor countries. The key message of this limited number of MPK-based studies is that revised estimates of conventional MPK estimates help us to better understand the MPK differences and to predict whether capital should flow from rich to poor countries.

The regression-based literature considers a wider set of variables as determinants of capital inflows, which cannot be easily accounted for in the MPK-based analysis. Considering the characteristics of the variables and their impacts on capital inflows, the large regression-based literature can be divided into three broad (not always

[4]Details concerning the construction of the revised MPK estimates reviewed in this chapter are provided in Chap. 3.

mutually exclusive) categories of factors, which is explained in greater detail below.[5] They are: *fundamentals* that directly influence the ex ante returns to capital in the absence of unexpected events (e.g., Clemens and Williamson 2004); *capital market imperfections/frictions* that contribute to the wedge between the expected returns and ex post returns to capital (e.g., Reinhardt et al. 2013); *institutions* that reduce political risks and the cost of doing business and influence the ex ante returns to capital and capital inflows (e.g., Alfaro et al. 2008).

Clemens and Williamson (2004), in a regression-based analysis, share a similar view to Lucas (1990) and Caselli and Feyrer (2007), point to the importance of economic fundamentals. In particular, Clemens and Williamson (2004) study the first era of financial integration (1870–1913) and the effects on British capital flows to 34 capital recipients. They find that countries with higher average schooling, urbanization, migration rates, and endowment of natural resources, which they categorize as fundamental factors, attract more foreign capital. Borensztein et al. (1998) share a similar view that fundamentals are important. They examine a specific type of capital flows (i.e., FDI) and find that once the host country achieves a certain level of absorptive capacity through a minimum threshold of human capital (a measure of fundamentals) it attracts more FDI inflows. Similarly, Noorbakhsh et al. (2001) find that human capital significantly increases FDI inflows. However, this view—-better fundamentals bring higher capital inflows—does not align with Gourinchas and Jeanne's (2013) empirical findings. Gourinchas and Jeanne (2013) find faster productivity growth, an outcome of higher fundamentals, negatively affects capital inflows, suggesting that capital does not flow to high-growth countries—a pattern opposite to the neoclassical prediction. In particular, Gourinchas and Jeanne examine the determinants of external debt (both private and public) for 65 non-OECD countries and find international lending is mainly driven by public lending and is negatively associated with productivity growth, whereas private lending is positively associated with productivity growth but has little impact on total international lending (i.e., private lending is only 6% of total lending). They use a standard Solow residual as a measure of productivity growth, which implicitly includes the productivity effect of human capital; however, their findings do not suggest better fundamentals increase capital inflows.

Several other studies empirically investigating the Lucas paradox have focused on capital market imperfections, such as lower barriers to international capital movements (i.e., capital account openness) and/or higher levels of financial integration with the world economy (Abiad et al. 2009; Reinhardt et al. 2013), as well as lack of financial development, such as the degree of credit allocated to the private sector as a fraction of GDP and/or stock market capitalization as a fraction of GDP (Forbes 2010; Von Hagen and Zhang 2010). For example, Abiad et al. (2009) find that a higher level of financial integration (measured by the sum of foreign assets

---

[5]A similar categorization of the determinants of capital flows is used in Clemens and Williamson (2004). However, they divide them into two broad categories, labelled as: the *global capital market failure* view, which includes factors listed in our *frictions* category, such as capital account restrictions, and the *unproductive domestic capital view*, which includes factors within our *fundamentals* and *institutions* categories, such as human capital and institutional quality.

and liabilities to GDP) causes capital to flow from rich to poor countries. They find, in Europe, a higher level of financial integration increases capital flows from rich to poor countries. Reinhardt et al. (2013) examine the interaction between capital account openness (e.g., allowing free capital mobility across borders) and economic development and find capital flows to poor countries if their capital accounts are open.

While these macro-level studies examine cross-country effects of capital market frictions on capital inflows, Kalemli-Ozcan et al. (2010) study a simple version of the standard neoclassical open economy model using within-country capital flow data for US states. They find that, in line with standard theory, their simple model explains a large proportion of within-country variation of capital flows, with capital flowing from slow-growing to fast-growing states, suggesting that barriers at the border prevent international capital flows. Several other studies find that other types of frictions, such as information asymmetries, matter for capital inflows (Portes and Rey 2005; Hashimoto and Wacker 2012). In particular, Hashimoto and Wacker (2012) examine the impact of countries' compliance with the International Monetary Fund's (IMF) Special Data Dissemination Standard (SDDS) on FDI and portfolio inflows. They find subscription to SDDS increases FDI inflows. Portes and Rey (2005) specifically point to information asymmetry, including information related to accounting practices, corporate culture, political events, and asset market structure, as important determinants of capital inflows.

Until recently, the empirical literature on capital inflows has not explicitly considered institutional quality as an important determinant. For example, Lucas (1990) rejects the idea that 'political risks' (a measure of institutional quality) have much influence on capital flows from rich to poor countries. However, the view that institutional quality matters receives support in the economic growth literature from cross-country correlations between measures of property rights and economic development (Knack and Keefer 1995; Hall and Jones 1999; Acemoglu et al. 2001). A more recent empirical literature (Alfaro et al. 2008; Papaioannou 2009) on international capital flows places more emphasis on institutional quality and argues that institutions have both direct and indirect effects on capital movements. In other words, they suggest institutions play a significant role in shaping the geography of international capital flows. Alfaro et al. (2008), for example, include an institutional quality index (reflecting property rights and good governance) in their cross-section regression model and argue that differences in the institutions index determine capital inflows and can fully account for the Lucas paradox. In particular, the positive and statistically significant correlation between capital inflows and income per capita disappears once institutional quality is controlled for.

Papaioannou (2009) investigates the determinants of bank flows (e.g., cross-border loans, debt investment etc. included in banks' on-balance sheet) using bilateral flow data and reaches a similar conclusion that institutional quality is a significant determinant of bank lending and also uncovers particular features of institutions that affect international bank flows. He finds property rights and legal institutions that protect foreign investors from expropriation and contract repudiation are the main determinants of bank lending. Other studies that examine specific aspects of institutional quality and find significant barriers to foreign investment include government corruption (Wei 2000), sovereign default (Reinhart and Rogoff 2004), and expropriation risk (Asiedu et al. 2009). Overall, these studies suggest that poor institutional quality (i.e., a higher level of various political risks) prevents capital flowing from rich to poor countries.

In contrast, Okada (2013) finds that institutional quality cannot, on its own, provide an answer to the Lucas paradox; instead the *interaction* between institutional quality and capital account openness can. More specifically, Okada finds that a higher level of institutional quality attracts capital inflows if capital account openness is ensured. Table 2.1 provides further details (e.g., sample of countries and sample period, methodologies, main variables of interest, and findings) considering for representative studies in this empirical literature.

Taken together, it is noteworthy to observe that the finding of this large empirical literature is inconclusive regarding which factor(s) matter most for capital inflows. This inconclusive finding is due, in part, to the variation in choices of the key dimension concerning the construction of revised-MPK estimates in the MPK-based literature, and the variation in model specification and econometric approaches in the regression-based literature. Moreover, in most cases, the regression-based studies tend to focus on only a narrow set of factors (e.g., an index that measures institutional quality or capital account openness or a specific factor that measures one or more fundamentals) as determinants of capital inflows, leaving open the question of whether the findings from the estimated regressions are robust to the inclusion of other covariates that may represent important investment incentives or whether the findings are robust to alternative empirical specifications and econometric approaches.

Based on this observation, an empirical investigation of the relative importance of factors from all three broad categories of factors (*fundamentals*, *institutions*, and *capital market imperfections*) is required that can potentially explain international capital flows and the Lucas paradox. Specifically, in modelling international capital flows, a wide variety of potential determinants spanning all categories are required to include in empirical models to examine the statistical significance of a measure of economic development (i.e., GDP per capita). Such a thorough empirical investigation can potentially account for the Lucas paradox i.e., the positive correlation between GDP per capita and capital inflows.

The empirical analysis of the Lucas paradox proceeds as follows. Chapter 3 provides the details concerning the construction of the revised MPK estimates and examines the extent to which the proposed revised MPK estimates are able to account for international capital flows. Chapters 4 and 5 critically analyse the regression-based studies, examine the robustness of their findings, and provide new empirical evidence on the Lucas paradox.

Table 2.1 Summary table of empirical literature of the determinants of capital inflows

Study	Sample and sample period	Methodology	Main variables of interest	Dependent variable	Standard controls	Main findings
Abiad et al. (2009)	Regional analysis: Europe, Western Hemisphere, Asia Pacific (1975–2004)	5-yearly panel Random effects model	Interaction between financial Integration (measured by net foreign asset holdings) and GDP per capita	Current account balance to GDP	GDP growth pc, fiscal balance, old age dependency, trade, net foreign assets to GDP	In Europe, increased financial integration causes capital flows from rich to poor countries
Alfaro et al. (2008)	98 countries (1970–2000)	Cross-section OLS	Institutional quality index	Private equity (direct and portfolio) inflows per capita	Schooling, distantness, capital account restrictions, etc.	Institutional quality explains why capital does not flow from rich to poor countries
Azémar and Desbordes (2013)	60 countries (1970–1998)	Cross-section OLS	Institutional quality index	Private equity inflows per capita	Schooling, distantness, capital account restrictions	Institutional quality does not explain the Lucas paradox
Caselli and Feyrer (2007)	52 countries, 1996	Parameter calibration from cross-section analysis	Separate reproducible capital share from total capital and re-estimate marginal product of capital (MPK)	N/A	N/A	MPK is lower in poor countries if MPK is properly calculated and this explains the Lucas paradox
Chirinko and Mallick (2008)	Caselli and Feyrer's (2007) sample	Parameter calibration from cross-section analysis	Adjustment cost added to MPK estimates	N/A	N/A	MPK is higher in poor countries if adjustment costs are included in MPK estimates

(continued)

Table 2.1 (continued)

Study	Sample and sample period	Methodology	Main variables of interest	Dependent variable	Standard controls	Main findings
Clemens and Willamson (2004)	34 countries (1870–1913)	OLS and Tobit regression	Uphill capital flows are due to either fundamentals or capital market imperfections	Capital flows as share of gross British capital using historical data	Different measures of fundamentals (migration, urbanization) and capital market imperfections (tariffs)	Fundamentals are stronger determinants of capital inflows than capital market imperfections
Forbes and Warnock (2012)	58 countries (1980–2009) quarterly data	Seemingly unrelated regression on 4 episodes (surges, stops, flight, retrenchment) with clustered standard errors	Identifying episodes (surges, stops, flight, retrenchment) of capital flows and their determinants	Quarterly gross capital inflows and outflows	Global risk, liquidity, growth and interest rates; regional trade and financial contagion factors; domestic factors	Global factors are more important determinant than domestic factors
Fernandez-Arias (1996)	13 countries quarterly data from 1989–1993	OLS estimation of reduced form equation	Relative effects of global factors (e.g. global shocks) on developing countries capital inflows	Portfolio inflows to GNP	Developed country interest rate, developing countries' debt price	Capital flows to developing countries results from a lower interest rates in developed countries
Gourinchas and Jeanne (2013)	60 non-OECD countries annual data	Cross-section OLS	Relationship between productivity catch-up and capital inflows	Sum of private and public capital inflows relative to initial GDP	Initial abundance of capital, population growth, openness	Capital does not tend to flow more toward countries with higher productivity growth and higher investment

(continued)

Table 2.1 (continued)

Study	Sample and sample period	Methodology	Main variables of interest	Dependent variable	Standard controls	Main findings
Hashimoto and Wacker (2012)	55 countries (1989–2008)	Fixed effects and random effects analysis	IMF's SDDS data subscription	Log of real FDI and portfolio inflows	Trade, real exchange rate volatility, political risk, GDP growth	Subscription to SDDScauses large increase in FDI inflows
Kalemli-Ozcan et al. (2010)	50 US states (1981–2000)	Simulation; cross-section and panel model approaches	Effects of change in output/income ratio on net capital flows	Change in output/income ratio	Lagged output/income ratio, growth of population, share of retirees in population	Capital flows from slow-growing to fast-growing states if there are no restrictions
Lowe et al. (2012)	Caselli and Feyrer's sample in 2006	Parameter calibration from cross-section analysis	Difference in MPK between private sector and public sector	N/A	N/A	Public sector MPK in rich countries is higher. This drives the overall MPK in rich countries and explains the Lucas paradox
Okada (2013)	112 countries (1985–2009)	5 yearly dynamic panel GMM	Interaction of capital account openness and institutions index	FDI per capita and Private equity per capita	GDP per capita, trade, education, inflation government expenditure	Higher levels of institutional quality increase capital inflows if capital account is open
Papaioannou (2009)	140 countries (1984–2002)	Cross-Section OLS, panel FE and gravity model approach	Institutions and particular features of institutions	Bilateral bank flow data	Gravity controls: GDP, distance	Institutions and particularly property rights, legal institutions are important determinants

(continued)

Table 2.1 (continued)

Study	Sample and sample period	Methodology	Main variables of interest	Dependent variable	Standard controls	Main findings
Portes and Rey (2005)	14 countries (1989–1996)	Between estimator on group means and gravity approach	Information asymmetries	Sum of sales and purchases of equities	Different types of determinants of information asymmetries: distance, financial transaction costs, index of insider trading	Information asymmetries have negative effects on capital inflows
Reinhardt et al. (2013)	109 countries (1980–2006)	5-yearly pooled OLS and panel FE	Interaction between capital account openness and GDP per capita	Net capital outflow to GDP proxied by current account balance	Fiscal balance, dependency ratio, per capita GDP growth, NFA to GDP	Capital flows are downhill if capital accounts are open
Reinhart and Rogoff (2004)	106 countries (since 1946)	Logistic regression	Debt default and capital inflows	Share of years in a default	Per capita income and share of years in a default	Default risks prevent capital flows form rich to poor
Swan (2008)	28 countries out of 52 in Caselli and Feyrer (2007)	Parameter calibration and 2SLS regression	Capital market imperfections	Private credit to GDP for 2SLS regression	Instrumental variables: legal origin dummies	Apparent high MPK in poor countries is due to capital market imperfections and the Lucas paradox is understood when capital market imperfections is included to the MPK estimates

References

Abiad A, Leigh D, Mody A (2009) Financial integration, capital mobility, and income convergence. Econ Policy 24(58):241–305

Acemoglu D, Johnson S, Robinson JA (2001) The colonial origins of comparative development: An empirical investigation. Am Econ Rev 91(5):1369–1401

Alfaro L, Kalemli-Ozcan S, Volosovych V (2008) Why doesn't capital flow from rich to poor countries? An empirical investigation. Rev Econ Stat 90(2):347–368

Asiedu E, Jin Y, Nandwa B (2009) Does foreign aid mitigate the adverse effect of expropriation risk on foreign direct investment? J Int Econ 78(2):268–275

Azémar C, Desbordes R (2013) Has the Lucas paradox been fully explained? Econ Lett 121(2):183–187

Barro RJ, Mankiw NG, Sala-i-Martin X (1995) Capital mobility in neoclassical models of growth. Am Econ Rev 85(1):103–115

Bhagwati J (1998) Capital myth-the difference between trade in widgets and dollars. Foreign Aff 77(3):7–12

Borensztein E, De Gregorio J, Lee JW (1998) How does foreign direct investment affect economic growth? J Int Econ 45(1):115–135

Caselli F, Feyrer J (2007) The marginal product of capital. Q J Econ 122(2):535–568

Chenery HB, Strout AM (1966) Foreign assistance and economic development. Am Econ Rev 56(4):679–733

Chirinko RS, Mallick D (2008) The marginal product of capital: a persistent international puzzle. CESifo working paper, no. 2399

Clemens MA, Williamson JG (2004) Wealth bias in the first global capital market boom, 1870–1913. Econ J 114(495):304–337

Eichengreen B (2001) Capital account liberalization: what do cross-country studies tell us? World Bank Econ Rev 15(3):341–365

Fernandez-Arias E (1996) The new wave of private capital inflows: push or pull? J Dev Econ 48(2):389–418

Forbes KJ (2010) Why do foreigners invest in the United States? J Int Econ 80(1):3–21

Forbes KJ, Warnock FE (2012) Capital flow waves: surges, stops, flight, and retrenchment. J Int Econ 88(2):235–251

Gourinchas PO, Jeanne O (2006) The elusive gains from international financial integration. Rev Econ Stud 73(3):715–741

Gourinchas PO, Jeanne O (2013) Capital flows to developing countries: the allocation puzzle. Rev Econ Stud 0:1–32

Hall RE, Jones CI (1999) Why do some countries produce so much more output per worker than others? Q J Econ 114(1):83–116

Hashimoto Y, Wacker KM (2012) The role of risk and information for international capital flows: new evidence from the SDDS. Courant Research Centre: poverty, equity and growth, discussion paper, no. 124

Kalemli-Ozcan S, Reshef A, Sørensen BE, Yosha O (2010) Why does capital flow to rich states? Rev Econ Stat 92(4):769–783

Knack S, Keefer P (1995) Institutions and economic performance: cross-country tests using alternative institutional measures. Econ Politics 7(3):207–227

Krueger AO (1968) Factor endowments and per capita income differences among countries. Econ J 78(311):641–659

Lowe M, Papageorgiou C, Perez-Sebastian F (2012) The public and private MPK. IMF. Mimeo, Washington, DC

Lucas RE (1990) Why doesn't capital flow from rich to poor countries? Am Econ Rev 80(2):92–96

Noorbakhsh F, Paloni A, Youssef A (2001) Human capital and FDI inflows to developing countries: new empirical evidence. World Dev 29(9):1593–1610

Okada K (2013) The interaction effects of financial openness and institutions on international capital flows. J Macroecon 35:131–143
Papaioannou E (2009) What drives international financial flows? Politics, institutions and other determinants. J Dev Econ 88(2):269–281
Portes R, Rey H (2005) The determinants of cross-border equity flows. J Int Econ 65(2):269–296
Reinhardt D, Ricci LA, Tressel T (2013) International capital flows and development: financial openness matters. J Int Econ 91(2):235–251
Reinhart CM, Rogoff KS (2004) Serial default and the paradox of rich-to-poor capital flows. Am Econ Rev 94(2):53–58
Rodrik, D. (1998) Who needs capital-account convertibility? In: Essays in international finance, International Finance Section, Department of Economics, Princeton University, Princeton, New Jersey, pp 55–65
Romer P (1986) Increasing returns and long-run growth. J Polit Econ 94(5):1002–1037
Solow RM (1956) A contribution to the theory of economic growth. Q J Econ 70(1):65–94
Summers LH (2000) International financial crises: causes, prevention, and cures. Am Econ Rev 90(2):1–16
Summers R, Heston A (1988) A new set of international comparisons of real product and price levels estimates for 130 countries, 1950–1985. Rev Income Wealth 34(1):1–25
Swan A (2008) New evidence on the marginal product of capital. Australian National University mimeo
Von Hagen J, Zhang H (2010) Financial development and the patterns of international capital flows. Singapore Management University, working paper, no. 02-2010
Wei SJ (2000) How taxing is corruption on international investors? Rev Econ Stat 82(1):1–11

Chapter 3
The Lucas Paradox: Review of Marginal Product of Capital and Net Versus Gross Capital Flows

Abstract This chapter reviews alternatives to conventional estimates of the marginal product of capital (MPK) and examines whether these revised estimates of MPK succeed in helping us understand observed international capital flows. Bivariate data analysis (i.e., using scatter plots of capital inflows and revised MPK estimates) conducted in this chapter suggests that the direction of capital flows points, if anything, towards relatively low-return countries, a pattern that runs opposite to the prediction of standard theory about the direction of capital flows. Instead of solving the Lucas paradox, these revised MPK estimates recast the puzzle from Lucas' original question of 'Why doesn't capital flow to poor countries?' to a new one: Why does capital flow to low-return countries? An explanation to this new puzzle is presented as that the revised MPK estimates do not capture adequately all the important factors that influence international capital flows. This chapter also brings a detailed discussion for better understanding the distinction between gross and net capital flows.

3.1 Introduction

This chapter provides a critical examination of MPK-based analysis of international capital flows, detailing the methods used to revise MPK estimates. In particular, different measurements of MPK estimates are considered in detail, such as MPK estimates proposed by Caselli and Feyrer (2007), Chirinko and Mallick (2008), Swan (2008), and Lowe et al. (2012). This chapter reviews the factors that they each use to augment the standard MPK estimates and examines whether these revised estimates help explain international capital data by examining the empirical relationship between the MPK estimates and the direction of capital flows. Observed international capital flows are inconsistent with the prediction of these revised MPK estimates, as the graphical analysis shows capital flowing from high-return to low-return countries.

M. Akhtaruzzaman, *International Capital Flows and the Lucas Paradox*,
https://doi.org/10.1007/978-981-13-9069-2_3

3.2 Revised Estimates of MPK

Caselli and Feyrer (2007) (hereafter, CF) start with a standard one-sector neoclassical model, as in Lucas (1990), with constant returns and perfectly competitive capital markets. Under these assumptions, the MPKs are calculated in the context of the following Cobb-Douglas production function:

$$Y = AK^{\alpha_w} L^{1-\alpha_w} \tag{3.1}$$

where Y is GDP, α_w is the gross measure of capital income share, $1-\alpha_w$ is the labour share, A is technology, and K and L are the capital and labour inputs, respectively. CF assume that human capital is included in A and they focus on methods for estimating the capital share parameter appropriately (α_w). The standard MPK measure, which CF refer to as a "*naïve estimate*" of MPK (MPKN), is:

$$MPKN = \alpha_w \frac{Y}{K} \tag{3.2}$$

They argue that use of the gross measure of capital share (α_w) will lead to an overestimate of the true MPK for reproducible capital (the type of capital that is actually mobile across international borders), if α_w is calculated as a residual from labour income. This biased estimate of the MPK becomes more inflated if there is a high share of the resource-based (i.e., non-reproducible) sector in total output, a common scenario in poor countries.[1] To address this problem, the authors estimate the capital share (α_w) by dividing capital into reproducible capital (e.g., equipment, machinery) and non-reproducible capital (e.g., land and natural resources). They then add non-reproducible capital as a possible input in the standard model and calculate the shares of output paid to reproducible (α_{rk}) and non-reproducible (α_{nk}) capital. They measure the share of reproducible capital in total capital income using natural and reproducible wealth data from the World Bank (2006), total capital share (α_w) data from Bernanke and Gürkaynak (2001), and data on GDP (Y), capital stock (K), output prices (P_y), and investment prices (P_k) from the Penn World Tables (PWT 6.1; Heston et al. 2002). Using these data, CF's revised MPK estimates for reproducible capital, denoted by MPKL, is as in Eq. (3.3), where α_{rk} represents the income share of reproducible capital only and is derived from the difference between the total capital share in GDP and the non-reproducible capital share in GDP, i.e., $\alpha_{rk} = \alpha_w - \alpha_{nk}$. After price adjustments, the revised MPK estimates for reproducible capital, denoted by PMPKL, is as in Eq. (3.4).

$$MPKL = \alpha_{rk} \frac{Y}{K} \tag{3.3}$$

[1]Countries are classified as poor or rich following the World Bank definition. This classification divides the sample into 30 poor countries and 22 rich countries. For the list of countries used in CF (2007), see Appendix D.

$$PMPKL = \alpha_{rk} \frac{P_y Y}{P_k K} \tag{3.4}$$

CF (2007) find that the reproducible capital share (α_{rk}) tends to be low and the price of capital goods (P_k) tends to be high in poor countries, which in turn contributes to lower marginal product of reproducible capital, MPK_{rk}. When adjustments for both reproducible capital share and prices are taken into account, MPK_{rk} are quite similar across countries and, if anything, the average reproducible MPK for poor countries is lower than that for rich countries. CF (2007) further assess whether credit market imperfections are responsible for differences in marginal product of capital and find that capital reallocation, to equalize the reproducible MPK across poor and rich countries, would not change the return differentials by much given the relatively high price of investment goods and the low share of reproducible capital in total capital in most poor countries.

In some respects, CF's finding is in line with Lucas' conclusions; however, the MPK estimation method is different from Lucas. More specifically, by demonstrating that the relative income share of reproducible capital is low in poor countries when properly measured, CF's (2007) findings suggest that the Lucas paradox can be accounted for by the lack of complementary factors which would otherwise raise the return to capital. CF (2007, p. 566) conclude arguing that "[i]ncreased aid flows to developing countries are unlikely to have much impact on capital stock and output, unless they are accompanied by a return to financial repression, and in particular to an effective ban on capital outflows in these countries". In sum, CF's revised MPK estimates suggest that the variation in reproducible capital MPK between rich and poor countries is much smaller than what is implied by conventional MPK estimates and, if anything, reproducible capital MPK is higher in the rich countries.

Chirinko and Mallick (2008) (hereafter, CM) take a similar approach as CF in estimating MPK differentials between rich and poor countries but their contribution is to parameterize capital adjustment costs (ς), and show that such costs account for MPK differentials across countries. CM explain that adjustment costs "…represent lost output from disruptions to the existing production process, as new capital goods are broken-in and 'fitted' and labour is diverted from production to 'bolting-down' new capital", (CM 2008, p. 3). This adjustment cost drives a wedge between gross output (Y^G) and net output (Y^N), which in turn influences the MPK estimates. In particular, published estimates in the United Nation's System of National Accounts (SNA) of aggregate output are net of adjustment costs (i.e., $Y^N = Y^G - \varsigma$). CM argue that by using Y^N, CF fail to consider this 'adjustment cost' in estimating MPK. CM therefore 'add back' adjustment costs in the MPK estimation.

CM, consistent with CF, calculate MPK estimates under the assumptions of constant returns and perfectly competitive capital markets and use the same dataset. CM estimate MPK as follows:

$$MPK = \frac{Y^N}{K}(\alpha_{rk} + 2\varsigma) \tag{3.5}$$

where $\varsigma \equiv \frac{A(I,K)}{Y^N}$, i.e., the adjustment cost function $A(I, K)$ depends on investment (I) and capital (K), and is homogeneous of degree one and separable from gross output. If the adjustment cost is absent ($\varsigma = 0$), then Eq. (3.5) coincides with CF's estimates of MPK. However, a challenging aspect of computing this revised MPK estimates is that no data source directly provides the 'adjustment cost' ratio. CM simulate adjustment costs (ς_R) for rich and poor countries. To parameterize adjustment costs, CM use a quadratic specification (e.g., Barro and Sala-i-Martin 2004):

$$A(I, K) = \left(\frac{\beta_R}{2}\right)\left(\frac{I^2}{K}\right) \tag{3.6}$$

The marginal adjustment cost is:

$$A_I = \beta_R\left(\frac{I}{K}\right) \tag{3.7}$$

where β_R is an adjustment parameter which can be estimated from available rich country data. Different studies (e.g., Hayashi 1982; Chirinko 1995; Abel and Blanchard 1986) predict different values for this adjustment parameter. For example, if $\beta_R = 23.641$ (the β_R estimates in Hayashi 1982), the adjustment costs/net output ratio using the US's investment share of capital ($I/K = 0.079$) and investment share of net output ($I/Y^N = 0.174$) is as follows:

$$\varsigma_R \equiv \frac{A(I, K)}{Y^N} = \frac{\beta_R\left(\frac{I}{K}\right)us\left(\frac{I}{Y^n}\right)us}{2} = \frac{(23.641)(0.079)(0.174)}{2} = 0.162 \tag{3.8}$$

Thus ς_R takes different values for different estimates of β_R and it ranges from a maximum of 52% to a minimum of 3%.[2] However, CM use the United States as a benchmark for the rich countries and assume a reasonably conservative range of values for the adjustment cost ratio for rich countries (ς_R) from 4 to 5%. For poor countries, they estimate the relative adjustment cost ratio, λ ($\lambda = \frac{\varsigma_p}{\varsigma_R}$, i.e., $\varsigma_p = \lambda \cdot \varsigma_R$) where ς_p is estimated using four proxies: 'cost and time' (from Djankov, et al. 2002) and 'Dealing with licenses', 'Registering Property', and 'Starting a Business' (from World Bank's Doing Business 2008). CM assume that these proxies adequately capture frictions and constraints to entrepreneurial activity and are proportional to true adjustment costs and consider a reasonable range of values of λ from 2.00 to 3.00. CM measure the MPK differential as a ratio of average MPK (computed by CF) plus adjustment costs for poor ($\lambda \cdot \varsigma_R$) to rich ($\varsigma_R$) countries, as follows:

$$\varphi(\varsigma_R, \lambda) \equiv \frac{Mean(MPK_P^{CF}) + \lambda \cdot \varsigma_R}{Mean\left(MPK_R^{CF}\right) + \varsigma_R} \tag{3.9}$$

$$= \frac{\text{CF's average MPK estimates for poor countries} + \text{adj.cost for poor countries}}{\text{CF's average MPK estimates for rich countries} + \text{adj.cost for rich countries}}$$

[2]CM find that the adjustment costs are inversely related to per capita income.

In Eq. (3.9), differences in MPK between rich and poor countries depend on averages of MPKs and the adjustment costs parameters ($\lambda \cdot \varsigma_R$ and ς_R). CM argue that equality between financial returns and MPK, which is implicitly assumed to hold by CF, does not hold in the face of adjustment costs. CM's result suggests that the MPK differential is 100–200% higher for poor countries than that reported by CF (2007). In other words, MPK in poor countries is much higher than that in rich countries. A puzzle for CM, in contrast to Lucas and CF, is that, despite such a higher MPK in poor countries, capital does not flow from rich to poor countries to eliminate this MPK difference. CM also assess the relative influence of two other explanations of MPK differentials: relative prices differences and financial frictions. They find that the impact of 'adjustment costs' on MPK is stronger than the other two explanations of MPK differentials. CM conclude that the Lucas paradox still persists when incorporating 'adjustments costs' into the MPK estimates.

Swan (2008) measures the MPK differentials of tradable capital goods, estimating the effects of capital market imperfections. His sample consists of only 28 countries, compared to a sample of 52 countries in CF (2007). Swan (2008) disagrees with CF's (2007) conclusion that capital market imperfections do not explain capital flows. He employs the Ricardian trade model of Eaton and Kortum (2001) to re-examine international capital movements and his key variable of interest is a measure of capital market imperfections (γ_n). He argues that the World Bank's ICP (international comparison program) price index of capital goods, used in CF, does not consider differences in the quality of capital goods. In particular, the ICP-based price index implies that Zambia and USA are producing the same quality of capital goods. Swan considers *quality adjusted capital goods* and finds that per capita income and capital goods prices are inversely related. In contrast to CF (2007), Swan estimates MPK for capital good j sourced from country i to destination country n as follows:

$$MPK_{ni}(j) = \frac{\alpha_n P_n^Y Y_n}{P_{ni}^K(j) K_n \gamma_n^{\omega}} \tag{3.10}$$

where γ_n is capital market imperfections in destination country ($\gamma_n \geq 1$) and ω measures the elasticity of MPK with respect to the measure of capital market imperfection ($\omega \geq 0$). The parameter ω is the key to this MPK estimation and an additional parameter to CF's MPK estimates. If $\omega = 0$, then capital market imperfections have no impact on MPK. Following CF, Swan uses the same data on output prices (P_n^Y) and GDP (Y_n) from PWT (6.2) and total capital share α_n^w ($\alpha_n = \frac{K_n}{W} \alpha_n^w$) estimates from Bernanke and Gürkaynak (2001). A key difference with CF is that K_n in Swan's treatment includes the stock of quality-adjusted capital goods while the capital good share in income, α_n includes only tradable items.

Swan constructs (tradable) capital stock (K_n) data using bilateral trade expenditure data on capital goods, from the Center for International Data at the University of California Davis, constructed by Feenstra et al. (2005). He also constructs a capital goods (tradable) price index, $P_{ni}^K(j)$, and compares it with an ICP-based capital goods price index and finds that quality capital goods prices are higher in poor countries. Swan argues that poor countries use low quality domestically produced capital goods since they are inefficient in producing quality capital goods and face high trade barriers. Poor countries that face these barriers end up with such small stocks of quality capital goods (K_n) that the denominator still remains small even after price adjustments $\left(\frac{P_n^Y Y_n}{P_{ni}^K(j)K_n}\right)$. As a consequence, his estimated trade-based MPK (with capital market imperfections embedded) is much higher in poor countries than corresponding ICP-based estimates.

Swan then examines how much of the variance in MPK estimates can be explained by capital market imperfections. Following Levine et al. (2000), Swan uses the inverse of the ratio of private credit to GDP as a measure of capital market imperfections (or financial intermediaries imperfections) and measures the response of MPK estimates with respect to these imperfections. The argument is that financial intermediaries lower the search costs of investments, manage risks, and mobilize savings, which in turn facilitate flows of capital to the highest return locations. To address the endogeneity of capital market imperfections, Swan follows Levine et al. (2000) in using *legal origin* to instrument for the inverse of private credit to GDP. Using a 2SLS approach, he finds that the estimated coefficient (ω) of capital market imperfections (γ) is around 1.2 and is statistically significant at the 1% level. Based on this estimate, Swan suggests that a 10% increase in capital market imperfections is predicted to increase MPK by 12%, ceteris paribus. Swan, contrary to CF (2007), argues that capital market imperfections matter and MPK would be equalized across countries if these imperfections were removed. He urges that foreign investors are concerned about capital market imperfections and this might be important in understanding the Lucas paradox.

Swan's finding provides support for the existence of the Lucas paradox and his finding is in line with Banerjee and Duflo (2005), who argue that imperfect credit markets cannot allocate resources efficiently due to a poor information system, lack of contract enforcement, and political pressure on borrowing. Baneerjee and Duflo argue that if these problems exist in the credit market, borrowers do not get equal treatment in borrowing and as a result none of interest rates, TFP (total factor productivity), and MPK are equalized across countries. They also argue that in the presence of imperfect credit markets, financial intermediaries, such as banks, charge much higher interest rates than the rates they pay to their depositors. Swan's finding thus supports the view of Baneerjee and Duflo that capital market failure is a potential explanation for the Lucas paradox.

More recently, Lowe et al. (2012) (hereafter, LPP) provide another perspective on the Lucas paradox, revising MPK estimates by refining further CF's reproducible capital (e.g., equipment, machinery) into public sector capital and private sector capital. They argue that MPK differs significantly between the two sectors and calculating MPK separately for private sector and public sector can explain cross-country variation in overall MPK, which in turn can provide an explanation of why capital does not flow from rich to poor countries. In particular, they revise CF's MPK estimates and calculate separately the MPK of private sector capital (MPKP) and public sector capital (PMPKG) under the same neoclassical assumptions (i.e., constant returns and perfectly competitive capital markets).

$$MPKP = \beta \frac{P_y Y}{P_k K_p} \tag{3.11}$$

$$MPKG = \gamma \frac{P_y Y}{P_k K_g} \tag{3.12}$$

where β and γ are the shares of private sector capital and public sector capital in income, respectively; K_p and K_g are the shares of private sector capital and public sector capital in total capital, respectively; and the notation for the other parameters is the same as described in CF's (2007) analysis. However, a distinctive feature of LPP's revised MPK estimates is the use of current local price data instead of purchasing power parity (PPP) data. In particular, in contrast to CF, LPP use GDP in current local prices ($P_y Y$), public capital in current local prices ($P_k K_g$), and private capital in current local prices ($P_k K_p$). They argue that the use of current local price data overcomes the limitations of and reliance on the PPP adjustments and extrapolated ICP data, which are not stable for the non-OECD countries.

LPP find that the average MPK of public sector capital is higher in rich countries compared to that in poor countries. However, the MPK of private sector capital does not vary much between rich and poor countries. More specifically, their finding suggests if a poor country has relatively low MPK in public sector capital, then this should not imply that MPK in the private sector is also low and hence capital should flow out of the poor countries to the rich countries. Based on their findings, they argue the Lucas paradox can be explained by differences in efficiencies in the public sectors between rich and poor countries. In particular, their finding suggests the possibility that overinvestment by government and a lack of checks and balances on public expenditures are responsible for a lower MPK in the public sector in poor countries. LPP's findings thus help us to understand the Lucas paradox and predict capital should flow from poor to rich countries if the overall MPK is considered (i.e., the higher overall MPK in rich countries is driven by the higher MPK in the public sector); however, we should not see capital flows out of poor countries if MPK of private sector capital is considered (i.e., MPK is almost identical between rich and poor countries). Further, LPP do not find that constraints in the financial frictions and/or differences in the complementary factors (e.g., human capital stock) between the rich and poor countries are responsible for the Lucas paradox.

Although these studies address several of the shortcomings associated with conventional MPK estimates; however, whether MPK is higher or lower in poor countries remains an open question. Even though the findings are inconclusive, this analysis has important implications for economic development in general and for capital flow guidelines for policymakers in developing countries in particular. If appropriate measures of the MPK across countries provide a convincing explanation for why capital does not flow, on average, from rich to poor countries, we should expect these revised estimates to also be useful in understanding the international reallocation of capital more generally. Specifically, if international capital flows to these relatively high MPK countries according to these revised estimates, then these revised estimates can be reasonably considered as offering an explanation to the Lucas paradox. The literature would then also inform international borrowers and lenders on which factors matter most for mutually beneficial cross-border investment flows. Following section examines whether the revised MPK estimates offer a reasonable explanation for the international capital flows actually observed.

3.3 Do Revised MPK Estimates Help Understand International Capital Flows?

3.3.1 Data and Descriptive Statistics

The revised estimates of CF's (2007) and LPP's (2012) are examined to check if the revised MPK estimates are positively correlated with international capital inflows over the period 1995–2007.[3] This time period spans the time periods examined by CF's 2007 and LPP's 2012 data sample. Scatter plot analysis are used to check whether international capital flows from low MPK to high MPK countries as suggested by CF (2007) and/or by LPP (2012). In particular, the scatter plots examine whether capital flows to countries with a higher PMPKL, i.e., the revised MPK after separation of reproducible capital and price adjustments suggested by CF, and/or with a higher MPKP, i.e., the revised MPK after separation of the private sector and public sector components of total reproducible capital suggested by LPP.

Two types of capital data are used in this scatter plot analysis: capital stock and capital flows. Lane and Milesi-Ferretti's (2007, updated 2012, hereafter, LM) capital stock data adjusted for valuation effects of capital are examined. LM (2007) construct stock data for foreign assets and liabilities and their subcomponents for 170 countries from 1970 to 2007. In particular, the valuation effects mean that they adjust the value of asset holdings (e.g., portfolio, FDI, other investment) at the end of year t, D_t, by a stock market price index, p_t (measured in dollars) and net purchases, d_t, as follows:

$$D_t = \frac{p_t}{p_{t-1}} D_{t-1} + \frac{p_t}{\bar{p}_t} d_t \tag{3.13}$$

where $\bar{p}_t$ is the average price of asset D during year t.

LM estimate stocks of FDI, portfolio, and debt based on the IMF's IFS flow data. Net foreign assets/liabilities (NFA/NFL) are calculated from the difference between total assets and total liabilities. In addition to aggregate capital data (i.e., NFA/NFL), individual types of capital are also examined: FDI, portfolio, and

[3]The revised MPK estimates of CM and Swan are not considered because CM report only the averages MPK for a rich-country-sample and a poor-country-sample and do not report country-specific MPK estimates. Swan reports MPK estimates for a small number of 28 countries only out of CF's 53 countries.

debt.[4] FDI is a category of cross-border investment associated with a resident in one country having control or a significant degree of influence (usually, 10% ownership or more of voting stock) on the management of the direct investment enterprise. FDI is the sum of equity capital, reinvested earnings, other long-term and short-term capital (e.g., intra-company loans) as shown in the balance of payments. Portfolio equity holdings measure ownership of voting stock below the 10% threshold and exclude liabilities constituting foreign authorities' reserves. Debt data include portfolio debt securities, plus bank loans and deposits and other debt instruments. LM use different data sources and construct stocks of these functional categories of data, such as IMF's (1993, 2003) International Financial Statistics (IFS) and Balance of Payments (BoP) Statistics, Bank for International Settlements (BIS), UNCTAD's (United Nations Conference on Trade and Development) World Investment Reports (various years), and also national sources.

The aim of this exercise is to understand the relationship between MPK differences and the allocation of capital across countries, which are summarized by stocks data for capital. However, MPK differences may also endogenously be determined by capital reallocation, and therefore it is also appropriate to look at short-term flows for capturing foreign investment responses to MPK differences. In doing so, averages of capital flow data over the same period 1995–2007 are used; averaging the data reduces volatility of year-specific capital flows data. FDI flows data are taken from the UNCTAD (2013) and the debt flows are calculated from the LM's debt stocks. The aggregate capital data (i.e., capital stocks or flows) and the data disaggregated by type (i.e., FDI, portfolio, and debt) included here are total net, that is, for example, net FDI (i.e., net of profit repatriation and other disinvestment) in the reporting economy from foreign sources less net FDI by the reporting economy to the rest of the world. Capital stocks and flows are expressed as percentages of GDP in order to improve the comparability of the data across countries.

In order to provide a consistent interpretation of capital stocks and capital flows in the scatter plots, the data are converted and labelled as follows. If the observation for a country lies above the zero-line this implies a net inward capital stock or flow and suggests that liabilities are greater than assets, indicating that capital flows into the country. If the observation for a country lies below the zero-line this suggests a net outward capital stock or flow and suggests that assets exceed liabilities, indicating that capital flows out of the country.

3.3.2 *Do CF's (2007) MPK Estimates Solve the Lucas Paradox? Capital Stock Data*

Net capital stock data (i.e., net external position) are plotted against MPKN, the naïve MPK (with no adjustments), and PMPKL, CF's revised MPK (reproducible capital

[4]Definitions of the types of capital are according to the IMF's Balance of Payments and International Investment Positions Manual (BPM6), Chap. 7.

share adjustment and price adjustment). MPK estimates are taken from Table II in CF and their estimates are for the year 1996. Of the 53 countries used in CF (2007), 52 are listed in the Table and used in this analysis. The exception is Hong Kong as adjusted values of MPK for Hong Kong are not reported by CF.

When net foreign liabilities holdings (NFL) are plotted against naïve MPK estimates (MPKN), the upward slope of the fitted line suggests that capital flows to relatively high-return countries (Fig. 3.1a). In contrast, if NFL are plotted against CF's revised MPK estimates (PMPKL), it appears that more international capital is accumulating in low-return countries (Fig. 3.1b), which have low-shares of reproducible capital, such as Burundi (BDI), Congo (COG), and Zambia (ZMB), compared to high-return countries that have high-shares of reproducible capital. This pattern is puzzling if we are to believe CF's revised MPK estimates help to explain the reallocation of international capital. For example, Fig. 3.1b reveals that the lowest estimated MPK (using CF's revised MPK estimates) is for Burundi, and yet Burundi is the third highest (after ZMB and COG) capital recipient. On the other hand, France is a relatively high MPK country and capital flows out from France (i.e., France is a net exporter of capital). However, this relationship may be driven by a larger share of debt in the NFL compared to stocks of aggregate capital (i.e. FDI and portfolio investments) for CF's sample. To examine this further, the two MPK estimates are plotted againsts the three types of capital: FDI, debt, and portfolio.

Examining net FDI stock data reveals a similar pattern. For the naïve MPK estimate, Fig. 3.2a shows that more FDI capital accumulates in some countries with a middle range of MPK values, with neither relatively high nor relatively low MPK receiving the bulk of foreign capital flows. On average, the relationship is positive though it appears non-linear and dispersion is relatively high, which may suggest that many factors other than MPK are important in determining FDI stock.[5] Figure 3.2b shows high-return countries accumulate less FDI capital; rather, more FDI accumulates in relatively low-return countries. Therefore, net FDI stocks also suggest that FDI accumulation is lower in CF's higher MPK countries.

Similarly, CF's revised estimates do not appear to help explain international lending patterns according to the prediction of standard theory. In particular, larger amounts of debt are accumulated by relatively low-return countries (Fig. 3.3b), based on the revised MPK estimates, on average, over the sample period. According to the naïve MPK estimates (Fig. 3.3a), however, the correlation between investment returns and debt accumulation is weak and positive. Portfolio capital shows that the volume of inflows is balanced by the outflows for most of the countries except Ireland, Finland, and Switzerland, which are dominant net portfolio capital importers, whereas Singapore and Belgium are net exporters. Portfolio capital (Figs. 3.4a, b) does not show any particular pattern of correlation. Based on the scatter plots, it is found that the relationship between international capital reallocation and capital returns (measured by MPK) does not follow the pattern predicted by standard theory

[5]This is consistent with the expectation that capital flow is heterogeneous across its types and depends on country-specific characteristics; for example, FDI targets the countries where factors complementary to capital (e.g., human capital stock) are higher.

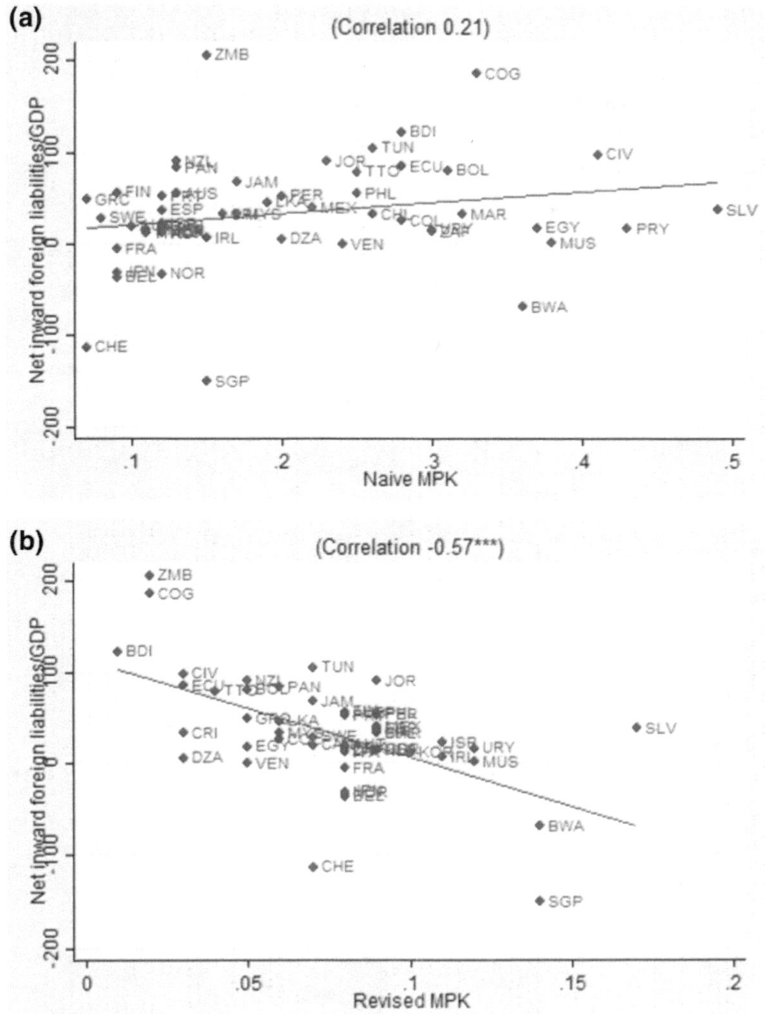

Fig. 3.1 Scatter plot analysis of capital inflows and revised MPK estimates. **a** Naive MPK and net inward foreign liabilities (NFL). **b** Revised MPK and net inward foreign liabilities (NFL)

(i.e., capital should flow to relatively higher MPK countries) if CF's revised MPK estimates are used.

CF further show how adjustments (for relative prices and reproducible capital share) reduce the variance of MPK between rich and poor countries (see Figure V in CF). They argue that MPK is high and highly variable in poor countries and low with small variance in rich countries when the naïve estimates of MPK are used (Fig. 3.5a). In particular, the differences between naïve and revised MPK estimates are larger for poor countries and the average MPK for poor countries drops from 27.2% (with a

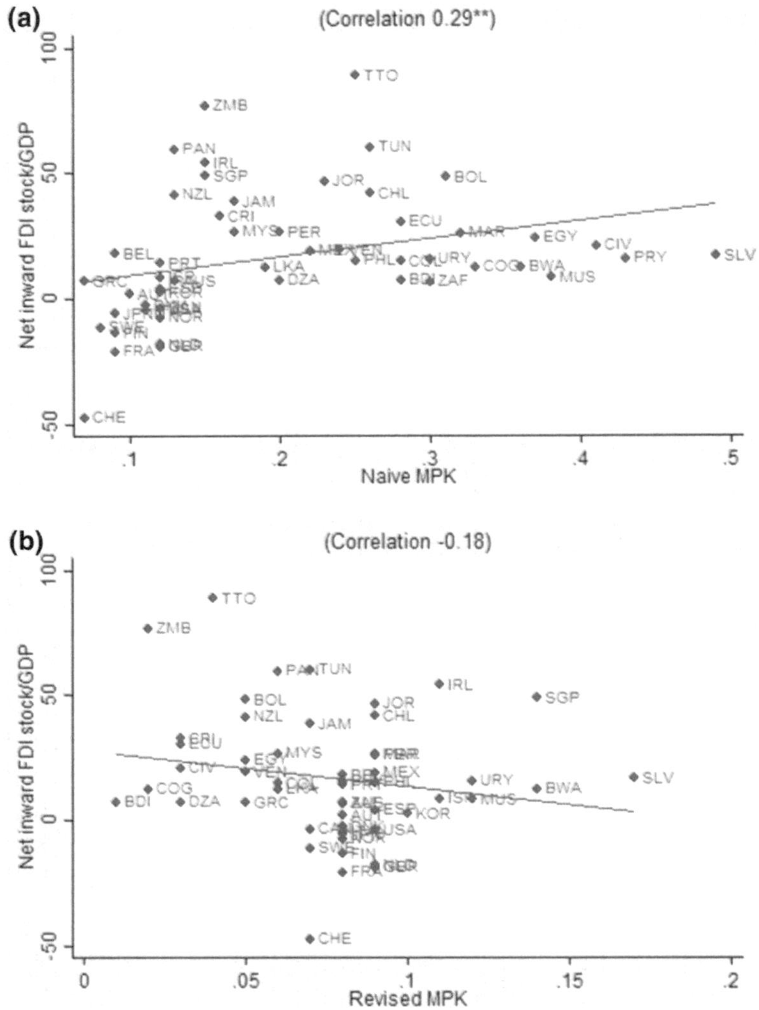

Fig. 3.2 Scatter plot analysis of capital inflows and revised MPK estimates. **a** Naive MPK and net inward FDI stock. **b** Revised MPK and net inward FDI stock

standard deviation of 9%) to 6.9% (with a standard deviation of 3.7%) if the revised MPK estimates are used. On the other hand, the reduction of average MPK for rich countries is much smaller, decreasing from 11.4% (with a standard deviation of 2.7%) to 8.4% (with a standard deviation of 1.9%) (see Table III in CF). Therefore, CF argue that if those corrections are taken into account, MPK is relatively higher in rich countries compared to poor countries (Fig. 3.5b). Their analysis appears to provide a convincing explanation of the Lucas puzzle. The relationship between the

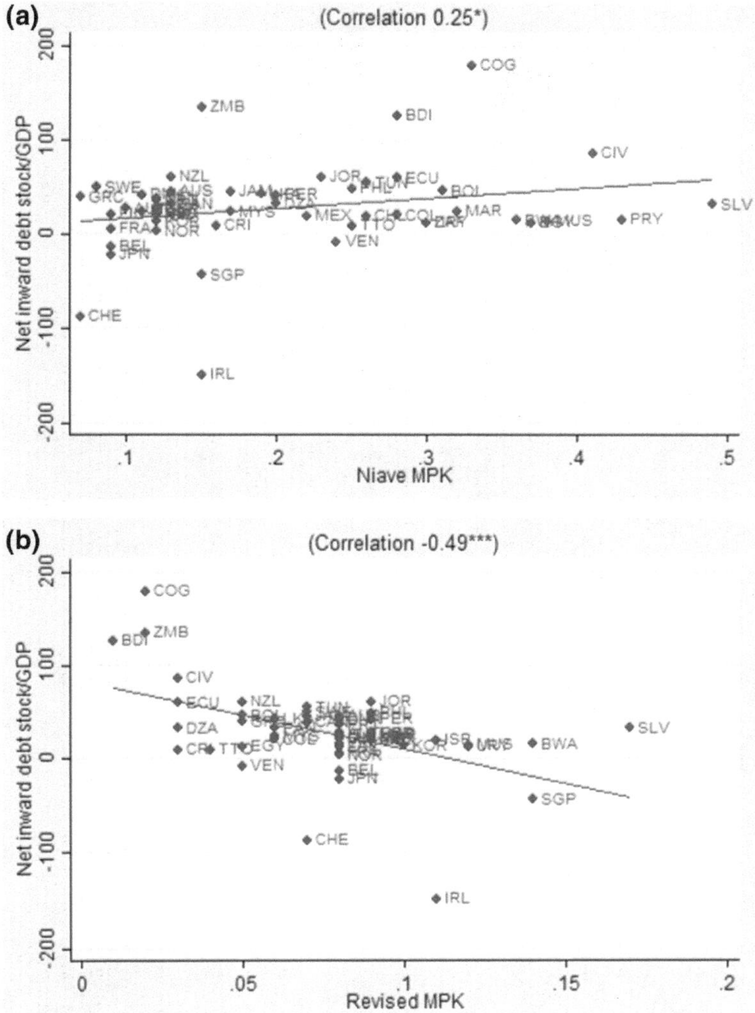

Fig. 3.3 Scatter plot analysis of capital inflows and revised MPK estimates. **a** Naive MPK and net inward debt stock. **b** Revised MPK and net inward debt stock

revised MPK estimates and capital flows rather generates a new puzzle: capital flows to low-return countries.

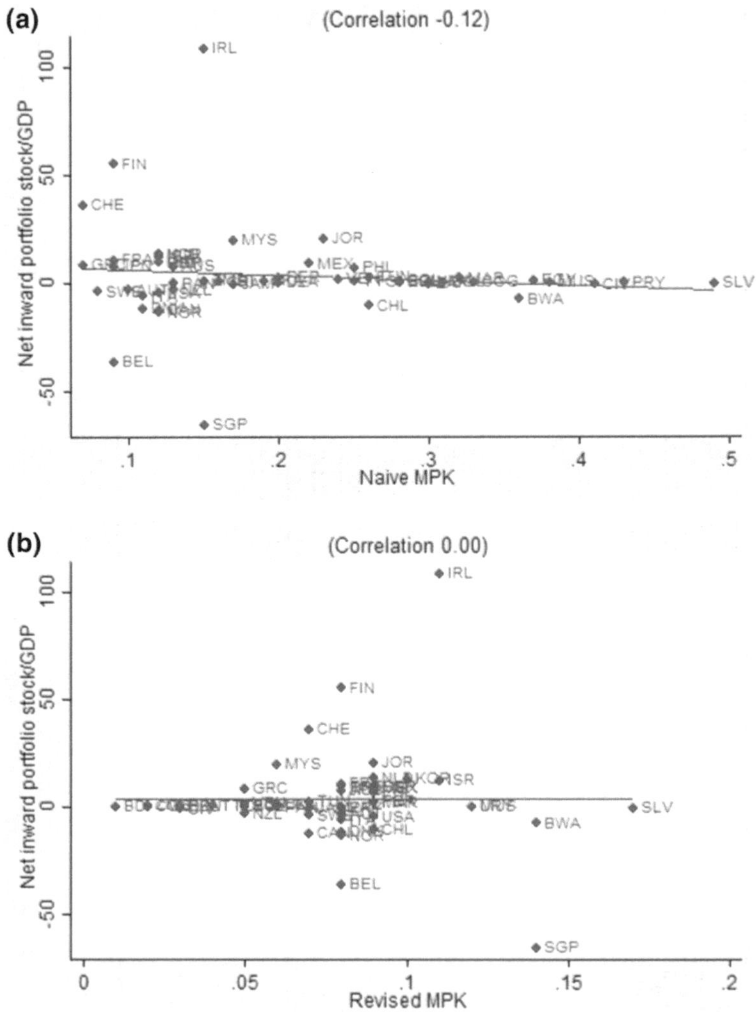

Fig. 3.4 Scatter plot analysis of capital inflows and revised MPK estimates. **a** Naive MPK and net inward portfolio stock. **b** Revised MPK and net inward portfolio stock

3.3.3 Do LPP's (2012) MPK Estimates Solve the Lucas Paradox? Capital Stock Data

We need to be cautious in analysing capital data based on LPP's revised MPK estimates. If we are to believe LPP's MPK estimates for the public sector, we should see that capital flows to countries with high MPK in their respective public sectors. However, the marginal productivity of capital in the Lucas paradox refers to private sector capital. This suggests that the Lucas paradox should not be explained by the

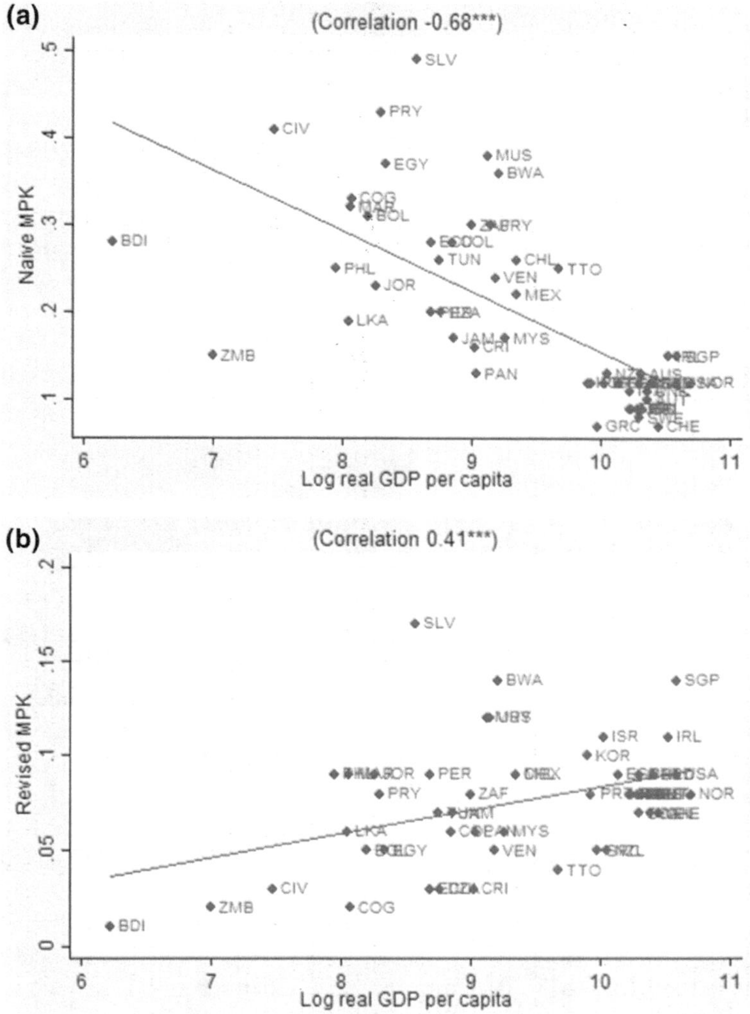

Fig. 3.5 Scatter plot analysis of capital inflows and revised MPK estimates. **a** Naive MPK and GDP per capita. **b** Revised MPK and GDP per capita

marginal productivity of public sector capital because many non-economic factors determine allocation of public sector capital. If we are to believe LPP's MPK estimates for private sector capital, we should see capital flows to countries with high private sector MPK. The revised MPK estimates of LPP's revised MPK are plotted against international capital accumulation to examine whether capital accumulates to countries with high MPK sectors. The same time span (1995–2007) for capital data is used so that we can compare LPP's scatterplot findings with that of CF.

Figure 3.6b shows a negative correlation between MPK in the private sector and net inward foreign liabilities (NFL) and suggests that more capital accumulates to low-return countries. Figure 3.6a shows a similar correlation between MPK in the public sector and net inward foreign liabilities and also suggests more capital accumulates in countries with low public sector MPK. For net inward FDI stock data (Figs. 3.7a, b), we see a weaker correlation between private sector MPK and net inward FDI. This weak correlation again points to other determinants of FDI that are potentially correlated with MPK. Debt stock data also conform to the same overall picture (Figs. 3.8a, b). It is also worth mentioning that more capital accumulating to countries with low-MPK public sectors (in Figs. 3.6a, 3.7a, and 3.8a) may suggest that official flows are determined by political considerations instead of returns to capital and more capital flows to countries with inefficient public sectors. The revised MPK estimates therefore suggests capital flows to low-return countries.

3.3.4 Do CF's and LPP's MPK Estimates Solve the Lucas Paradox? Capital Flow Data

Capital flow data are also examined against the naïve MPK and revised MPK estimates. The interpretation of capital flow data is consistent with that for capital stock data: if the observation for a country lies above the zero line this implies inflows are greater than outflows, indicating capital flows to the country; if the observation for a country lies below the zero line this implies outflows are greater than inflows, indicating capital flows out of the country.

The correlation between net inward FDI flow and the naïve MPK estimates (in Fig. 3.9a) suggests that capital flows to high-return countries, such as Congo (COG) and El-Salvador (SLV), which is consistent with the predictions of standard theory. On the other hand, when CF's revised MPK estimates are used, FDI appears to flow towards relatively low-return countries (Fig. 3.9b), including Zambia (ZMB), and Trinidad and Tobago (TTO). However, the correlation between the revised MPK estimates and FDI flows is weak (−0.18). International lending flows suggest, if CF's revised MPK estimates are used, more debt flows to low-return countries (Fig. 3.10b), such as Congo (COG), compared to high-return countries, such as Botswana (BWA).

The correlation between FDI flows and LPP's revised MPK estimates is weak. More specifically, there is no significant correlation between the revised private sector MPK and FDI flows (Fig. 3.11b). Revised public sector MPK estimates (Fig. 3.11b) suggest that FDI flows to low-return countries, such as Jordan (JOR), Bolivia (BOL), and Zambia (ZMB). Similarly, international lending flows suggest capital flows to low-return countries (Figs. 3.12a, b) whether it is public sector or private sector capital.

To summarize, a conclusion can be drawn from these scatter plot analysis for capital stocks and capital flows: the revised MPK estimates, whether these are revised based on the separation of natural capital from reproducible capital and/or separation

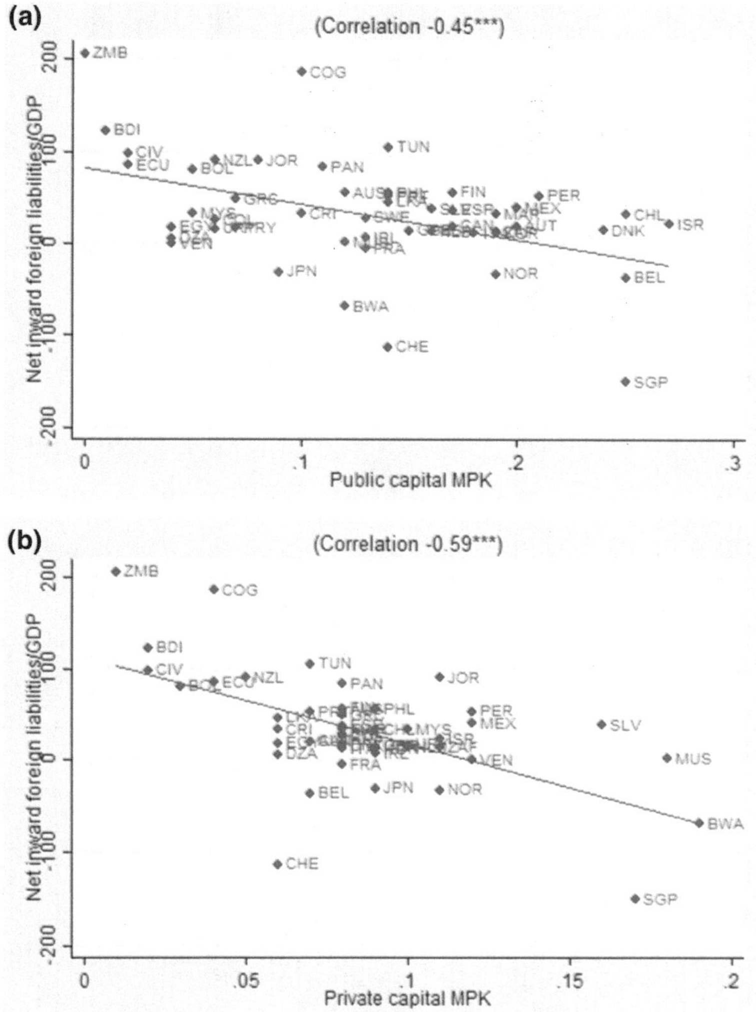

Fig. 3.6 Scatter plot analysis of capital inflows and revised MPK estimates. **a** Public MPK and net inward foreign liabilities (NFL). **b** Private MPK and net inward foreign liabilities (NFL)

of public capital and private capital from total reproducible capital, are unable to predict international capital flows. Specifically, the correlation between the revised MPK estimates and capital flow data shows capital flows to low-return countries, a pattern opposite to what standard theory suggests.

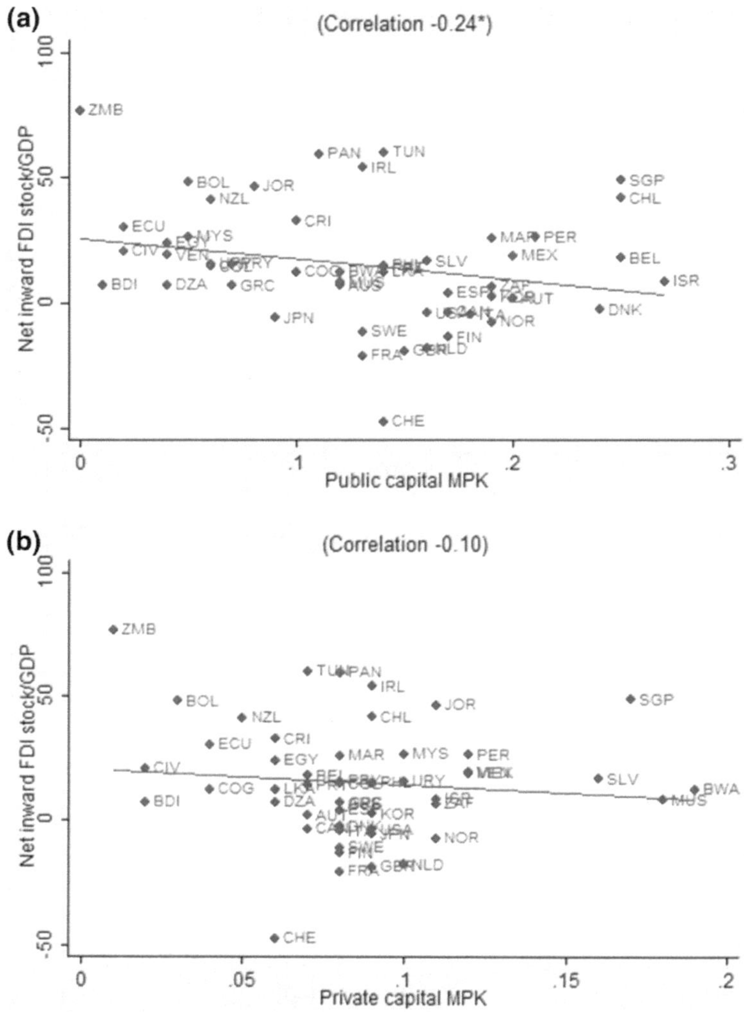

Fig. 3.7 Scatter plot analysis of capital inflows and revised MPK estimates. **a** Public capital MPK and net inward FDI stock. **b** Private capital MPK and net inward FDI stock

3.4 What Do We Learn from this Exercise?

The revised MPK estimates provided by the studies reviewed in this chapter suggest that MPK is higher in rich countries. In particular, these studies argue that if the MPK is appropriately calculated, then the average MPK is higher in rich countries and this is why we observe the lack of capital flow from rich to poor countries. The revised MPK estimates are examined against capital flow and stock data to improve our understanding of observed international capital flows. The findings suggest that

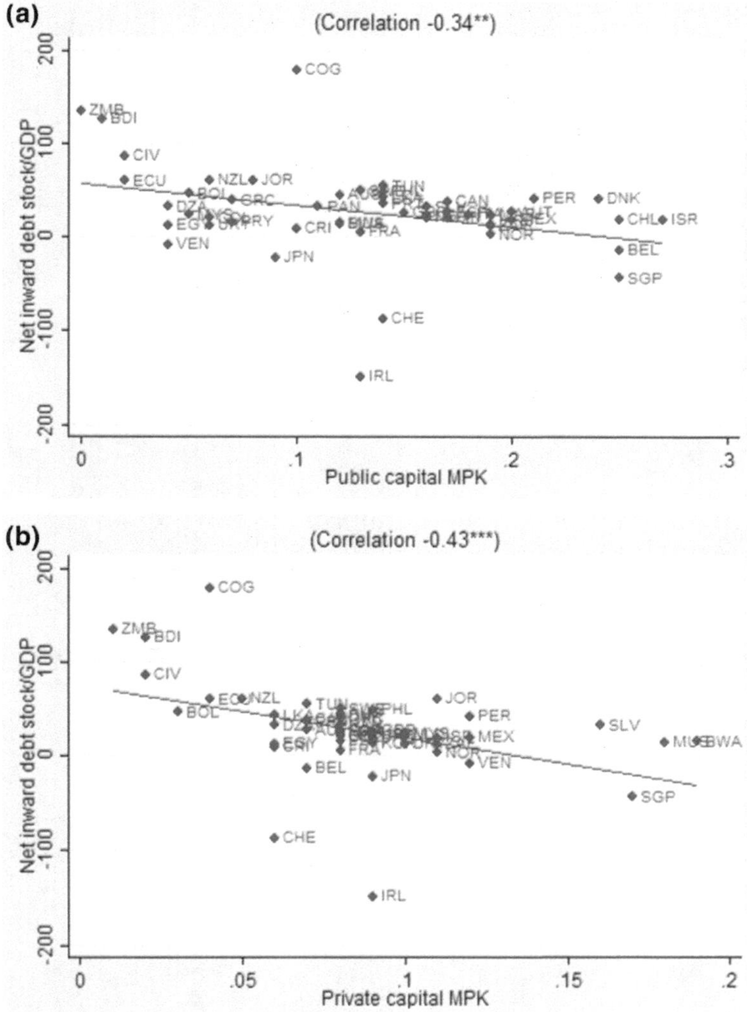

Fig. 3.8 Scatter plot analysis of capital inflows and revised MPK estimates. **a** Public capital MPK and net inward debt stock. **b** Private capital MPK and net inward debt stock

international capital, if anything, flows to relatively low-return countries based on these revised MPK estimates. Specifically, the revised estimates of CF (2007) and LPP (2012) recast the puzzle from "why doesn't capital flow to poor countries?" to a new puzzle: "why does capital flow to low-return countries?"

There are many possible explanations for this new puzzle. First, the revised MPK estimates likely do not adequately capture all factors that determine international capital flows. In particular, many other factors influencing returns on capital and eventually driving capital inflows are not explicitly taken into account in these revised

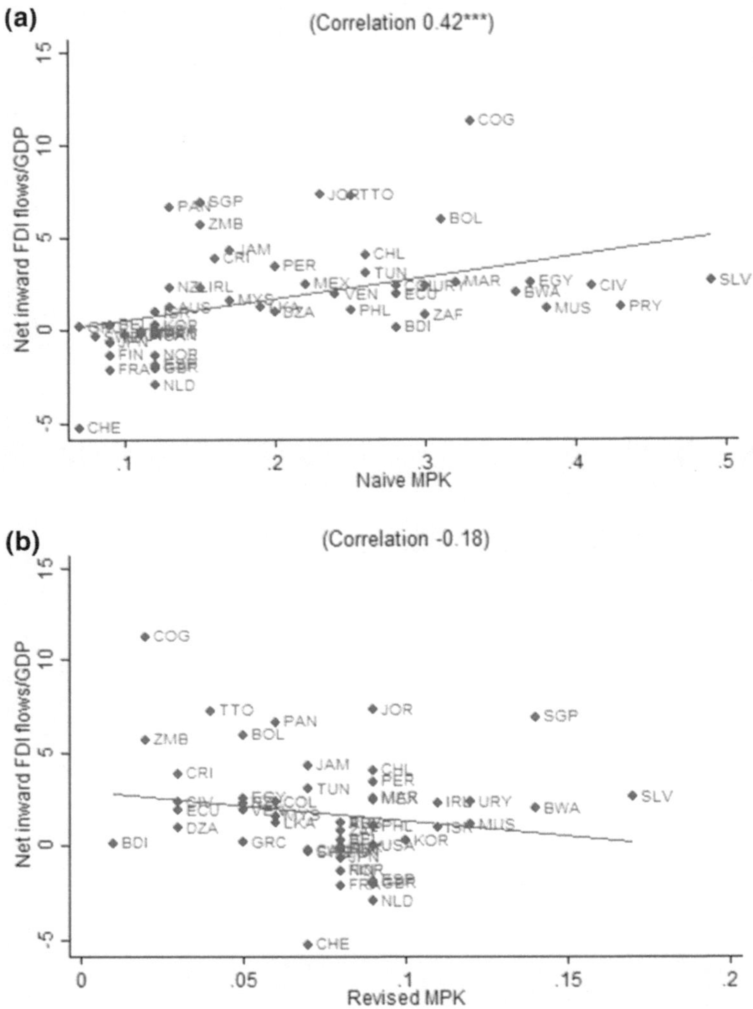

Fig. 3.9 Scatter plot analysis of capital inflows and revised MPK estimates. **a** Naive MPK and net inward FDI flows. **b** Revised MPK and net inward FDI flows

MPK estimates. More specifically, the revised MPK estimates are unable to capture fully country-specific investment incentives or investment constraints affecting *ex post* returns on capital. A discussion on the importance of these factors as potential determinants of capital inflows in the theoretical model analysis is provided in Chap. 2. Separation of the reproducible capital share from total capital and/or separation of public sector and private sector capital from total reproducible capital cannot account for these influences. However, the two dimensional scatter plots employed in this chapter are also unable to capture the effects of these multi-dimensional

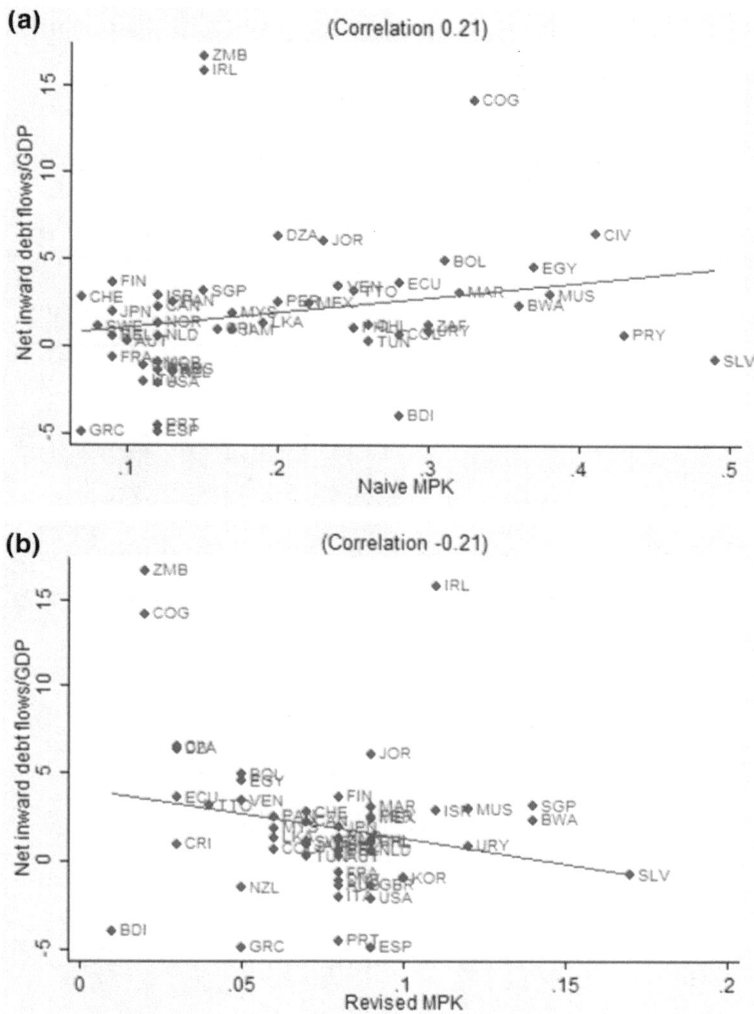

Fig. 3.10 **a** Naive MPK and net inward debt flows. **b** Revised MPK and net inward debt flows

factors. These drawbacks suggest a need for a more comprehensive framework that can capture a more diverse set of possible explanations of the Lucas paradox. The most promising avenue for addressing this need appears to be multivariate regression analysis, which is the focus of the following chapters.

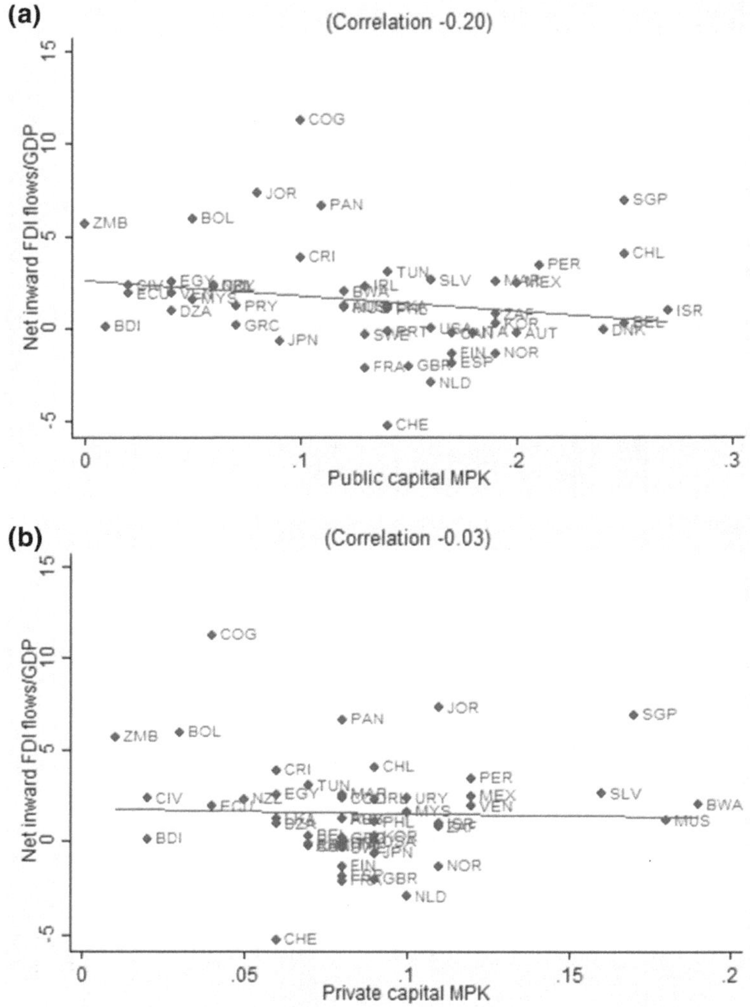

Fig. 3.11 Scatter plot analysis of capital inflows and revised MPK estimates. **a** Public capital MPK and net inward FDI flows. **b** Private capital MPK and net inward FDI flows

3.5 Net Versus Gross Capital Flows

The regression based empirical literature offers different choices of capital flows as the dependent variable, which is one of the important reasons for contrasting findings in the existing literature. More importantly, a justification for the precise choice of dependent variable is usually not provided, as the relationships being tested are not derived from a particular model. For example, in case of foreign direct investment (FDI), gross FDI inflows and net FDI inflows (defined as inward minus outward

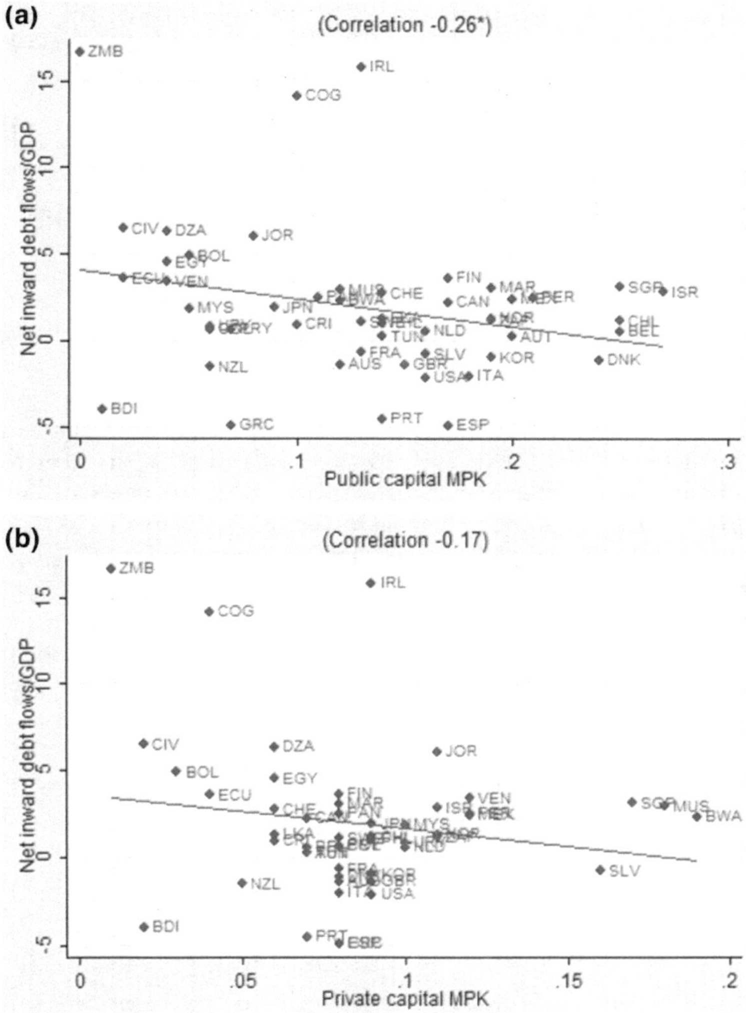

Fig. 3.12 Scatter plot analysis of capital inflows and revised MPK estimates. **a** Public capital MPK and net inward debt flows. **b** Private capital MPK and net inward debt flows

gross FDI flows) are both often used and different arguments can be made in favour of each, depending on the context. Although gross inflows appear to be more often used in the empirical literature, net FDI inflows are also used (See, for example, Asiedu 2002; Asiedu et al. 2009; Asiedu and Lein 2011; Busse and Hekefer 2007; Globerman and Shapiro 2002; Schneider and Frey 1985). Compounding ambiguity about what precisely is being measured in models with different dependent variables is the terminology of *flows* versus *inflows*: in some authors' terminology, "net FDI flows" (or "net FDI") does not mean the same thing as "net FDI inflows". Foreign direct investment itself refers to net inflows of financial capital used by a foreign owner to acquire a lasting controlling stake (usually defined as 10% or more of the voting equity shares, although reporting standards vary somewhat across countries and this threshold is sometimes higher).

According to definitions used by the World Bank's *World Development Indicators* (WDI) and the United Nations Conference on Trade and Development (UNCTAD) "net FDI inflows" corresponds to the IMF International Financial Statistics' (IFS) definition of FDI liabilities, which is the sum of direct investment equity capital, reinvestment of earnings, and other long-term and short-term capital as shown in the balance of payments net of any disinvestment by, or any claims of the foreign affiliate against, the direct investor. In other words, net FDI inflows is gross inward flows after "netting out" other financial flows such as depreciation on FDI investment in the recipient country, profit repatriation and other disinvestment (apart from FDI outflows). In contrast, "net FDI flows" refers to inflows (net) minus outflows (net): that is, the host country's liabilities (to foreign owners) net of its foreign assets (i.e., claims on assets in foreign countries). Details spelling out these definitions are found only in a small number of empirical studies (e.g., Alfaro et al. 2008; Kolstad and Villanger 2008; Jensen 2003), which clearly indicate that net FDI inflows (i.e. gross liabilities) is the dependent variable in the empirical model.[6] The terms "FDI" and "gross inflows" are used synonymously to refer to "net FDI inflows": (fully appreciating the potentially confusing clash of our "gross inflows" referring to what the World Bank and UNCTAD define as "net FDI inflows"). The terms "net FDI" and "net flows" are used to refer synonymously to "net FDI flows" (i.e., inflows minus outflows). In Chap. 6, an empirical specification is developed and discussed in detailed to show how net versus gross FDI could change empirical results and which one is more appropriate to use.

References

Abel AB, Blanchard OJ (1986) The present value of profits and cyclical movements in investment. Econometrica 54(2):249–273

Alfaro L, Kalemli-Ozcan S, Volosovych V (2008) Why doesn't capital flow from rich to poor countries? An empirical investigation. Rev Econ Stat 90(2):347–368

Asiedu E (2002) On the determinants of foreign direct investment to developing countries: is Africa different? World Dev 30(1):107–119

Asiedu E, Lien D (2011) Democracy, foreign direct investment and natural resources. J Int Econ 84(1):99–111

Asiedu E, Jin Y, Nandwa B (2009) Does foreign aid mitigate the adverse effect of expropriation risk on foreign direct investment? J Int Econ 78(2):268–275

[6]Jensen (2003) for example, uses the term "net FDI inflows" to refer to data obtained from the WDI, stating that it "…should not confused with overall net FDI flows. Net FDI flows are total FDI inflows of foreign capital minus total FDI outflows of domestic capital" (p. 597). Busse and Hefeker (2007) refer to their dependent variable as "FDI net inflows", but they explicitly define this as inflows net of outflows (or "net FDI flows" as defined in our discussion above.

Banerjee AV, Duflo E (2005) Growth theory through the lens of development economics. In: Aghion P, Durlauf SN (eds) Handbook of economic growth. Amseterdam, North-Holland Press, vol 1, pp 473–552
Barro RJ, Sala-i-Martin X (2004) Economic growth. MIT Press, Cambridge, Massachusetts
Bernanke BS, Gürkaynak RS (2001) Is growth exogenous? Taking Mankiw, Romer, and Weil seriously. Nat Bur Econ Res Macroecon Annu 16
Busse M, Hefeker C (2007) Political risk, institutions and foreign direct investment. Eur J Polit Econ 23(2):397–415
Caselli F, Feyrer J (2007) The marginal product of capital. Q J Econ 122(2):535–568
Chirinko RS (1995) Nonconvexities, labor hoarding, technology shocks, and procyclical productivity a structural econometric analysis. J Econ 66(1):61–98
Chirinko RS, Mallick D (2008) The marginal product of capital: a persistent international puzzle. CESifo working paper, no. 2399
Djankov S, La Porta R, Lopez-de-Silanes F, Shleifer A (2002) The regulation of entry. Q J Econ 117(1):1–37
Eaton J, Kortum S (2001) Trade in capital goods. Eur Econ Rev 45(7):1195–1235
Feenstra RC, Lipsey RE, Deng H, Ma AC, Mo H (2005) World trade flows: 1962–2000. National Bureau of Economic Research, working paper, no. 11040
Globerman S, Shapiro D (2002) Global foreign direct investment flows: the role of governance infrastructure. World Dev 30(11):1899–1919
Hayashi F (1982) Tobin's marginal q and average q: a neoclassical interpretation. Econometrica 50(1):213–224
Heston A, Summers R, Aten B (2002) Penn world table version 6.1. Center for International Comparisons at the University of Pennsylvania
International Monetary Fund (1993) Balance of Payments Manual, vol 5, International Monetary Fund, Washington
International Monetary Fund (2003) Foreign Direct Investment Statistics: How Countries Measure FDI, Washington, DC
Jensen NM (2003) Democratic governance and multinational corporations: political regimes and inflows of foreign direct investment. Int Org 57(03):587–616
Kolstad I, Villanger E (2008) Determinants of foreign direct investment in services. Eur J Polit Econ 24(2):518–533
Lane PR, Milesi-Ferretti GM (2007) The external wealth of nations mark II: revised and extended estimates of foreign assets and liabilities, 1970–2004. J Int Econ 73(2):223–250
Levine R, Loayza N, Beck T (2000) Financial intermediation and growth: causality and causes. J Monet Econ 46(1):31–77
Lowe M, Papageorgiou C, Perez-Sebastian F (2012) The public and private MPK. IMF. Mimeo, Washington, DC
Lucas RE (1990) Why doesn't capital flow from rich to poor countries? Am Econ Rev 80(2):92–96
UNCTAD (2013) Foreign direct investment database. Online data retrieved on March, 2013. New York and Geneva: United Nations
Schneider F, Frey BS (1985) Economic and political determinants of foreign direct investment. World Dev 13(2):161–175
Swan A (2008) New evidence on the marginal product of capital. Australian National University Mimeo
World Bank (2004) World development indicators, CD-ROM. World Bank, Washington, DC
World Bank (2008) Doing business. World Bank, Washington, DC

Chapter 4
Estimating the Determinants of Capital Inflows Using Cross Sectional Data

Abstract This chapter re-investigates the empirical studies claimed for a solution to the Lucas paradox using cross-sectional regression analysis with new specifications of the conditional mean capital inflow function. By replicating a closely related empirical work (Alfaro et al. 2008), this empirical chapter shows that differences in institutional quality (e.g., property rights) between rich and poor countries are not sufficient to explain fully why such large capital flows are observed flowing from poor to rich countries. This finding implies that, when the empirical model is specified more appropriately, differences in institutional quality cannot fully explain why capital flows to rich countries. This chapter confirms this finding using an updated dataset on capital inflows covering the most recent decade. This updated analysis shows that institutional quality alone does not solve the Lucas paradox because capital is still observed flowing to rich countries.

4.1 Introduction

Chapter 3 examined whether MPK-based analysis helps us to understand international capital flows and to explain the Lucas paradox and found that international capital flows do not follow predictions based on the revised MPK estimates. Following the failure of the MPK analysis to provide compelling answers, an alternative empirical and much larger literature based on regression analysis is considered in this chapter to examine if this empirical approach could provide a solution to the Lucas paradox. An advantage of this regression-based analysis compared to the two-dimensional scatter plot analysis is that it can utilize more data and information using a larger set of variables considered as potentially important determinants of capital inflows. The analysis begin by examining cross-section regression models and employ cross-section OLS (ordinary least squares) estimation using full-sample averages of the variables of interest. In principle, this cross-section average regression analysis is especially relevant for the variables at low frequencies, such as an index of the quality of institutions.

In the cross-section analysis, Sect. 4.2 replicates the empirical analysis of Alfaro et al. (2008), a closely related investigation into the determinants of the Lucas para-

M. Akhtaruzzaman, *International Capital Flows and the Lucas Paradox*,
https://doi.org/10.1007/978-981-13-9069-2_4

dox, and examine the robustness of their empirical findings. It is found that when the empirical model specification is adjusted to better fit the data, or when data outliers (i.e., observations that are substantially different from all other observations) are removed, Alfaro et al.'s model is no longer able to fully explain the Lucas paradox. Section 4.3 examines the Lucas paradox using this alternative empirical specification on an updated dataset and reach the same conclusion. Section 4.4 addresses identification issues (i.e., causal effects of the variables of interest) using an instrumental variables (IV) approach.

4.2 Does Institutional Quality Explain the Lucas Paradox?

Alfaro et al. (2008) investigate the determinants of capital flows for a sample of 98 countries from 1970 to 2000.[1] They provide empirical evidence suggesting that differences in institutional qualities between rich and poor countries help to explain the Lucas paradox. In particular, their main argument is that the positive and significant correlation between per capita income and per capita inflows disappears if an index of institutional quality is included in the regression model. Alfaro et al. (2008) use a cross-section approach as they argue that most of the explanatory variables in their model are slowly changing over time; in particular, their main variable of interest, an institutions index (the International Country Risk Guide's measure of institutional quality), shows almost no time variation during the sample period.

The basic specification of their empirical model is:

$$F_i = \mu + \beta_1 logY_i + \beta_2 I_i + \gamma X_i + \varepsilon_i \tag{4.1}$$

where F_i, average per capita inflows of direct and portfolio equity investment, is a function of the log of initial GDP per capita (Y_i), the institutions index (I_i), controls (X_i), and a stochastic error term (ε_i).

Capital inflows (F_i) are the sum of FDI inflows and portfolio equity inflows. Alfaro et al. (2008) use capital inflows data from the International Financial Statistics (IFS) of the International Monetary Fund (IMF). FDI is the sum of equity capital, reinvested earnings, other long-term capital, and short-term capital as shown in the balance of payments.[2] Portfolio investment excludes liabilities constituting foreign authorities' reserves and covers transactions in equity securities and debt securities. The institutions index is taken from Political Risk Services (PRS) group's 'political risk' rating, which is their aggregate International Country Risk Guide (ICRG) index. Alfaro et al. (2008) use initial year's (1970) purchasing power parity (PPP) adjusted

[1]Alfaro et al. (2008) is one of the most highly cited works in the empirical literature on the determinants of capital inflows that uses a cross-section approach and this chapter reviews their work.

[2]According to the IMF (BPM6), an investment is considered as direct if a foreigner holds a controlling stake of at least 10% of the local firm's equity. Portfolio equity holdings measure ownership of voting stock below the 10% threshold.

GDP per capita from the Penn World Table 6.1 (Heston et al. 2002) and constant US dollars GDP per capita deflated by US CPI (1996) from World Development Indicators (WDI), World Bank (2004). Alfaro et al. (2008) also include additional controls (X_i): average years of schooling from Barro and Lee (2001) to measure levels of human capital; IMF's (2001) de jure measure of legal restrictions on cross-border capital flows to measure capital account restrictions; and construct a distantness index to measure remoteness and information frictions.

Alfaro et al. (2008) claim that cross-country differences in institutional quality alone can account for the Lucas paradox; more specifically, they suggest that other factors, such as human capital and capital account restrictions, are far less important than property rights security, absence of corruption, and political stability in explaining the vast discrepancies in cross-country capital flows. They also claim that the institutions index has an exogenous causal effect on capital inflows on the basis of their instrumental variable (IV) estimation. These findings suggest a definitive solution to the Lucas paradox and merit further investigation.

Carefully observing their empirical approach and the properties of their data, standard diagnostic checking were applied to their results and found that their findings are not entirely convincing. Firstly, a histogram plot reveals that their dependent variable is highly skewed (Fig. 4.1a) and has a long right tail. Transforming a highly skewed variable can often produce a relatively more symmetric distribution and, in this particular case, a log-transformed dependent variable (per capital inflows) is used.[3] A logarithmic transformation is often employed to obtain a more homogenous variance of the variable of interest and increases forecast precision (Lütkepohl and Xu 2011). Following this argument, a log-transformed version of their dependent variable is used and is found as much more symmetric and more closely approximates a normal distribution (Fig. 4.1b).

Alfaro et al.'s cross-section OLS results are replicated with the log-transformed dependent variable, and mixed results.[4] Alfaro et al.'s Tables 3 and 4 are reproduced using their specification (i.e., Eq. 4.1) and compare their estimates to those obtained from estimating the log-transformed specification (i.e., Eq. 4.2):

$$log^*(F_i) = \mu + \beta_1 log Y_i + \beta_2 I_i + \gamma X_i + \varepsilon_i \qquad (4.2)$$

Table 4.1 replicates Alfaro et al.'s Table 3 using both untransformed and log-transformed dependent variables. Column 2 replicates Alfaro et al.'s original model (i.e., with an untransformed dependent variable, which is labelled as linear model) using their data set and shows that inclusion of an index of institutions fully explains the Lucas paradox, meaning that the positive and statistically significant effect of GDP per capita becomes insignificant after inclusion of institutional quality in the

[3] A transformation method is followed as is used by Burbidge et al. (1988) and is known as inverse hyperbolic sine (IHS) transformation: $y = \ln\left(x + \sqrt{x^2+1}\right)$. For simplicity, it is referred as log* and this transformation is used throughout the thesis unless otherwise stated. Busse and Hefeker (2007) also used this transformation. See details of this transformation in Appendix A.

[4] The author is grateful to the Alfaro et al. for sharing their dataset.

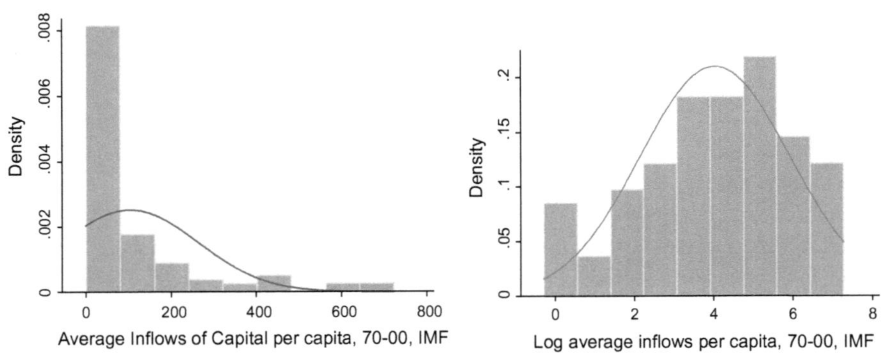

(a) Untransformed variable (b) Log-transformed variable

Fig. 4.1 Histogram plots of dependent variable: per capita inflows, 1970–2000

model. However, inclusion of the institutions index does not change the statistical significance of GDP per capita in model with the log-transformed dependent variable (i.e., the log model), suggesting that inclusion of the institutions index can no longer solve the Lucas puzzle of uphill capital flows (Column 2*).

The Lucas paradox is stronger (in terms of statistical significance) in the log model with outliers removed (Column 2**).[5] Moreover, the estimates of Alfaro et al.'s linear model are sensitive to outliers.[6] In particular, if their model (i.e., without log-transformation) is run removing five outlier observations (Sweden, Denmark, Finland, Great Britain, and Netherlands from their 98-country Whole World Sample), GDP per capita retains its statistical significance even though index of institutions is controlled for (Column 2′). A similar result is obtained for Alfaro et al.'s Base Sample (Columns 3–7), i.e., inclusion of the index of institutions does not solve the Lucas puzzle in their Base Sample of 81 countries. In particular, the log transformation for the Base Sample (Column 4*) gives the same result as in the Whole World Sample (Column 2*). If GDP per capita data are taken from the WDI (i.e., constant US dollars instead of PPP adjusted), the log model for the Base Sample (Column 7*) gives the same result and suggests that including an index of institutional quality cannot solve the Lucas paradox even if the outliers are not removed.

A critical point is then to determine whether log*-model is a more appropriate specification than the linear specification employed in Alfaro et al. (2008). Histogram plot suggests that the untransformed dependent variable used by Alfaro et al. is highly skewed (Fig. 4.1a) compared to the log*-transformed dependent variable (Fig. 4.1b); however, the residuals (from Column 2 in Table 4.1) appear to be approximately

[5]Outlier observations have large residuals. To identify outliers, studentized residuals are used. Eight outliers in the log* model (2**) are: Singapore, South Africa, Trinidad and Tobago, Sweden, Ukraine, Senegal, Iran, and Zimbabwe.

[6]The studentized residual plot shows that there are five outliers in linear model and sorting the 10 largest and the 10 smallest residuals, the residuals of Sweden exceeds −2.5 and those of Finland, Denmark, Netherlands, and Great Britain exceed 2.5.

Table 4.1 Replication of Alfaro et al.'s Table 3, N = 98 countries, 1970–2000[a]

Variables		Whole world	Whole world	Whole world	Whole world	Whole world	Base sample	Base sample	Base sample	Base sample	Base sample	Base sample	Base sample
		Linear	Linear	Log*	Linear	Log*	Linear	Linear	Log*	Linear	Linear	Linear	Log*
		(1)	(2)	(2*)	(2/)	(2**)	(3)	(4)	(4*)	(5)	(6)	(7)	(7*)
Log GDP per capita (PPP), 1970		**1.05***** (0.17)	**0.20** (0.13)	**0.69**** (0.27)	**0.24**** (0.11)	**0.97***** (0.18)	**1.18***** (0.19	**0.14** (0.20)	**0.85***** (0.22)				
Log GDP per capita, 1970											**0.84** (0.13)	**0.20** (0.13)	**0.49**** **(.23)**
Av institutional quality, 1984–2000			**0.68***** (0.14)	**0.51***** (0.18)	**0.49***** (0.10)	**0.47***** (0.10)		**0.75***** (0.17)	**0.51***** (0.12)	**0.82***** (0.12)		**0.67***** (0.15)	**0.47**** (0.23)
R-squared		0.37	0.52	0.47	0.54	0.78	0.39	0.52	0.81	0.52	0.44	0.53	0.46
Observations		98	98	98	93	90	81	81	73	81	81	81	81
Normality test	Doornik-Hansen	0.00	0.00	0.00	0.00	0.64	0.00	0.00	0.50	0.00	0.00	0.00	0.00
	Shapiro-Wilk	0.00	0.00	0.00	0.00	0.28	0.00	0.00	0.11	0.00	0.00	0.00	0.00
Heteroscedasticity	White	0.00	0.00	0.74	0.00	0.17	0.00	0.00	0.18	0.00	0.00	0.00	0.77
	Breusch-Pagan	0.00	0.00	0.36	0.00	0.02	0.00	0.00	0.16	0.00	0.00	0.00	0.36
RESET		0.00	0.00	0.62	0.00	0.08	0.00	0.00	0.03	0.00	0.00	0.00	0.73
RMSE		1.26	1.11	1.39	0.76	0.78	1.33	1.19	0.74	1.18	1.70	1.18	1.44

Notes Columns 2* and 7* use log* (per capita inflows) as dependent variables, Columns 2** and 4* use log* (per capita inflows) as dependent variables and remove outliers, Column 2/ removes outliers but does not use log* dependent variable, and the other remaining models use per capita inflows as dependent variable. Robust standard errors are in parentheses, ***$p<0.01$, **$p<0.05$, *$p<0.1$. Diagnostic tests: p-values are reported. For comparability of our coefficient estimates with those of the authors

[a]As with Alfaro et al., the 98-country Whole World Sample includes all countries with data available for per capita inflows, GDP per capita, and the index of institutions and excludes countries with population less than a million. The Base Sample is composed of 81 countries out of 98 countries for which all the main explanatory variables are available

normally distributed based on inspection of Fig. 4.2a. To dig a bit deeper into why the residual density plot of the untransformed model used by Alfaro et al. looks normal, it might be that the outlier observations in their sample may have contributed to this finding. The influence of these outliers on the residuals emerges in the residual density plot from the fitted regression (i.e., Column 2′) in Table 4.1. Excluding these outliers, the apparent residual normality of their untransformed model is largely reduced (Fig. 4.2b). The residual density plot is closest to being normally distributed (Fig. 4.2d) if log* model is used with outliers removed (i.e., Model 2** in Table 4.1).

A formal diagnostic tests is conducted for normality, homoscedasticity, and functional form to test whether Alfaro et al.'s linear model or the log* model better fit the data.[7] Specifically, the diagnostic tests examine which of the two alternative specifications (i.e., linear or log*) is closer to satisfying the underlying assumptions required for desirable statistical properties and validity of inference. The diagnostic tests results suggest that the log* models (e.g., Model 2* in Table 4.1) satisfies more of the formal tests but still exhibits residual non-normality.

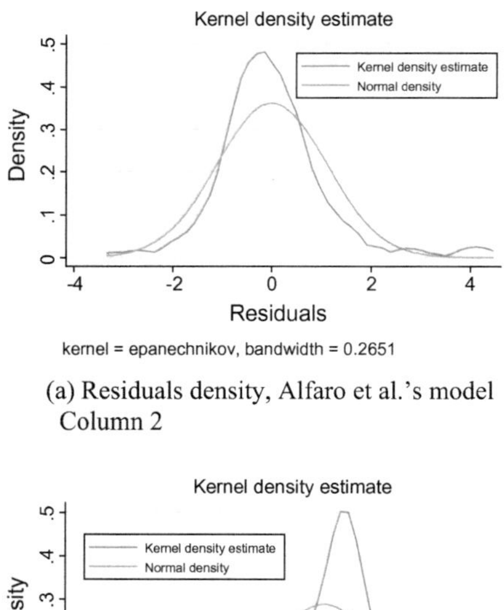

(a) Residuals density, Alfaro et al.'s model Column 2

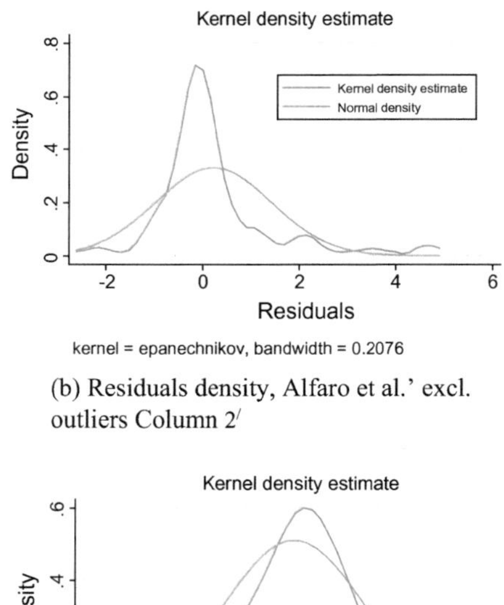

(b) Residuals density, Alfaro et al.' excl. outliers Column 2′

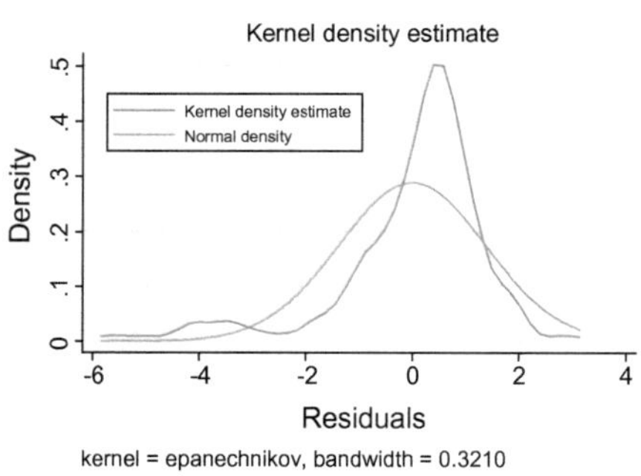

(c) Residuals density, log*-model incl. outliers Column 2*

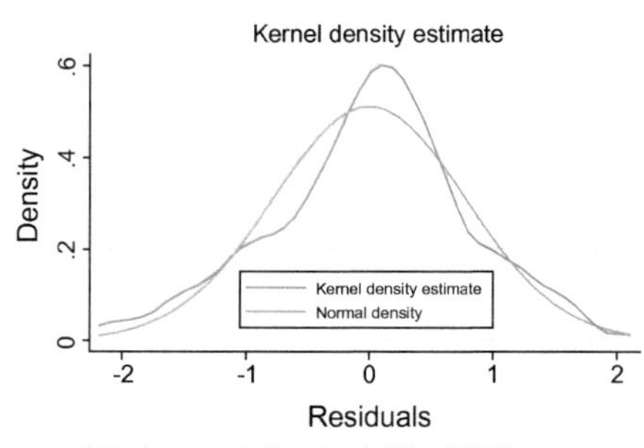

(d) Residuals density, log*-model excl. outliersColumn 2**

Fig. 4.2 Kernel density and normal density of estimated residuals: 1970–2000

---

[7] See details of the diagnostic tests in Appendix A.

However, the fitted model performs better with respect to the diagnostic tests if the eight outliers are removed from the log* model (Model 2** in Table 4.1).[8] Examining the residual density plots for the log* model with outliers removed (i.e., Fig. 4.2d) shows that this model is closer to being normally distributed compared to the log* model including outliers (Fig. 4.2c).

In addition, a graphical presentation of heteroscedasticity in the residuals of the estimated regressions also suggests that the log* model better fits the data. A model with homoscedastic errors should not show any pattern to the residuals plotted against fitted values. The plotted residuals from our log* model against fitted values (Fig. 4.3b) show that there is no such pattern, whereas in Alfaro et al.'s linear model the residuals are more widely spread at higher fitted values (Fig. 4.3a). Alfaro et al. use White's heteroscedasticity-corrected standard errors to treat the symptoms of the problem; however, this cannot solve the underlying problem if heteroscedasticity is due to model misspecification. Moreover, there is a larger difference between robust and conventional standard errors if linear model is used.[9] However, the standard errors are almost the same in the log* model. In particular, for the coefficient of GDP per capita, conventional standard errors (0.20) are almost twice as large as robust standard errors (0.13) in the linear model (Model 2, Table 4.1) whereas they are 0.25 and 0.27 respectively in the log* model (Model 2*, Table 4.1). This difference between conventional and robust standard errors also suggests model misspecification if the linear model is used.

Table 4.2 replicates Alfaro et al.'s Table 4 and examines other proposed explanations of the Lucas paradox, such as years of schooling, distantness, and capital

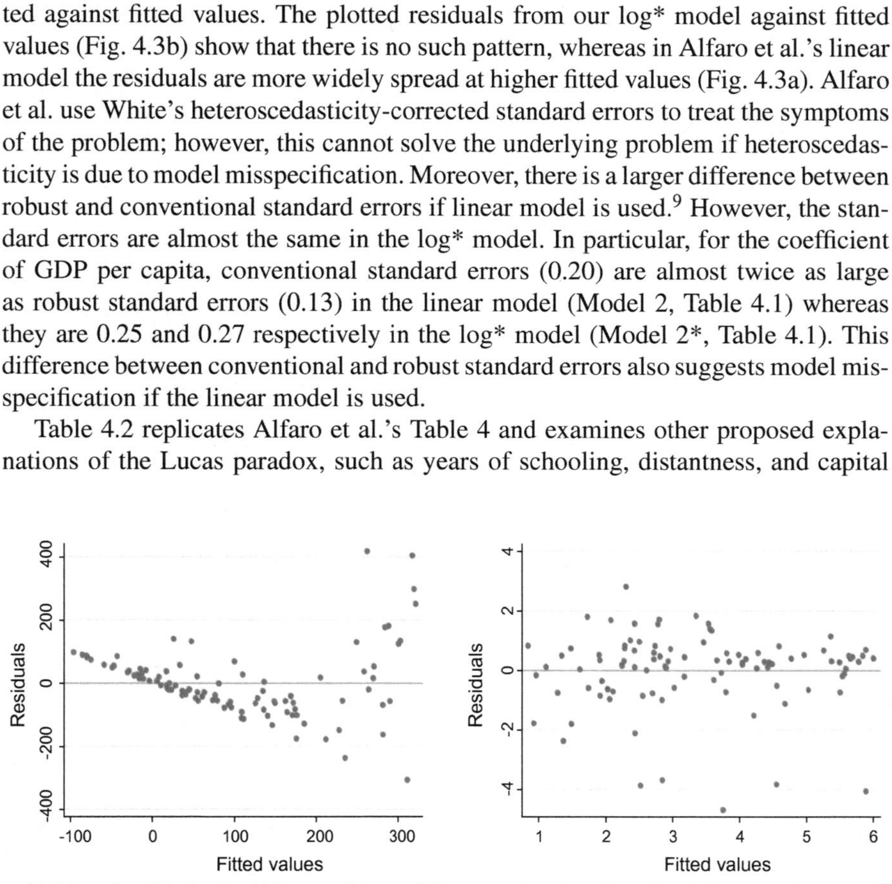

(a) Plot of residuals for Alfaro et al.'s model (b) Plot of residuals for the log* model

Fig. 4.3 Heteroscedasticity of residuals: 1970–2000

[8]Outliers are also identified by using studentized residuals and it is necessary to remove eight outliers that exceed +2 and −2; otherwise the estimates do not satisfy the diagnostic tests.

[9]King and Roberts (2014) argue that a large difference between conventional and robust standard errors is a 'bright red flag' of model misspecification.

controls.[10] A similar conclusion is reached for their full model; when the dependent variable is log* transformed, institutions no longer solve the Lucas paradox (Columns 7* and 8*, Table 4.2). In particular, among the alternative explanations of the Lucas paradox, only the capital account restrictions variable is statistically significant and has a negative impact on capital inflows in the linear model. In the log* model, by contrast, in addition to GDP per capita and institutional quality, years of schooling (i.e., human capital) is a statistically significant determinant and increases capital inflows, while restrictions to the capital account become statistically insignificant. Our preferred specification (i.e., the log* model) also suggests that institutions cannot solve the Lucas paradox even after adding additional controls. Moreover, the log* models removing outliers (Models 7* and 8*) pass the diagnostic tests and confirm that institutions cannot solve the Lucas paradox if an appropriately specified model is employed.

Alfaro et al. (2008, p. 355) argue that "....[r]ecent research on institutions and development shows that these two variables are highly collinear because the historically determined component of institutions is a very good predictor for income in 1970. Nevertheless, our index of institutions is significant at the 1% level, while the log GDP per capita is not". In contrast, our results suggest that the statistical insignificance of GDP per capita is due to model misspecification or is dependent on outliers. Rather, the Lucas paradox is still alive and the institutions index, while a significant determinant of capital inflows, does not fully account for why capital tends to predominantly flow to relatively rich countries.

Keskinsoy (2012) examined if the institutional quality can explain the Lucas paradox using cross-section averaged data of a sample of 47 developing countries from 1970 to 2006. The author found that institutional quality cannot explain the Lucas paradox if the Lucas paradox is examined on developing economies. However, Keskinsoy's work cannot be considered as investigating to find a solution to the Lucas paradox. The sample should include both developed and developing countries in order to identify whether capital flows follow the prediction of neoclassical model or consistent to the Lucas paradox.

Azémar and Desbordes (2013) (hereafter, AD) also reconsider the model estimated by Alfaro et al. and reach a similar conclusion. Our analysis, which was carried out independently of their work, differs in several ways from AD. First, this replication uses Alfaro et al.'s original data set and shows how Alfaro et al.'s estimates are changed with alternative specifications. Alfaro et al. use the IMF's IFS capital flow data for their main analysis and also use Lane and Milesi-Ferretti's (2007, updated 2012, hereafter, LM) capital stock data for robustness checking, whereas AD's analysis is based solely on the LM data. AD use a different method (S-estimator by Verardi and Croux 2008) to identify outlier observations and find six outliers: Botswana, India, Kuwait, Panama, Singapore, and Zimbabwe for the LM data. Our studentized residual test using the authors' original IFS data suggests the

[10]The Barro and Lee (2010) data set provides schooling data for 82 countries out of Alfaro et al.'s 98 country sample, although Alfaro et al. report that N = 92 in their Table 4. Alfaro et al.'s own data set also contains schooling data for only 82 countries.

Table 4.2 Replication of Alfaro et al.'s Table 4, N = 98 countries, 1970–2000

Variables		Whole world	Whole world	Whole world	Base sample	Base sample	Base sample	Base sample	Base sample	Base sample	Base sample
		Log*	Log*	Log*	Log*	Log*	Log*	Log*	Log*	Log*	Log*
		(1)	(2)	(3)	(4)	(5)	(6)	(7)	(7*)	(8)	(8*)
Log GDP per capita (PPP) 1970		1.12***	0.99***	0.82***	1.14***	1.11***	0.91***	0.13	0.56**	0.21	0.47***
Log GDP per capita ($1996) 1970		(0.24)	(0.17)	(0.14)	(0.24)	(0.19)	(0.16)	(0.19)	(0.23)	(0.16)	(0.16)
Average institutional quality, 1984–2000								0.65*** (0.16)	0.48*** (0.11)	0.59*** (0.14)	0.43*** (0.12)
Log average schooling 1970–2000		0.09 (0.18)			0.06 (0.18)			−0.10 (0.15)	0.47** (0.16)	−0.19 (0.20)	0.40** (0.17)
Log average distantness			−0.68 (0.71)			−0.58 (0.73)		−0.29 (0.60)	0.50* (0.30)	−0.28 (0.60)	0.48 (0.30)
Average restrictions to capital mobility				−1.54*** (0.53)			−1.83*** (0.61)	−1.23** (0.48)	−0.62 (0.41)	−1.18** (0.46)	−0.60 (0.37)
R-squared		0.39	0.38	0.42	0.39	0.39	0.45	0.54	0.83	0.55	0.84
Observations		82	97	97	81	81	81	81	73	81	73
Normality test	Doornik-Hansen	0.00	0.00	0.00	0.00	0.00	0.00	0.00	0.61	0.00	0.34
	Shapiro-Wilk	0.00	0.00	0.00	0.00	0.00	0.00	0.00	0.62	0.00	0.33
Heteroscedasticity	White's	0.00	0.00	0.00	0.00	0.00	0.00	0.01	0.05	0.01	0.15
	Breusch-Pagan	0.00	0.00	0.00	0.00	0.00	0.00	0.00	0.29	0.00	0.42
RESET		0.00	0.00	0.00	0.00	0.00	0.00	0.00	0.31	0.00	0.23
RMSE		1.34	1.26	1.22	1.34	1.33	1.27	1.18	0.69	1.28	0.67

Notes 7* and 8* are the log* models excluding outliers. The insignificance of GDP per capita in Model 7 is due to the existence of outliers in the log* model, which does not satisfy any of the diagnostic tests, suggesting Model 7* is a preferred model. Robust standard errors are in parentheses, $***p < 0.01$, $**p < 0.05$, $*p < 0.1$. Diagnostic tests: p-values are reported. See Appendix B for detailed explanations of all variables and sources outlier observations are Sweden, Denmark, Netherlands, Great Britain, and Finland for the linear model. AD's choice of preferred models is based purely on goodness-of-fit. Unlike AD, our selection of model specification is based on diagnostic testing of normality, homoscedasticity, and functional form.

More importantly, a basic difference between our exercise and that of AD is a difference in motivation. Our replication exercise is motivated by the broader objective of arriving at a more general empirical model of capital inflows and to provide a more comprehensive test of the Lucas paradox. In doing so, replication of Alfaro et al. is just a first step. In the next sections, the Lucas paradox is examined using an updated dataset and alternative sources of data for capital inflows, and consider alternative types of capital flows (public flows and private flows) as robustness checks of our findings. Further, Chap. 4 examines other empirical model-based explanations of the Lucas paradox (e.g., interaction effects of two independent determinants) using alternative econometric approaches (i.e., panel fixed effects and dynamic models). Therefore, empirical findings of this analysis are based on a broader perspective that allows us to formulate a more general appropriately specified empirical model of the determinants of capital inflows that helps us to address the question: what factors (if any) are sufficient to explain the Lucas paradox?

4.3 Cross Section Analysis Using an Updated Dataset, 1984–2017

The determinants of capital inflows are examined in cross-section model using an updated dataset from 1984 to 2017 for Alfaro et al.'s Whole World Sample.[11] Cross-section OLS is run on the log* model (i.e., Eq. 4.2) using averages of the variables over the full sample period (1984–2017) and the results are compared to Alfaro et al. as a benchmark. The following section first explains which specific variables are considered in measuring the key determinants (fundamentals, institutions, and frictions), the dependent variable, and the controls.[12] This section also provides detailed definitions and discusses the challenges of properly measuring key variables. The following discussion proceeds based on the broad categories of the determinants of capital inflows as discussed in the literature review section.

[11]Alfaro et al.'s (2008) country sample was retained as it contains a sufficiently large number of countries excluding outlier countries and countries with population less than a million. Moreover, using the same country sample for the updated data helps us to understand better the empirical findings compared to a benchmark estimation result.

[12]For additional descriptions of sources of data and data construction, see Appendix B.

4.3.1 Data and Descriptive Statistics

Dependent Variable

The dependent variable is the sum of direct (i.e., FDI) and portfolio equity inflows, which is common (e.g., Alfaro et al. 2008) in this regression-based literature.[13] The inflows here are *gross* inflows net of disinvestment and profit repatriation NOT *net* inflows (i.e., inflows minus outflows).[14] More specifically, the dependent variable in our empirical model is *gross* inflows of FDI and portfolio equity NOT *net* equity inflows (i.e., inflows minus outflows). *Gross* inflows was used instead of *net* inflows because this is in line with most of the literature on the Lucas paradox, allowing for maximal comparability of the findings. The reasons of why *gross* measure is preferred over net is explained in Chap. 3 (Sect. 3.4) and will be discussed in more detail in Chap. 6 (Sect. 6.3.1). Gross inflows per capita (i.e., dividing by a country's population) is calculated and is used as the dependent variable. The terms 'capital inflows', 'per capita inflows', and 'capital inflows per capita' are used in this chapter to refer synonymously to this dependent variable throughout this book, if not mentioned otherwise.

The data are taken from two different sources: annual inflows data of direct and portfolio equity are taken from the International Financial Statistics (IFS) of the International Monetary Fund (IMF), which is a standard source for capital data in this literature (e.g., used in Alfaro et al. 2008; Papaioannou 2009). For an alternative source of capital data, annual inflows data are calculated from LM's (2007, updated 2012) direct and portfolio equity stock data set.

Fundamentals

In the regression-based literature (e.g., Noorbakhsh et al. 2001; Alfaro et al. 2008; Papaioannou 2009), a commonly used variable in the set of fundamentals is the stock of human capital, measured by the average years of schooling from Barro and Lee (1996, updated 2010). Barro and Lee's data show the average years of schooling of persons of age 25 or above, based on information from the United Nation's Educational, Scientific and Cultural Organization (UNESCO) Statistical Yearbook, U.N. Demographic Yearbooks and some other sources.[15] An issue with these schooling data as a measure for fundamentals is that they do not adjust for the quality of edu-

[13]In this chapter, sum of direct and portfolio equity inflows are used as capital inflows and as the dependent variable; because, including debt might complicate the results because private debt may be partially substitutable for public debt and in this case private debt may be influenced by factors beyond the scope of this analysis. See Sect. 4.3.4 for further discussion on this point.

[14]The IMF's Balance of Payments manual suggests that, the net recording in the financial account means aggregations whereby all debit entries of a particular asset type are netted against all credit entries in the same asset type or in the same liability type. However, changes in financial assets should not be netted against changes in liabilities (IMF BPM6 p. 134, Chap. 8). That said, net capital inflows (inflows with a positive sign) arise when new bonds issued to foreign residents are netted against redemption of bonds issued but acquisition of bond assets is not netted against incurrence of bond liabilities.

[15]Barro and Lee schooling data are measured at five-year intervals.

cation, which suggests that this is a poor proxy for fundamental differences across countries. Relying on human capital as a measure of fundamentals and considering it as a main determinant for capital inflows is not unanimous in the regression-based literature. Clemens and Williamson (2004) for example, use the demographic composition by age as a proxy for fundamentals; they argue that as a country develops the youth dependency ratio lowers and the more mature adult population increases the productivity of labour, which in turn requires more investment and more capital inflows if domestic savings are insufficient. In addition to the working age population, Clemens and Williamson (2004) use the population growth rate, net migration rate, primary product exports, and urbanization as proxies for fundamentals. Hashimoto and Wacker (2012) show that conventional indicators of fundamentals (e.g., schooling measures of human capital) are statistically insignificant determinants of capital inflows, supporting the view that one should not rely solely on schooling data as a proxy for fundamentals.

The logarithm of average years of schooling from Barro and Lee (1996, updated 2010) is used as a measure of fundamentals. Following the arguments by Clemens and Williamson (2004) and Hashimoto and Wacker (2012), in addition to Barro and Lee's schooling data, the proportion of working age population (% of WP) is used as an additional proxy for fundamentals. In addition, a TFP (total factor productivity) index is constructed for use as a direct measure of differences in fundamentals across countries.[16]

Institutional Quality

A commonly used source for a measure of institutional quality is Political Risk Services (PRS) Group's 'political risk' rating, namely the International Country Risk Guide (ICRG).[17] Among many others, Alfaro et al. (2008) and Papaioannou (2009) utilize this source to measure differences in institutional qualities across countries. Their empirical findings are based solely on ICRG's index of institutions. However, other indices are also available and often used to measure differences in institutional qualities, such as the Freedom House Index, Transparency International's CPI (corruption perception index), the World Bank's CPIA (Country policy and institutions assessments) index, and the World Bank Institute's (WBI) Governance Indicators (Kaufmann et al. 2004, updated 2013). For example, Globerman and Shapiro (2002) and Daude and Stein (2007) use Governance Indicators to measure differences in institutional qualities. It is reasonable to argue that a perfect measure for institutional quality will undoubtedly never exist and there are limitations of using such indices for cross-country comparisons. An alternative measures of institutional quality is considered and therefore institutional quality is not rely solely on a single index measure. In particular, the ICRG's index from PRS Group and Governance Index

[16]Details of the construction of the TFP measure are given in Appendix B.

[17]Since 1979, the PRS provided 'political risk' services and was developed by Coplin and O'Leary; in 1993. The ICRG rating is used for forecasting financial, economic, and political risk. For details of each sub-index of the ICRG measure of the institutions index, see Appendix B.

based on the World Bank Institute's Governance Indicators are used as measures for the differences in institutional qualities.[18]

Some other studies use specific components of institutional quality as determinants of specific types of capital inflows (predominantly for FDI inflows). For example, Wei (2000) uses measures of corruption from three different sources: ICRG, Transparency International, and Price Waterhouse. Asiedu et al. (2009) consider expropriation risk as a determinant of FDI and use ICRG's measure of expropriation risk. Busse (2004) uses a measure of democracy from Freedom House. In Chap. 6, a robust exercise, similar to these studies, is conducted and examined each individual aspect of institutional quality for FDI flows.

Capital Account Openness or Capital Controls

A commonly used approach to measuring capital controls (e.g., in Alfaro et al. 2008) is the IMF's de jure measure of legal restrictions on cross-border capital flows. It is based on the IMF's Annual Report on Exchange Arrangements and Exchange Restrictions (AREAER). A limitation of this measure of capital controls is its binary nature; it treats all countries as either completely closed (if its value is 1) or completely open (if its value is 0). It does not allow for varying degrees of intensity of openness or closure, which is likely to be more useful information in analysing international capital flows. The Quinn index (1997, updated to 2006) is the other widely used de jure index for capital control that addresses this problem. Quinn uses qualitative descriptions from the AREAER reports and also includes additional information on whether a country under consideration has entered into international integration agreements. The Quinn index explains government policy stance towards capital account liberalization and current account liberalization by offering a measurement of the existence of restrictions and the severity or magnitude of these restrictions. However, the IMF's AREAER measure and the Quinn index measure are both not publicly available.

An alternative approach to de jure measurement of capital account openness is the de facto measure that exhibits how much a country is integrated with the world economy in practice (Prasad et al. 2003; Kose et al. 2006). Prasad et al. (2003) argue that many countries with extensive capital controls experience large volumes of capital outflows and some countries with open capital accounts experience low volumes of capital inflows or outflows. Prasad et al. (2003) mention that the de jure capital account restrictions may be ineffective in controlling capital flows and find that some Latin American countries experienced financial integration in the 70s and 80s though they were de jure closed to financial flows. China has not been able to stop speculative capital inflows though it has an extensive regime of capital controls (Prasad and Wei 2007).

A publicly available de jure measure of capital account openness constructed by Chinn and Ito (2008, updated 2012) is used to examine the effectiveness of free capital movement policies on capital inflows. This measure is also used in Reinhardt et al. (2013) and Hashimoto and Wacker (2012). The Chinn and Ito index, by construction, measures the extensity of capital controls as it may not directly measure

[18] See details of the World Bank Institute's Governance Indicators in Appendix B.

the stringency of restrictions on cross-border capital transactions. The correlation between the Quinn-index and the Chinn and Ito index is 0.839 (Chinn and Ito 2008), suggesting that Chinn and Ito's index is also a good proxy for intensity of capital controls. For robustness checking, a de facto measure of capital account openness is also used in our empirical analysis. Following Baltagi et al. (2009), a de facto measure is used based on the estimated gross stocks of assets and liabilities of direct investment and portfolio investment as a share of GDP from the data constructed by LM (2007, updated 2012).

Economic Development

Measurement of economic development does not differ much across the studies in this literature. For example, Alfaro et al. (2008) use initial year's (1970) PPP adjusted GDP per capita from PWT6.1 (Heston et al. 2002) and constant GDP per capita in 1970 deflated by US CPI from WDI, World Bank (2004), whereas Reinhardt et al. (2013) use GDP per capita relative to the US from PWT 7.0 (Heston et al. 2011). GDP per capita (PPP) in the base year period (1984) is used as a measure of economic development and the data are taken from both sources: the Penn World Table (PWT 7.1) and the WDI, World Bank (2013a, b). The sign of the relationship between GDP per capita and capital inflows from the estimated regression helps us to characterize the Lucas paradox. In particular, from Eq. (4.2) a positive and statistically significant coefficient estimate of GDP per capita demonstrates higher GDP per capita increases capital inflows and suggests the existence of the Lucas paradox. If inclusion of any factor (i.e., a factor that measures one or more fundamentals or an index that measures capital account openness or institutional quality), or a combination of factors, makes this relationship disappear (i.e., the coefficient becomes insignificant), then this will provide a potential explanation to the Lucas paradox. A negative and statistically significant coefficient of this variable, on the other hand, suggests capital flows are downhill, as the standard neoclassical model predicts.

Other Controls

For robustness checking of the empirical findings a set of standard controls are used. In particular, it is examined whether the findings from estimated regressions are changed in the presence of these alternative explanations of the Lucas paradox. The standard controls are: distantness, financial development, trade openness, and macroeconomic stability.[19] These controls are also commonly used in this literature. Distantness (measured by distance from the capital city of a country to capital cities of other countries) is a proxy for remoteness that has a negative impact on capital inflows resulting from information asymmetry. In particular, information asymmetry that has an impact on capital inflows includes information related to accounting practices, corporate culture, political events, and asset market structure (Portes and Rey 2005). Trade openness (measured by sum of export and imports as a proportion of GDP) is a relevant factor in the decision making of foreign investors as an economy more open to trade offers higher opportunities for revenues from production in the tradable sector. A highly developed financial market (measured by credit to the

[19]See details of the variables used to measure each controls and the data sources in Appendix B.

private sector as a proportion of GDP) increases capital inflows. The argument for this relationship suggests that financial intermediaries lower the costs of researching potential investments, manage the risks, mobilize savings, and conduct exchange (Greenwood and Jovanovic 1990; King and Levine 1993b). Macroeconomic stability and fiscal discipline of an economy is captured by average inflation. An economy with large capital inflows and less volatility in exchange rates and inflation rates may reflect the absorptive capacity of the economy and the capability of utilizing foreign capital more efficiently. High inflation rates provide negative signals to potential investors about the macroeconomic stability of the country.

4.3.2 Cross Section Findings

Table 4.3 reports cross-sectional model estimates using the updated dataset. Linear model (i.e., with untransformed dependent variable) as well as log model (i.e., with a log*-transformed dependent variable) are estimated, as done for the Alfaro et al. replication. The results are consistent with our findings using Alfaro et al.'s dataset and suggest that the index of institutions solves the Lucas paradox (Model 2) only if the dependent variable is not log*-transformed. By contrast, the index of institutions cannot fully explain the Lucas paradox and the log of per capita income retains a positive and statistically significant effect on capital inflows in the log*-transformed model (Model 3). Interestingly, an alternative measure of institutional quality—the WBI's Governance Index—suggests institutional quality cannot solve the Lucas paradox even when the dependent variable is not log*-transformed (Model 4).[20] In the log* model (Model 5), the evidence for the Lucas paradox is even stronger in the sense that the statistical significance of the coefficient of GDP per capita is higher. Model 6 adds additional control variables (e.g. distantness, capital controls, and years of schooling) proposed by Alfaro et al. and finds the paradox does not go away. If other standard determinants of capital inflows are added, the Lucas paradox remains pertinent. In particular, other commonly used determinants examined of are capital inflows, such as trade openness, financial development, and macroeconomic stability. Lucas paradox still persists (Models 6–9) despite the presence of these additional determinants.[21] These findings suggest that the conclusions that institutions do not solve the Lucas paradox in the log* model also applies to the updated data. Our empirical finding is in line with the more micro-level study by Caner et al. (2011), which examines the Lucas paradox using data from the Norwegian Sovereign Wealth Fund (NSWF) and finds that the quality of institutions does not fully account for the importance of per capita income for investment of the NSWF.

---

[20] An index measure is used based on six Governance Indicators, see Appendix B.

[21] Based on coefficient estimates (Table 4.3) and sample mean and sample standard deviation (Summary Statistics 1), a one standard deviation improvement in log* of per capita income, going from the income level of Ecuador to Estonia, has a similar impact on per capita inflows as a 0.36 standard

Table 4.3 Cross section analysis: N = 98 countries, 1984–2017

Variables		Linear	Linear	Log*	Linear	Log*	Log*	Log*	Log*	Log
		(1)	(2)	(3)	(4)	(5)	(6)	(7)	(8)	(9)
Log GDP per capita (PPP), 1984		3.611*** (0.910)	0.215 (0.452)	0.301*** (0.068)	0.325 (0.311)	0.331*** (0.044)	0.281*** (0.082)	0.302*** (0.087)	0.273*** (0.064)	0.605*** (0.112)
Av institutional quality, 1984–2017			0.309*** (0.098)	0.045*** (0.006)			0.043*** (0.006)	0.034*** (0.007)	0.035*** (0.007)	0.046*** (0.009)
Average governance index, 1996–2017					0.964*** (0.275)	0.138*** (0.015)				
Average capital account openness, 1984–2017							0.106** (0.053)	0.088* (0.052)	0.077 (0.049)	0.045 (0.066)
Log average schooling, 1985–2010							−0.026 (0.144)	−0.045 (0.158)		
Log average distantness							−0.211 (0.226)	−0.162 (0.229)	−0.227 (0.223)	0.027 (0.253)
Log average trade								0.316* (0.188)	0.303* (0.171)	0.654*** (0.152)
Log average financial development								0.159 (0.123)	0.115 (0.114)	0.179 (0.130)
Log average inflation								−0.064 (0.045)	−0.058 (0.036)	0.052 (0.052)
Observations		98	98	98	98	98	89	87	96	96
R-squared		0.211	0.301	0.801	0.336	0.840	0.806	0.832	0.830	0.878
Normality test	Doornik-Hansen	0.00	0.00	0.00	0.00	0.00	0.00	0.11	0.13	0.00
	Shapiro-Wilk	0.00	0.00	0.01	0.00	0.00	0.00	0.32	0.39	0.00
Heteroscedasticity	White	0.11	0.56	0.67	0.42	0.81	0.03	0.01	0.02	0.46
	Breusch-Pagan	0.09	0.08	0.21	0.04	0.40	0.10	0.10	0.23	0.22
RESET		0.00	0.00	0.00	0.00	0.00	0.01	0.00	0.00	0.80
RMSE		4.34	3.92	0.50	3.74	0.44	0.47	0.46	0.48	0.92

Notes Alfaro et al.'s (2008) Whole World (98) country sample is used. Robust standard errors are in parentheses, $^{***}p < 0.01$, $^{**}p < 0.05$, $^{*}p < 0.10$
Diagnostic tests: p-values are reported for each test

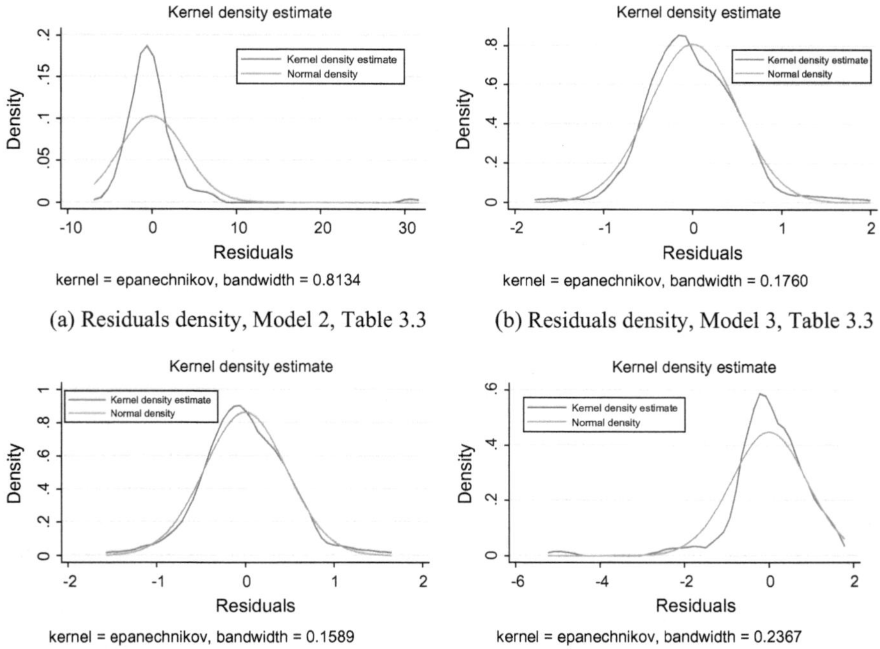

(a) Residuals density, Model 2, Table 3.3

(b) Residuals density, Model 3, Table 3.3

(c) Residuals density, Model 8, Table 4.3

(d) Residuals density, Model 9, Table 4.3

Fig. 4.4 Kernel density and normal density of estimated residuals: 1984–2017

To determine whether our log* model is a better fit for the data than the linear specification, formal diagnostic tests are conducted and kernel densities of the residuals are plotted from the estimated regressions for the two alternative specifications. The density plots of the residuals (Fig. 4.4) indicate that the log* model (Fig. 4.4b) is closer to having normally distributed residuals whereas the residuals from the linear model (Fig. 4.4a) appear to depart from the normality assumption to a much greater extent, suggesting the log* model is closer to satisfying the underlying assumption of normal errors. Formal diagnostic tests, such as normality, homoscedasticity, and functional form for the two alternative specifications for each estimated regression are reported in the last rows of Table 4.3. Model 8 in Table 4.3, which utilizes the maximum number of observations (due to dropping schooling), gives us a model that satisfies more statistical properties compared to Model 7 in terms of the results of the formal diagnostic tests and its residual density plot (Fig. 4.4c). More specifically, the majority of the tests are satisfied for the log* models, suggesting that the log* models are a better fit to the data than the linear model. In Models 8 and 9, total observations are 96 due to missing data on Trade Trinidad and Tobago and inflation for Argentina in World Development Indicators.

deviation improvement in institutions, such as going form a level of institutional development of Ecuador to Italy.

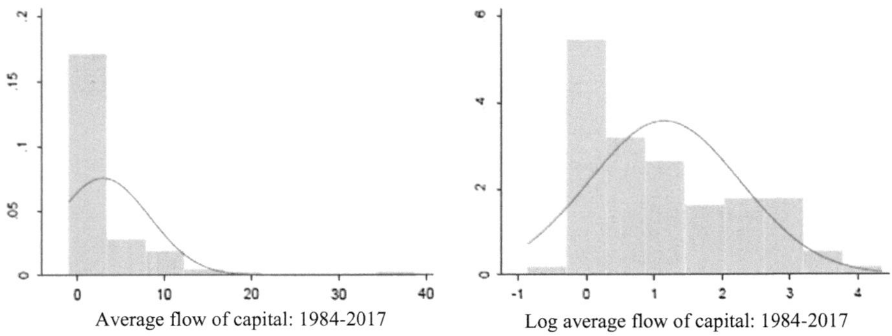

(a) Untransformed variable (b) Log*-transformed variable

Fig. 4.5 Histogram plots of dependent variable: per capita inflows: 1984–2017

A concern from the diagnostic tests is that the model that uses our specific log*-transformed dependent variable (i.e., IHS-transformation) does not satisfy the functional form test (Ramsey RESET test) whereas a simple log-transformed (Model 9, Table 4.3) model does. However, the residual density plot from Model 8 that uses our preferred log-transformation (i.e., Fig. 4.4c based on Model 8, Table 4.3) is more closely normally distributed than that of Model 9, which uses a simple log-transformation (i.e., Fig. 4.4d based on Model 9, Table 4.3), suggesting that the log*-transformation better fits the data.[22] The distributions of the dependent variables for the updated data also suggest that the log*-transformed per capita inflows (Fig. 4.5b) are closer to being normally distributed than the untransformed per capita inflows (Fig. 4.5a).

Following King and Roberts' (2014) suggestion on checking the difference between robust and conventional standard errors, a larger difference is found between robust and conventional standard errors if linear model is employed, as was found in Alfaro et al.'s (2008) replication. In particular, for the coefficient of log GDP per capita, conventional standard errors (0.59) are almost two and a half times larger than robust standard errors (0.27) in the linear model (Model 2, Table 4.3) whereas there is little difference between the conventional and robust standard errors in the log* model (Model 3, Table 4.3). This difference between conventional and robust standard errors also lends support to a diagnosis of model misspecification if the linear model is used.

To sum, the results of the regression models in Table 4.3 and argue that lack of statistical significance of log GDP per capita (Model 2) is associated with model misspecification and is also observed using the updated data. Capital still flows to the rich countries. The log* model is a better fit for the data than the linear model. It also appears in this updated dataset that the lack of significance of log GDP per

[22]Simple log-transformation means y = log(x) whereas our preferred log-transformation follows IHS's transformation (log*).

capita is not robust to the measure of institutions employed (Model 4 compared to Model 2).

4.3.3 Decomposition of GDP Per Capita

Having confirmed that the Lucas paradox persists in the updated cross-section dataset and that the log* model provides a better fit for the data, the cross-section analysis is extended to examine the independent effect of capital stock per worker. In particular, the income variable (GDP per capita) is decomposed into capital stock per worker and total factor productivity (TFP) and examine independent effects of the two potential determinants (i.e., capital stock per worker and total factor productivity) on capital inflows.[23] A motivation for this analysis is that if one could hypothetically account for variation in TFP across countries, then according to neoclassical model we should find a negative relationship between capital stock per worker and capital inflows. That is, if the solution to the Lucas paradox is found in accounting for differences in the marginal product of capital across countries (for a given level of capital), then the positive association between per capita income and capital inflows should be driven entirely by factors leading to country TFP differences. This decomposition of per capita income therefore suggests to us whether Lucas paradox extends beyond productivity differences. More specifically, if the coefficient of capital stock per worker is negative and statistically significant, then this would suggest that capital is indeed flowing downhill in the neoclassical sense. This would then verify that the Lucas paradox is all about *high* productivity of investment in capital-abundant rich countries.

Table 4.4 reports the results from regressing capital inflows on decomposed per capita income (i.e., on TFP and capital stock per worker). Model 1 reproduces the benchmark regression result using per capita income for comparison. Model 2 reports the marginal effect of capital stock per worker on capital inflows after accounting for TFP differences across countries. A positive and statistically significant effect of capital stock per worker suggests the Lucas paradox extends beyond productivity differences across countries. More specifically, capital does not flow to poor countries and either frictions/barriers are preventing capital from flowing to relatively capital-scarce poor countries or else the productivity of capital is relatively high in countries that are already relatively capital-abundant.

---

[23]Cross country capital stock data are constructed to measure TFP following the approach in Hall and Jones (1999), details of the construction of the TFP and capital stock are given in Appendix B. Hall and Jones's (1999) TFP index also uses Barro and Lee's human capital data, which seems more appropriate than the standard Solow residual estimates of TFP, as used in Alfaro et al. (2008), that include human capital in the residual. Assume that the functional form of the model is appropriate, the potential measurement error in estimating TFP and that TFP differences may be sensitive to parameter estimates. Also acknowledged, that this decomposition may not capture completely the effects of the income variable on capital inflows and that the income variable is affected by other factors as well.

Table 4.4 Cross section analysis decomposition of GDP per capita, N = 98 countries, 1984–2017

Variables		(1)	(2)	(3)	(4)	(5)	(6)
Log GDP per capita (PPP), 1984		0.801*** (0.061)					
Log capital stock per worker, 1984			0.470*** (0.068)	0.146** (0.056)	0.371*** (0.057)	0.146** (0.056)	0.158*** (0.052)
Log TFP, 1984			0.277** (0.126)	0.108* (0.063)	0.172* (0.099)	0.085 (0.060)	0.051 (0.069)
Average institutional quality				0.051*** (0.006)		0.045*** (0.006)	0.034*** (0.008)
Average capital account openness					0.336*** (0.061)	0.140** (0.054)	0.133** (0.055)
Log average distantness							−0.115 (0.235)
Log average trade							0.354* (0.190)
Log average financial development							0.199 (0.148)
Log average inflation							−0.044 (0.043)
Observations		98	82	82	82	82	80
R-squared		0.675	0.580	0.789	0.675	0.802	0.831
Normality test	Doornik-Hansen	0.04	0.31	0.03	0.58	0.02	0.32
	Shapiro-Wilk	0.20	0.41	0.04	0.92	0.04	0.47
Heteroscedasticity	White	0.01	0.06	0.09	0.31	0.22	0.02
	Breusch-Pagan	0.00	0.03	0.13	0.24	0.05	0.08
RESET		0.00	0.00	0.02	0.00	0.03	0.00
RMSE		0.62	0.73	0.51	0.62	0.48	0.46

Notes The dependent variable is log capital inflows per capita (log*F). The observations of the Models 2–5 are reduced to 82 due to the limited availability of cross-country schooling (used in the TFP index) and capital stock data; of Model 6 is reduced to 80 due to missing data on Inflation (for Argentina) and on Trade (for Trinidad and Tobago). Robust standard errors are in parentheses, ***$p < 0.01$, **$p < 0.05$, *$p < 0.10$. Diagnostic tests: p-values are reported for each corresponding test

Models 3 and 4 is estimated in order to isolate the relative influence of the key barriers and frictions (i.e., institutional or capital markets) in explaining the Lucas. The result suggests that differences in institutional qualities capture the Lucas paradox more precisely than differences in capital account openness. In other words, the strong (in terms of statistical significance) and the positive significant effects of capital stock per worker on capital inflows is reduced to a larger extent if accounting for differences in institutional qualities (Model 3) compared to differences in capital account openness (Model 4). However, no evidence is found that the relative effect of the institutions index on capital inflows is larger than capital account openness when they are both included in the model (Model 5). This finding remains the same if other potential explanations of the Lucas paradox are controlled for (Model 6). This finding suggests that the Lucas paradox extends beyond differences between rich and poor countries with respect to TFP, institutional quality, and capital market imperfections.

4.3.4 Robustness Checks

Table 4.5 repeats the exercise examining the Lucas paradox but using an alternative source of capital inflows: the LM data obtained by first differencing the stock data of direct and portfolio equity. The LM data source allows us to verify the robustness of our estimates to alternative measure of the dependent variable. An issue with using the IMF's IFS capital flow data is that it does not incorporate potentially large valuation effects.[24] Capital stock data measure the long-run asset holding positions of a country and LM's estimates adjust for the valuation effects of capital.

Models 1 and 2 report the estimates from the linear model, suggesting that the results are unchanged from the estimates based on the IMF's capital flow data. In particular, in a linear model, the Lucas paradox disappears if an index of institutional quality is included (Model 2). However, GDP per capita retains its statistical significance in the log* model (Model 3) indicating that our earlier findings are robust to the use of alternative sources of capital data. This finding is also robust to other proposed explanations of the Lucas paradox as shown in Model 4. In particular, the full model with log*-transformation of the dependent variable (Model 4) is closer to satisfying the underlying assumptions of statistical adequacy. This result is comparable to the results to AD's (2013) findings; for example, Models 5 and 6 in Table 4.5 are similar to AD's Models 5/ and 6/ in their Table 4. As in AD, the index of institutional quality cannot solve the Lucas paradox. Interestingly, most of the log* models fail to satisfy the normality test but they pass the RESET test for the LM capital data, whereas for the IMF's IFS capital data the log*-models pass normality and fail RESET. However, looking at the normality of the residuals of the estimated regression suggests that the log* model is more appropriate because the residuals density plots suggest a log*-transformed dependent variable is approximately normally distributed (e.g., Fig. 4.4b).[25]

Table 4.6 adds several controls that are commonly considered in the literature as robustness checks and also includes additional controls for robustness checking of the findings. Existing literature argues that countries with well-developed infrastructure attract foreign investments because it reduces transaction costs associated with these investments. A commonly used measure of infrastructure (e.g., in Alfaro et al. 2008) is the percentage of paved roads in total roads. A new measure of infrastructure

---

[24]Valuation effects are discussed in more detail in Chap. 4 (Sect. 4.3.1).

[25]Moreover, LM's capital data also suggests that the histogram plots (see Fig. C.1 in Appendix C) of the log*-transformed dependent variable is approximately normally distributed compared to untransformed dependent variable.

Table 4.5 Cross section using LM flow data: N = 98 countries, 1984–2017

Variables		Linear	Linear	Log*	Log*	Log*	Log*
		(1)	(2)	(3)	(4)	(5)	(6)
Log GDP per capita (PPP), 1984		3.323*** (0.658)	0.508 (0.323)	0.794*** (0.112)	0.750*** (0.129)	0.880*** (0.100)	0.652*** (0.143)
Average inst. quality, 1984–2017			0.252*** (0.053)	0.050*** (0.009)	0.044*** (0.009)		
Av. capital account openness					0.066 (0.079)		0.029 (0.089)
Log average distantness					−0.038 (0.255)		−0.201 (0.305)
Log average trade					0.722*** (0.161)		
Log average fin development					0.025 (0.130)		
Log average inflation					−0.016 (0.054)		
Average Governance index, 1996–2017						0.139*** (0.022)	0.149*** (0.027)
Log average school 1985–2010							0.424** (0.222)
Observations		98	98	98	98	98	89
R-squared		0.279	0.376	0.832	0.869	0.835	0.837
Normality test	Doornik-Hansen	0.00	0.00	0.00	0.00	0.00	0.00
	Shapiro-Wilk	0.00	0.00	0.01	0.05	0.00	0.00
Heteroscedasticity	White	0.17	0.61	0.37	0.55	0.27	0.51
	Breusch-Pagan	0.13	0.10	0.15	0.01	0.07	0.07
RESET		0.00	0.00	0.33	0.75	0.28	0.04
RMSE		6.38	5.97	0.76	0.69	0.75	0.76

Notes Robust standard errors are in parentheses, $^{***}p < 0.01$, $^{**}p < 0.05$, $^{*}p < 0.10$. Diagnostic tests: p-values are reported for each corresponding test

is used that can potentially tell us more about the relationship between infrastructure and capital inflows. This new infrastructure variable is the World Bank's logistic performance index, which is based on the quality of trade and transport related infrastructure, such as ports, railroads, and information technology. A country with a higher value of the logistic performance index is more likely to attract higher capital inflows. Model 2 reports the effect of infrastructure measured by the percentage of paved roads in total roads and finds it to be positive but statistically not significant. In Model 3 the World Bank's logistic performance index of infrastructure has a statis-

Table 4.6 Cross section analysis additional robustness checks, N = 98 countries, 1984–2017

Variables	(1)	(2)	(3)	(4)	(5)	(6)	(7)	(8)	(9)
Log initial GDP per capita (PPP)	0.301*** (0.078)	0.293*** (0.063)	0.228*** (0.066)	0.323*** (0.092)	0.294*** (0.079)	0.283*** (0.077)	0.325*** (0.083)	0.310*** (0.074)	0.304*** (0.072)
Index of institutions	0.045*** (0.006)	0.045*** (0.006)	0.036*** (0.006)	0.041*** (0.007)	0.046*** (0.007)	0.045*** (0.006)	0.043*** (0.007)	0.045*** (0.006)	0.046*** (0.006)
Paved roads (% of total roads)		0.071 (0.181)							
Logistic performance index			0.390** (0.158)						
Stock market value				0.543* (0.282)					
Tax on profits					0.298 (0.256)				
Log working age population						−0.002 (0.004)			
Oil dummy							−0.140 (0.181)		
Sahara dummy								0.042 (0.117)	
English speaking population									0.050 (0.211)
Observations	98	98	97	76	89	98	98	98	89
R-squared	0.801	0.801	0.817	0.799	0.805	0.801	0.802	0.801	0.811

Notes Dependent variable is log capital inflows per capita (log*F). Robust standard errors are in parentheses. ***$p < 0.01$, **$p < 0.05$, *$p < 0.1$

tically significant positive effect on capital inflows.[26] However, there is no change in the overall picture of the results, i.e., GDP per capita is still statistically significant.

Examining the effects of financial development on capital inflows, existing literature uses various measures, such as credit to the private sector as a proportion of GDP and M2/GDP (World Bank 1989; King and Levine 1993a). Beck et al. (2000, updated 2013) include several other indicators of financial development, such as liquid liabilities/GDP, stock market capitalization/GDP, stock market turnover/GDP, private bond market capitalization/GDP, and growth of stock market capitalization/GDP. Among these alternative financial development indicators, private stock market capitalization/GDP is used as a robustness check for the effect of financial development. Model 4 finds that market capitalization has an insignificant effect on capital inflows.[27] Heavy tax rates are considered as a barrier to capital inflows, particularly for FDI (Gastanaga et al. 1998; Wei 2000). Model 5 examines this variable including average tax rates on profits and capital gains and finds the effect on capital inflows is also not statistically significant.

It is argued in the literature that demographic composition can proxy for fundamentals and determines capital inflows (e.g., Clemens and Williamson 2004). The log of the age dependency ratio (% of working age population) is examined to check whether inclusion of the differences in this fundamental change the Lucas paradox and found that working age population has a statistically significant effect on capital inflows (Model 6). Models 7, 8, and 9 include an oil-country dummy, a sub-Saharan Africa country dummy, and a dummy for the fraction of the population speaking English (as a proxy for the effects of shared language), respectively; however, they also are statistically insignificant determinants of capital inflows, and, more importantly, the overall results are robust to the inclusion of these dummies.

Table 4.7 reports the robustness of our findings to consideration of different types of capital inflows. In particular, the dependent variable investigated so far is private capital inflows, which includes only direct and portfolio equity. Some studies include other types of flows (debt) or use net flows (i.e., current account balance to GDP) as the dependent variable. It is worth mentioning that Lucas (1990) questioned the observed pattern of private capital flows so the empirical investigation of the Lucas paradox should, in principle, focus on private capital flows. The result is checked whether the Lucas paradox is robust to consideration of debt flows (both public and private) or net flows as the dependent variable.

Both private and public debt flows are considered because many developing countries also receive a large amount of public debt from different sources both bilaterally (e.g., between two national governments) and from multilateral agencies (e.g., the World Bank, IMF). These public debt inflows usually target infrastructure sectors in developing countries, which may reduce potential private investments (e.g., FDI) to these sectors in developing countries. This suggests there might be a substitutability

[26] This new infrastructure index is only available in recent periods with a maximum of two time series observations available in the WDI.

[27] Other indicators of financial development are also examined (results not reported) and similar results obtained.

Table 4.7 Cross section analysis additional robustness checks for types of flows, N = 98 countries, 1984–2017

Variables	FDI and portfolio	FDI and portfolio	FDI and portfolio and private debt	FDI and portfolio and private debt	FDI and portfolio and public debt	FDI and portfolio and public debt	Net flows	Net flows	FDI and portfolio, PPP adjusted
	(1)	(2)	(3)	(4)	(5)	(6)	(7)	(8)	(9)
Log initial GDP pc (PPP)	0.294*** (0.081)	0.261*** (0.079)	0.281*** (0.078)	0.249*** (0.077)	0.0271*** (0.078)	0.227*** (0.075)	5.186*** (1.233)	5.495*** (1.449)	0.332*** (0.091)
Index of institutions	0.042*** (0.006)	0.030*** (0.006)	0.039*** (0.006)	0.030*** (0.006)	0.040*** (0.006)	0.029*** (0.006)	−0.236** (0.095)	−0.236** (0.110)	0.022*** (0.006)
Capital account openness		0.116** (0.049)		0.109** (0.048)		0.120** (0.046)		−0.668 (0.754)	0.124** (0.052)
Log distantness		−0.102 (0.188)		−0.010 (0.186)		−0.066 (0.191)		3.213 (3.158)	−0.023 (0.183)
Log trade		0.176 (0.140)		0.237* (0.133)		0.198 (0.142)		2.783 (2.017)	0.404* (0.131)
Log financial development		0.113 (0.077)		0.072 (0.072)		0.120 (0.074)		−0.231 (1.762)	0.043 (0.076)
Log inflation		0.096** (0.042)		0.071* (0.040)		0.069 (0.042)		2.124 (4.613)	0.092** (0.042)
Log per capita GDP growth		0.119** (0.054)		0.103** (0.050)		0.075 (0.048)		0.545 (1.149)	0.227** (0.060)
Observations	98	98	98	98	98	98	96	96	98
R-squared	0.812	0.844	0.799	0.833	0.799	0.832	0.176	0.213	0.840

Notes Dependent variable: log capital inflows per capita (log*F) in Models 1–6 and 9; Net flows (current account balance to GDP) in Models 7 and 8. Robust standard errors are in parentheses

$^{***}p < 0.01$, $^{**}p < 0.05$, $^{*}p < 0.1$

relationship between private capital inflows and public debt inflows. This suggests it may not be appropriate to consider private debt flows in isolation. Moreover, considering net flows as the dependent variable suggests including official transfers (i.e., government to government payments, such as various kinds of aid) and private transfers (e.g., made in response to individual's initiatives, such as remittances). It is noteworthy that if we use net flows as the dependent variable, we are including government to government flows and current transfers and these findings should be interpreted carefully as an empirical test of neoclassical model predictions or as an empirical test of the Lucas paradox. This is because government to government flows, aid, and remittances are not determined by the marginal productivity of capital, a tenet of capital flows from rich to poor countries as suggested by the neoclassical model or lack of capital flows from rich to poor countries as suggested by Lucas.

In Table 4.7, Models 1 and 2 present a benchmark result based on capital inflows (FDI and portfolio) as the dependent variables. Adding private debt to the dependent variable does not resolve the Lucas paradox (Models 3 and 4). In other words, private debt also flows to rich countries as does FDI or portfolio flows. The results in Models 5 and 6 are driven by FDI and portfolio flows but no statistically significant result is found if the dependent variable is debt flows (results are not reported).

The regression results using net flows (Models 7 and 8) suggest capital flows out if the country is rich (i.e., a positive coefficient implies the current account balance is surplus). The results in Models 7 and 8 might be driven by aid or grant flows, or by private transfers. The net flows (i.e., the current account balance) may represent large flows of aid and grants from rich countries. Moreover, the growth (as measured by log per capita GDP growth) effect is not significantly associated with net flows (Model 8), whereas it is a statistically significant determinant of private capital inflows (Models 2 and 4).

So far, the dependent variable examined is (real) capital inflows (deflated by the US CPI, 2005) per capita, which is common in the literature. However, there may be an issue that a dollar of capital flow from a rich country (say, US) to a poor country (say, Ethiopia) can buy more goods and services compared to the same flow to another rich country (say, Germany). This suggests it is worth examining whether the findings remain the same if we use purchasing power parity (PPP) adjusted capital inflows.[28] Model 9 uses PPP adjusted capital inflows as the dependent variable and finds the results remain unchanged. Indeed, the Lucas paradox is stronger in terms of statistical significance with the PPP adjustment. To sum, the findings from this comprehensive robustness checking as implying that (private) capital flows to rich countries, i.e., the Lucas paradox persists.

[28]PPP adjusted capital inflows are defined as: capital inflows × (GDP per capita, PPP/GDP per capita, constant US dollars).

4.4 Instrumental Variable (IV) Estimates

It is possible that capital inflows can affect institutional quality with more capital inflows creating incentives to reform, which suggests a potential reverse causality problem in our cross-section analysis. An instrumental variables approach is used to account for any bias and inconsistency resulting from reverse causality between capital inflows and the institutions index, considering the European settler mortality rate as an instrument for the institutions index, as in Alfaro et al. (2008). Alfaro et al. (2008), following Acemoglu et al. (2001, 2002), argue that European settlers faced different mortality rates in different colonies and they set up 'extractive institutions' in the places where mortality rates were high; they use historical mortality rates of European settlers as an instrument for current institutions of former colonies. Alfaro et al. find institutional quality, when instrumented, has a causal effect on capital inflows.

The IV approach is widely used in the growth literature (e.g., La Porta et al. 1998, 1999; Hall and Jones 1999) and other instruments are used for institutional quality in the growth literature instead of relying on a single instrument. For example, La Porta et al. (1998, 1999) use legal origin as an instrument for current institutions arguing that a country's legal system has long-standing consequences for contractual institutions and that legal origin was determined by the colonizers during the 18th and 19th century. La Porta et al. find common-law countries and former British colonies have better property rights and thus argue for influences of colonial experience on current institutions.

Distance from the equator (the absolute value of latitude) influenced Western European settlers to migrate and settle (Hall and Jones 1999). Hall and Jones argue that Western European settlers were more likely to settle in locations with less population and similar climate to Western Europe and shipped Adam's Smith's 'property rights' ideas to these locations; therefore they use latitude as an instrument for 'social infrastructure' in explaining differences in income per capita.[29] Hall and Jones (1999) also use the fraction of the population speaking one of the five main Western European languages (English, French, German, Portuguese, and Spanish) as the primary language and measure exogenous effects of 'social infrastructure' on income per capita.

Djankov et al. (2002) find evidence that former British colonies have less intrusive regulatory systems and more dispute resolution than other former colonies. Bockstette et al. (2002) argue that a long history of a state is associated with greater ethnic homogeneity and with more stability implying an effective government, which improves institutional quality that eventually fosters economic development. Bockstette et al. (2002) show that 'state antiquity' is an effective instrument for 'social infrastructure' in Hall and Jones (1999).

This suggests there is a long list of alternative instruments considered in the literature, which can be utilized as potential alternative instruments to identify exogenous

[29] Hall and Jones (1999) use the term 'social infrastructure' to incorporate institutions and openness to trade.

effects of the variables of interests (i.e., the institutions index or income per capita). The IV analysis assumes that, following Alfaro et al. (2008), the institutions index is the only endogenous variable in the structural model (Eq. 4.2), and examine the robustness of the exogenous effects of the institutions index on capital inflows across alternative instruments. Even though Alfaro et al. (2008) consider GDP per capita as exogenous, this research considers that GDP per capita to be endogenous (see Sect. 4.4.3). The following section discusses the necessary criteria for a valid instrument before the results from IV estimation is presented.

4.4.1 Over-Identifying Restrictions and Week Identification

Assume for the moment, as in Alfaro et al. (2008), that the institutions index is the only endogenous variable in the structural model (Eq. 4.2). For this specific instance, Z is the instrument for institutions index where the equation is exactly identified (i.e., the number of IVs is exactly equal to the number of endogenous explanatory variables). The Z instruments in the reduced form equation (Eq. 4.3), for Institutions I, must satisfy the conditions: instrument relevance (as shown in 4.4a) and instrument exogeneity (as shown in 4.4b)[30]:

$$I_i = \mu + \pi Z_i + \varepsilon_i \tag{4.3}$$

$$Cov(Z_i, I_i) \neq 0 \tag{4.4a}$$

$$Cov(Z_i, \varepsilon_i) = 0 \tag{4.4b}$$

The relevance of instruments suggests the more the variation of the endogenous variable that is associated with the variation in the instrument, the more relevant the instrument is. Otherwise, an instrument that explains little of the variance of the endogenous explanatory variable is called a weak instrument. If the instrument is weak, then 2SLS estimates are badly biased even if the sample size is large.

The relevance condition of the instrument can be tested from the first-stage regression, specifically, if the coefficient of the instrument is marginally statistically significantly different from zero, the IV estimates are likely to be less informative (i.e., less-relevant to the variable of interest). It is also true that having a large number of instruments, relative to sample size, results in potentially serious bias if some or all of the instruments are weakly correlated with the variables of interest. Stock and Yogo's (2005) simulations provide critical values for Cragg and Donald's (1993) F-statistics, which give an indication of the strength (i.e., weak or strong) of this identification.

Over-identification restrictions are examined, which is essentially testing whether the additional instruments are valid, in the sense of being uncorrelated with the

[30]For details of these requirements and the discussion, see Stock and Watson (2003).

error term. The IV equation is exactly identified in regression Table 4.8 where a set of alternative instruments are used for the institutions index in turn. Later, more instruments are considered than the number of endogenous explanatory variables (see Sect. 4.4.3 where six instruments are considered for two endogenous variables) to check the validity of the over-identification restrictions. This approach implicitly assumes that there is at least one subset of valid instruments that is sufficient to obtain exact identification. Practically, the null tests whether the coefficients on all the instruments and the included exogenous variables in an auxiliary regression of the 2SLS residuals on all exogenous variables should be zero. Non-rejection of the null is taken as support that the over-identification restrictions are valid.

4.4.2 IV Results for Endogenous Institutions Index

The IV analysis starts with instrumenting the institutions index by European settler mortality. One may wonder about how robust Alfaro et al.'s IV estimates are to alternative choice of instruments since it is not guaranteed that European settler mortality is the ideal instrument for current institutions.[31] In the growth literature, alternative instruments for institutions are used but they are not usually used in the capital flow literature and the findings in the growth literature are usually based on IV estimates using a single instrument. Given this observation, in addition to European settler mortality, alternative instruments are utilized for current institutions to explore whether the exogenous effects of the institutions index are robust. Moreover, diagnostic tests are conducted for the IV regressions to examine which of the instruments meet the criteria for a valid instrument.

Table 4.8 reports the IV estimation results. Out of the six instruments examined, settler mortality and latitude exhibit strong associations with institutional quality. The first stage regression of Model 1 suggests that mortality rates more than 100 years ago are a major determinant of early institutional development and there is a strong correlation between early institutions and the current level of institutional development. The result from the second stage regression suggests that a higher level of institutional quality has a significant effect on capital inflows and the effect is exogenous (Model 1). This finding supports Alfaro et al. (2008) and suggests that the institutions index has a statistically significant positive exogenous effect on capital inflows. But an important caveat is that this finding is based on a small sample size of 45 countries due to limitations on the availability of data on European settler mortality. On the other hand, latitude also shows a strong positive influence on the current level of institutional quality in the first stage but there is no statistically significant effect of the institutions index on capital inflows in the second stage (Model 2). Note that

[31] Acknowledging the Acemoglu et al.'s (2001, 2002) argument that European setter mortality as a preferred instrument over others; however, it is worth examining how robust our findings are across other available instruments. More importantly, relying on European settler mortality as the only instrument reduces the number of observations in our sample by almost 50%.

Table 4.8 IV regressions: only institutions index is instrumented: N = 98 countries, 1984–2017

	(1)	(2)	(3)	(4)	(5)	(6)
First stage: institutions index						
log initial GDP per capita	7.861*** (1.802)	10.357*** (1.061)	11.228*** (0.875)	10.940*** (0.964)	11.230*** (0.884)	11.096*** (0.898)
Log mortality	−4.312** (1.764)					
Latitude		17.528*** (6.234)				
Former Brit colony			1.847 (2.066)			
Eng. language speaking				5.700 (3.954)		
Brit legal origin					2.109 (2.165)	
State antiquity						2.539 (4.308)
R^2 first	0.681	0.748	0.676	0.680	0.678	0.680
Weak identification—F	5.98	7.91	0.79	2.08	0.99	0.35
Observations	45	89	98	89	98	95
Second stage: DV: log capital inflows per capita*						
Institutions index	0.042*** (0.015)	0.039 (0.024)	0.094 (0.094)	0.045 (0.031)	0.126 (0.108)	0.102 (0.116)
Log initial GDP per capita	0.198 (0.166)	0.318 (0.321)	−0.296 (1.062)	0.259 (0.373)	−0.642 (1.201)	−0.381 (1.295)
Observations	45	89	98	89	98	95
R^2 s	0.861	0.816	0.648	0.827	0.379	0.616
Weak identification—F	5.98	7.91	0.79	2.08	0.99	0.35

Notes Robust standard errors are in parentheses, ***$p < 0.01$, **$p < 0.05$, *$p < 0.1$

the sample size has increased from 45 to 89 when latitude is used as an alternative instrument for institutional quality. The other instrumental variables examined do not lead to statistically significant effects of institutions on capital inflows (Models 3–6) and these instruments are not statistically significant in the first-stage regressions for institutions.

Model 1 and Model 2 show Cragg–Donald's weak instrument test values (weak identification F) are the closest to the critical value (8.96) and the highest (7.91) if latitude is used as an instrument for the institutions.[32] Other instruments used in the single IV estimates all suggest weak instrumentation of the endogenous explanatory variable. Based on this result, Model 2 is picked and latitude is considered as a preferred instrument out of the six single instruments used in the single IV estimation. Following Angrist and Pischke's (2008) observation, this exactly-identified estimate is median-unbiased and therefore unlikely to be subject to a weak instruments problem. However, Alfaro et al. (2008) and/or Acemoglu et al. (2001) would argue that latitude is not a good instrument and that settler mortality can better explain the exogenous variation in the institutions index.

4.4.3 IV Results for Endogenous Institutions Index and Endogenous GDP Per Capita

Alfaro et al. (2008) treat GDP per capita as exogenous when they instrument institutional quality by settler mortality. This implies that they consider GDP per capita as part of the instrument set in the first-stage estimation. This approach was followed in the previous exercise (Table 4.8) and observed that in the first-stage, when the institutions index is instrumented, GDP per capita carries a heavy weight in explaining the variation in institutions (with a coefficient that is statistically significant at the 1% level). When GDP per capita is included in the second stage, the predicted value of the institutions index is highly correlated with GDP per capita, which may contribute to GDP per capita being not statistically significant and the institutions index significant in the second stage (Model 1, Table 4.8).

Reverse causality could also be a potential problem between capital inflows and GDP per capita if capital inflows have a positive effect on GDP per capita. More specifically,

GDP per capita in the model considered here is the base-year value, which arguably would reduce this problem. However, in a pure cross-section analysis, the variation being exploited is across countries and there is a high correlation between base-year GDP per capita and current GDP per capita, suggesting a potential reverse causality even if GDP per capita is measured in the base-year. Moreover, the deep determinants literature argues that differences in institutional quality are a key factor in determining differences in economic development, which suggests GDP per capita is endogenous and using GDP per capita as part of the instrument set for the institutions index violates an essential exogeneity condition for justification as a valid instrument. This suggests there is also a contradiction between Alfaro et al.'s approach and the existing growth literature if GDP per capita is considered as exogenous. Therefore, if there is a concern about reverse causality between capital inflows and the institutions index,

[32]When the number of endogenous explanatory variables, $n = 1$, the number of instruments, $K = 1$, and maximal size, $r = 15\%$, then the critical value is 8.96. See critical values in Stock and Yogo's (2005), Table 2, p. 40.

then there should be a similar concern that capital inflows affect GDP per capita as well.

In this context, the first-stage (reduced form) equation for the endogenous explanatory variables GDP per capita (Y_i) and the institutional quality index (I_i) both instrumented by Z, are given by:

$$I_i = \mu_1 + \pi_1 Z_i + u_{1i} \tag{4.5a}$$

$$log(Y_i) = \mu_2 + \pi_2 Z_i + u_{2i} \tag{4.5b}$$

Table 4.9 reports the IV estimation results using six instruments (Z) for the two endogenous variables. All six instruments are examined for the two endogenous variables in Model 1. In the first stage, Model 1 suggests that all of the instruments used, except former British colony and latitude, are statistically significantly associated with institutional quality; all of the instruments used, except former British colony, are statistically significantly associated with GDP per capita. If settler mortality is dropped (Model 2) to maximize sample size, then the fraction of English-speaking and latitude are significant instruments for both GDP per capita and the institutions index. Model 3 includes four instruments and the fraction of English-speaking population and latitude are again significantly associated with the institutions index and/or GDP per capita in the first-stage.

In the second-stage, the institutions index shows a significant exogenous effect on capital inflows if settler mortality is included in the instrument set (Model 1). The institutions index also shows a significant exogenous effect on capital inflows if settler mortality is excluded from the instrument set (Model 2). This suggests average institutional quality has a causal effect on average capital inflows and current institutions can be adequately explained either by distance from the equator or by the fraction of English-speaking population. In Model 2, latitude and fraction of English speaking population are both highly statistically significant instruments in the first-stage. Notably, findings from Model 2 that excludes settler mortality is based on a larger sample (79) compared to Model 1, which is based on a smaller (40) sample. The explained variation (in terms of R^2 value) in the institutions index and GDP per capita by the instruments in Model 1 is larger than in Model 2; however, R^2 are not strictly comparable since samples vary between the two models. In Model 3, institutions index or GDP per capita does not show significant impact for this set of instruments, even though the fraction of English-speaking population and latitude are highly significant in the first-stage.

The weak-identification test results in the multiple endogenous explanatory variables regression models suggest all the models suffer from severe weak identification. In particular, although several IVs are statistically significant in the first stage, the Cragg–Donald's weak instrument test values suggest that weak identification is a problem in all models. This may lead to potentially serious bias resulting from a larger number of instruments in the Models. The *p*-values for the Hansen test how-

Table 4.9 IV regression: GDP pc and institutions index are instrumented: N = 98 countries, 1984–2017

		6IV	5IV	4IV
		(1)	(2)	(3)
Log initial GDP per capita	Former Brit colony	−0.0443 (0.477)	−0.033 (0.695)	
	Log mortality	−0.717*** (0.128)		
	Eng. speaking	1.693*** (0.480)	1.725*** (0.491)	1.725*** (0.495)
	State antiquity	−0.899*** (0.348)	0.122 (0.549)	0.123 (0.550)
	Latitude	0.373 (0.642)	3.158*** (0.605)	3.159*** (0.613)
	Brit legal	−1.291*** (0.460)	−0.504 (0.755)	−0.507 (0.381)
	R^2 first	0.765	0.445	0.445
Institutions index	Former Brit colony	−4.263 (3.172)	3.388 (5.091)	
	Log mortality	−9.272*** (1.699)		
	Eng. speaking	18.22*** (6.062)	21.269*** (6.229)	21.43*** (6.285)
	State antiquity	−12.67* (7.621)	3.092 (7.104)	3.210 (7.157)
	Latitude	18.09** (8.862)	51.710*** (9.683)	51.13*** (9.611)
	Brit legal	−6.397* (3.747)	−4.889 (5.025)	−2.150 (5.070)
	Observations	40	79	79
	R^2 first	0.708	0.491	0.489
Second stage (log* capital inflows per capita)	Log initial GDP per capita	0.068 (0.178)	−0.440 (0.650)	−0.796 (1.075)
	Institutions index	0.054*** (0.012)	0.088** (0.040)	0.111 (0.068)
	Observations	40	79	79
	R^2 second	0.820	0.686	0.498
	Weak identification F	1.676	0.860	0.538
	Over identification test (Hansen-p)	0.559	0.373	0.590

Notes Robust standard errors are in parentheses, ***$p < 0.01$, **$p < 0.05$, *$p < 0.1$

ever suggest that the over-identification restrictions are valid and the instruments are uncorrelated with the error term.

Overall, the IV findings suggest that the significant exogenous effect of the institutions index on capital inflows is not robust to the choice of alternative instruments. This may, in part, reflect sensitivity to sample size, which varies across the choice of instruments. However, based on tests for weak instrumentation, latitude was a preferred instrument for the institutions index instead of settler mortality. If the institutions index and GDP per capita are both considered as endogenous, and more instruments are used than the endogenous variables, then the exogenous effect of average institutional quality on average capital inflows is better explained either by distance from the equator or by the fraction of English-speaking population (i.e., based on Model 2 in Table 4.9). Weak instrumentation is a pervasive problem in this case as well. A reason for choosing latitude or fraction of English-speaking population as instruments instead of settler mortality for institutions is that the findings are based on a much larger observation of countries (see Model 2 in Table 4.8 or in Table 4.9).

4.5 Summary of Cross Section Analysis

This section examines alternative explanations to the Lucas paradox focussing specifically on the role of institutional quality. In modelling international capital flows, the role of institutions are examined using alternative empirical specifications on cross-section data averaged over a sufficiently long sample period (1984–2017) for a relatively large (98) sample of countries. The findings suggest that the institutions index alone cannot solve the Lucas paradox. The level of economic development has a statistically significant effect on capital inflows. This finding from our cross-section analysis is in sharp contrast to the claim in Alfaro et al. (2008), one of the most cited empirical works in the cross-section literature on the determinants of capital inflows. This finding suggests that Alfaro et al.'s finding is due to model misspecification and/or dependent on outlier observations. If a more appropriately specified model is employed, the institutions index does not fully account for the Lucas paradox, although it is a statistically significant determinant of capital inflows.

This empirical analysis is extended to an updated dataset covering the most recent decade and reach the same conclusion on the determinants of international capital flows. The cross-section analysis was further advanced by examining the Lucas paradox specifically whether it relates to initial capital stock per worker and productivity differences. The findings suggest that the Lucas paradox extends beyond mere productivity differences. In other words, this finding suggests that capital does not flow to poor countries even if differences between rich and poor countries with respect to TFP are controlled for, in addition to differences with respect to institutional quality and capital market imperfections. No robust evidence is found from the estimated regression that differences in institutional quality explain lack of capital flows from rich to poor countries more precisely than differences in capital account openness.

The empirical findings are robust to controls that are commonly used in this literature and remain the same for additional robustness checks. Different types of capital inflows are examined to check the sensitivity of the results. The instrumental variables analysis suggest that the exogenous effect of the institutions index on capital inflows is not robust to the choice of alternative instruments and does not pass instrument validity tests.

References

Acemoglu D, Johnson S, Robinson JA (2001) The colonial origins of comparative development: An empirical investigation. Am Econ Rev 91(5):1369–1401

Acemoglu D, Johnson S, Robinson JA (2002) Reversal of fortune: geography and institutions in the making of the modern world income distribution. Q J Econ 117(4):1231–1294

Alfaro L, Kalemli-Ozcan S, Volosovych V (2008) Why doesn't capital flow from rich to poor countries? An empirical investigation. Rev Econ Stat 90(2):347–368

Angrist JD, Pischke JS (2008) Mostly harmless econometrics: an empiricist's companion. Princeton University Press, New Jersey

Asiedu E, Jin Y, Nandwa B (2009) Does foreign aid mitigate the adverse effect of expropriation risk on foreign direct investment? J Int Econ 78(2):268–275

Azémar C, Desbordes R (2013) Has the Lucas paradox been fully explained? Econ Lett 121(2):183–187

Baltagi BH, Demetriades PO, Law SH (2009) Financial development and openness: evidence from panel data. J Dev Econ 89(2):285–296

Barro RJ, Lee JW (1996) International measures of schooling years and schooling quality. Am Econ Rev 86(2):218–223

Barro RJ, Lee JW (2001) International data on educational attainment: updates and implications. Oxford Econ Papers 53(3):541–563

Barro RJ, Lee JW (2010) A new data set of educational attainment in the world, 1950–2010. J Dev Econ 104:184–198

Beck T, Demirgüç-Kunt A, Levine R (2000, updated 2013). A new database on financial development and structure. World Bank Econ Rev 14(3):597–605

Bockstette V, Chanda A, Putterman L (2002) States and markets: the advantage of an early start. J Econ Growth 7(4):347–369

Burbidge JB, Magee L, Robb AL (1988) Alternative transformations to handle extreme values of the dependent variable. J Am Stat Assoc 83(401):123–127

Busse M (2004) Transnational corporations and repression of political rights and civil liberties: an empirical analysis. Kyklos 57(1):45–65

Busse M, Hefeker C (2007) Political risk, institutions and foreign direct investment. Eur J Polit Econ 23(2):397–415

Caner M, Caner T, Grennes TJ (2011) Determinants of investment by the Norwegian Sovereign Wealth Fund: GDP vs. Institutions. Global Econ J 11(1)

Chinn MD, Ito H (2008) A new measure of financial openness. J Comp Policy Anal 10(3):309–322

Clemens MA, Williamson JG (2004) Wealth bias in the first global capital market boom, 1870–1913. Econ J 114(495):304–337

Cragg JG, Donald SG (1993) Testing identifiability and specification in instrumental variable models. Econ Theory 9(2):222–240

Daude C, Stein E (2007) The quality of institutions and foreign direct investment. Econ Politics 19(3):317–344

Djankov S, La Porta R, Lopez-de-Silanes F, Shleifer A (2002) The regulation of entry. Q J Econ 117(1):1–37
Gastanaga VM, Nugent JB, Pashamova B (1998) Host country reforms and FDI inflows: how much difference do they make? World Dev 26(7):1299–1314
Globerman S, Shapiro D (2002) Global foreign direct investment flows: the role of governance infrastructure. World Dev 30(11):1899–1919
Greenwood J, Jovanovic B (1990) Financial development, growth, and the distribution of income. J Polit Econ 98(5):1076–1107
Hall RE, Jones CI (1999) Why do some countries produce so much more output per worker than others? Q J Econ 114(1):83–116
Hashimoto Y, Wacker KM (2012) The role of risk and information for international capital flows: new evidence from the SDDS. Courant Research Centre: poverty, equity and growth, discussion paper, no. 124
Heston A, Summers R, Aten B (2002) Penn world table version 6.1. Center for International Comparisons at the University of Pennsylvania
Heston A, Summers R, Aten B (2011). Penn world table version 7.0. Center for International Comparisons at the University of Pennsylvania
Kaufmann D, Kraay A, Mastruzzi M (2004) Governance matters III: governance indicators for 1996, 1998, 2000, and 2002. World Bank Econ Rev 18(2):253–287
Keskinsoy B (2012) Essays on international capital flows to developing countries (Doctoral dissertation, University of Nottingham)
King RG, Levine R (1993a) Finance and growth: schumpeter might be right. Q J Econ 108(3):717–737
King RG, Levine R (1993b) Finance, entrepreneurship and growth. J Monet Econ 32(3):513–542
King G, Roberts ME (2014) How robust standard errors expose methodological problems they do not fix, and what to do about it. Polit Anal 1–21
Kose MA, Prasad E, Rogoff KS, Wei SJ (2006) Financial globalization: a reappraisal. National Bureau of Economic Research, working paper, no. 12484
La Porta R, Lopez-de-Silanes F, Shleifer A, Vishny RW (1998) Law and finance. J Polit Econ 106(6):1113–1155
La Porta R, Lopez-de-Silanes F, Shleifer A, Vishny R (1999) The quality of government. J Law Econ Organ 15(1):222–279
Lane PR, Milesi-Ferretti GM (2007) The external wealth of nations mark II: revised and extended estimates of foreign assets and liabilities, 1970–2004. J Int Econ 73(2):223–250
Lucas RE (1990) Why doesn't capital flow from rich to poor countries? Am Econ Rev 80(2):92–96
Lütkepohl H, Xu F (2011) Forecasting annual inflation with seasonal monthly data: Using levels versus logs of the underlying price index. J Time Ser Econ
Noorbakhsh F, Paloni A, Youssef A (2001) Human capital and FDI inflows to developing countries: new empirical evidence. World Dev 29(9):1593–1610
Papaioannou E (2009) What drives international financial flows? Politics, institutions and other determinants. J Dev Econ 88(2):269–281
Portes R, Rey H (2005) The determinants of cross-border equity flows. J Int Econ 65(2):269–296
Prasad E, Wei SJ (2007) The Chinese approach to capital inflows: patterns and possible explanations. In: Edwards S (ed) Capital controls and capital flows in emerging economies: policies, practices and consequences. University of Chicago Press, Chicago, Illinoi
Prasad E, Rogoff K, Wei SJ, Kose MA (2003) Effects of financial globalisation on developing countries: some empirical evidence. Econ Polit Weekly 38(41):4319–4330
Quinn D (1997) The correlates of change in international financial regulation. Am Polit Sci Rev 91(03):531–551
Reinhardt D, Ricci LA, Tressel T (2013) International capital flows and development: financial openness matters. J Int Econ 91(2):235–251
Stock J, Watson MW (2003) Introduction to econometrics. Pearson Education, New York

Stock JH, Yogo M (2005) Testing for weak instruments in linear IV regression. In: Andrews DWK, Stock JH (eds) Identification and inference for econometric models: essays in Honor of Thomas Rothenberg. Cambridge, Massachusetts, Cambridge University Press

Verardi V, Croux C (2008) Robust regression in Stata. Stata J 9(3):439–453

Wei SJ (2000) How taxing is corruption on international investors? Rev Econ Stat 82(1):1–11

World Bank (1989) World Development Report 1989: Financial systems and development. Oxford University Press for the World Bank, New York

World Bank (2004) World development indicators. World Bank, CD-ROM, Washington, DC

World Bank (2013a) World development indicators, Online data retrieved on 30 March 2013. World Bank, Washington, DC

World Bank (2013b) Global development horizon: capital for the future: savings and investment in an interdependent world. World Bank, Washington, DC

Chapter 5
Panel and Non-linear Models of Capital Inflows

Abstract This chapter examines whether international capital flows can be explained using panel data and panel model estimators to filter out effects of more complex intertemporal dependencies while controlling for country-specific omitted variables and addressing the potential endogeneity of these determinants. The conclusion of this empirical analysis remained the same that differences in institutional quality between rich and poor countries cannot fully explain why capital does not flow from rich to poor countries. Moreover, panel-data estimates suggest that generous policies relating to capital account convertibility (i.e., lower levels of restrictions on capital movements) are relatively more influential than differences in institutional quality in determining international capital flows. This chapter also examines the claims in the literature that interaction effects (i.e., multiplicative effects of two independent determinants) are required to explain or account for the Lucas paradox. Having analysed several specifications allowing such interaction effects, the findings on the explanation of the Lucas paradox remain unchanged. Capital tends to flow to rich countries and economic development (measured by GDP per capita) is a primary determinant of capital inflows. Institutional quality, capital account openness, the stock of human capital, and/or other potential factors examined also appear as significant determinants, although the size and statistical significance of estimated marginal effects depend on the estimation approach. These factors do not, however, fully capture the effect of economic development. The Lucas paradox therefore stands, as yet, unresolved.

5.1 Introduction

A potential concern with the cross-section results in Chap. 4 is that the data could miss important dynamic effects in the capital flow process by taking averages over longer periods. An argument in favour of using cross-section model in the existing literature (e.g., Alfaro et al. 2008) is that the variable of interest (e.g., the institutions index) is slowly-moving and therefore the vast majority of variation to be explained is across countries rather than over time. However, it is not uncommon to employ panel data analysis when variables of interest, such as the institutions index, are

M. Akhtaruzzaman, *International Capital Flows and the Lucas Paradox*,
https://doi.org/10.1007/978-981-13-9069-2_5

slowly-moving. The existing empirical literature investigating the determinants of capital flows looking for a solution to the Lucas paradox makes use of panel data and panel estimators. Papaioannou (2009), for example, examines the effects of an institutions index on bilateral bank flows in a model with fixed effects; Okada (2013) examines interaction effects (i.e., includes a multiplicative term of two determinants) between an institutions index and capital account openness on private equity flows in a dynamic panel model estimated using a GMM (generalized methods of moments) approach.

Panel model analysis exploits both the cross-section and time-series aspects of the data to understand variation across countries and over time. Moreover, our country sample is obviously heterogeneous, containing both rich and poor countries, and country-specific (unobservable) characteristics should have effects on capital inflows. More specifically, the fixed effects (FE) estimator is more likely to reduce the bias in the estimates resulting from unobserved cross-sectional heterogeneity and to provide more convincing estimates of the true effect of the time-varying variables of interest (e.g., the institutions index, capital account openness). On the other hand, the OLS cross-section estimates are unable to control for unobserved country-specific characteristics; relegating them to the error term may produce biased and inconsistent estimates as a consequence of omitted variables. A panel fixed effect analysis is therefore able to make use of time-series variation in the data as well as control for unobserved country-specific characteristics (e.g., social norms, culture, and geography) that are time invariant but affect capital inflows.

An additional advantage of using panel data is that in addition to the key determinants of capital inflows we can control for common time shocks including year dummies in the regression model. For example, if a two-way (i.e., country dummies and year dummies) FE estimator is used, it controls for country-specific fixed effects and country-irrespective common time shocks as well (i.e., inclusion of year dummies captures all types of common time effects, such as a global financial crisis or global economic booms). In particular, common global shocks are attributed to the year-specific dummies. The panel model estimates help us to compare our findings with the results of studies (e.g., Fernandez-Arias 1996; Forbes and Warnock 2012) that suggest common global factors account for more variation in capital flows and domestic factors (e.g., capital account openness or institutional quality) are less important.

On the basis of these additional advantageous features of panel model analysis, the Lucas paradox is examined in this chapter using panel data to observe if a solution to the Lucas paradox is found. In other words, the panel model estimators check whether the results from cross-section analysis are changed if the time-series variation is utilized in the data and address the limitations of the cross-sectional OLS estimator. Before the empirical estimation, a discussion is added about econometric issues related to panel data analysis in Sect. 5.2. In Sects. 5.3 and 5.4, the results are presented and checked whether the main findings in the cross-section analysis of the previous chapter are robust when panel estimators are used. Lastly, Sect. 5.5 examines whether an interaction between two different determinants in the panel context is sufficient to explain the Lucas paradox.

5.2 Econometric Issues in Panel Models

In this section, using standard notation, FE model is used considering the advantages of estimating a FE model over cross-sectional OLS. Most of the econometric discussion for panel FE is based on Wooldridge (2003) and the notation is adopted from Soderbom (2011). By discussing briefly the concerns related to dynamic panel model estimation, a dynamic panel model is outlined later in this section. Consider a panel model with a single explanatory variable, for each individual unit *i*:

$$y_{it} = x_{it}\beta + (c_i + \varepsilon_{it}), t = 1, 2 \ldots \text{T and } i = 1, 2 \ldots \text{N} \tag{5.1}$$

where y_{it} is the dependent variable, x_{it} is a $1 \times K$ vector of observables, c_i and ε_{it} are unobserved, and β is a $K \times 1$ vector of parameters to be estimated. A problem is that we do not observe c_i which is constant over time for each individual unit (here, country) but varies across individuals. Hence, if we estimate the model in levels using pooled OLS then c_i will be allocated to the error term ($v_{it} = c_i + \varepsilon_{it}$). Then OLS will not be BLUE (best linear unbiased estimator), because the error term $v_{it}^{OLS} = c_i + \varepsilon_{it}$ is serially correlated:

$$Corr\left(v_{it}^{OLS}, v_{i,t-s}^{OLS}\right) = \frac{\sigma_c^2}{\sigma_c^2 + \sigma_\varepsilon^2} \tag{5.2}$$

for $s = 1, 2 \ldots$ T, where σ_c^2 is the variance of errors within individuals (c_i) and σ_ε^2 is the variance of (overall) errors (ε_i), and assuming that ε_{it} is not autocorrelated. This suggests the need for a feasible generalized least square estimator or clustering of the standard errors on the individual units, to improve efficiency. OLS estimates would be consistent. However, a problem with relying on OLS for this model is that the standard formula for calculating the standard errors is inappropriate. In particular, with positive serial correlation, the OLS estimates of the standard errors will be smaller than the true standard errors. This will lead to the conclusion that the parameter estimates are more precise than they really are and there will be a tendency to reject the null hypothesis when it should not be rejected.

However, if c_i is correlated with x_{it} (i.e., *corr* $(c_i, x_{it}) \neq 0$) then assigning c_i to the error term can result in an omitted variable problem, which is more serious. If we apply OLS to panel data assuming that $E(\varepsilon_{it}|x_{it}) = 0$ where c_i is correlated with x_{it}, then OLS will provide biased and inconsistent estimates of the parameters. This is seen by considering the following result for a single regressor model:

$$plim\hat{\beta} = \beta + \frac{cov(x_{it}, c_i)}{\sigma_x^2} \tag{5.3}$$

If X_{it} is positively correlated with c_i, then there is an upward bias and if negatively correlated, a downward bias even if the sample size is large.

In the face of these issues for panel data, FE methods transform the model and estimate the unobserved fixed effects (c_i) controlling for the country-specific characteristics that are invariant over time. The FE model thus allows us to estimate a model using panel data replacing the assumption $E(\varepsilon_{it}|x_{it}) = E(c_i + v_{it}|x_{it}) = 0$ with a weaker assumption that $E(v_{it}|x_{it}) = 0$, and results in consistent estimators while allowing c_i to be freely correlated with x_{it}. The FE model including a country-specific dummy (accounting for country-specific characteristics) is therefore as follows:

$$y_{it} = x_{it}\beta + \mu_i + \varepsilon_{it} \text{ where } \mu_i = \alpha + c_i \tag{5.4}$$

The panel FE model estimating the country-specific fixed parameters does not allow dynamics in the process which may be crucial for understanding the dynamic nature of the data. Inclusion of a lagged dependent variable (LDV) in Eq. (5.4), however, violates an important assumption of exogeneity (i.e., $E(\varepsilon_{it}|x_{it}, \mu_i) = 0$) of the regressors of the FE estimation. Consider the dynamic panel model:

$$y_{it} = \rho y_{i,t-1} + x_{it}\beta + \mu_i + \varepsilon_{it} \tag{5.5}$$

where y_{it} is a function of μ_i, which immediately follows that $y_{i,t-1}$ is also a function of μ_i, resulting in a correlation between country-specific fixed effects (μ_i) and the LDV (i.e., $E(y_{i,t-1}, \mu_i) \neq 0$). Similarly, the LDV is correlated with the error term (i.e., $E(y_{i,t-1}, \varepsilon_{i,t-1}) \neq 0$). Inclusion of the LDV ($y_{i,t-1}$) in the model thus violates the strict exogeneity assumption. The FE estimator is then biased and inconsistent even if the ε_{it} are not serially correlated. More specifically, Nickell (1981) shows that this bias arises from the demeaning process, which subtracts the individual's mean values of the dependent variable and regressors from the respective variables, creating a correlation between regressors and errors. The mean of the LDV contains observations 0 through (T − 1) on y, and the mean error contains contemporaneous values of the error for t = 1… T. The resulting correlation creates a bias, known as the Nickell bias, in the estimate of the coefficient of the LDV that cannot be reduced even if the sample size is very large. Nickell shows that, for a fixed T, the FE estimator is inconsistent as $N \to \infty$ (i.e., cross-section dimension of the panel becomes large) but is consistent as $T \to \infty$ (i.e., the time-dimension of the panel becomes large), suggesting that the bias is severe when the autoregressive coefficient, ρ, is high and the number of time periods T is low.[1]

One solution to this problem is first differencing the model Eq. (5.5) that wipes out the country-specific fixed effects (μ_i) and yields:

$$\Delta y_{it} = \rho \Delta y_{it-1} + \Delta x_{it}\beta + \Delta\varepsilon_{it} \tag{5.6}$$

However, the y_{it-1} in Δy_{it-1} is a function of ε_{it-1} which is also in $\Delta\varepsilon_{it}$. So, Δy_{it-1} is correlated with $\Delta\varepsilon_{it}$, by construction. For a consistent estimator, Anderson and Hsiao (1981) suggest an IV (instrumental variable) estimator based on further lags of

[1]See Nickell (1981) for further details.

Δy_{it} as instruments for Δy_{it-1}. For example, Δy_{it-2} would be a valid instrument for Δy_{it-1} if ε_{it} is serially uncorrelated. Anderson and Hsiao (1981) also suggest an IV estimator based on lagged levels of Δy_{it} as instruments for Δy_{it-1}. For example, y_{it-2} would be a valid instrument for Δy_{it-1}. This IV method leads to consistent but not necessarily efficient estimates of the parameters in the model because it does not make use of all the available moment conditions whereas GMM allows more moment conditions than parameters. Arellano and Bond's (1991) difference-GMM approach is then used to obtain efficient estimates. One criticism of this standard-GMM approach is that lagged levels are often poor instruments for first differenced variables. Specifically, if the autoregressive process is too persistent, then the lagged levels are weak instruments. The system-GMM (Blundell and Bond 1998) approach mitigates this problem using additional moment conditions in which lagged differences of the dependent variable are orthogonal to levels of the errors $\left(E\left[\Delta y_{it-1}\varepsilon_{it}\right]\right) = 0$ for each $t \geq 3$. System GMM extends difference-GMM by estimating simultaneously in differences and in levels. In particular, system-GMM uses both the level version of the dynamic panel model in addition to the differenced version and the effects of the unobserved fixed effect can be estimated; however, system-GMM requires more assumptions than difference GMM. System-GMM requires that lagged changes in the dependent variable are valid instruments for the level of lagged dependent variable in the level equation.

As we move from difference to system GMM, the same redundancy will apply and only one lag is usually used for each time period and instrumenting variable; however, that leads to the number of instruments increasing linearly in T, the number of time periods (Roodman 2009). Moreover, Roodman (2009) suggests that there is a concern of instrument proliferation in system-GMM in that the instrument counts become large relative to the sample size making some asymptotic results and relevant specification tests (e.g., the Hansen test) misleading. In particular, numerous instruments can over-fit endogenous variables in the sense of failing to remove their endogenous components and biasing coefficient estimates towards those from non-instrumenting estimators.

Acknowledging the limitations of alternative estimators, panel model estimation is applied to the investigation of the Lucas paradox. Initially, a panel fixed effects (FE) model is employed and then a system-GMM estimator is used to understand the feedback effect of capital inflows and to examine if there is a solution to the Lucas paradox when endogeneity of the regressors is controlled for. In order to smooth out the impact of short-run fluctuations, a panel of non-overlapping 4-year averages (similar to Chinn and Prasad 2003; Reinhardt et al. 2013) over the period 1984–2015 are used and the sample of 98 countries is used; there are eight time observations for most countries and our preferred model includes a log*-transformed dependent variable. The empirical specifications of the panel FE model (including country fixed effects and time fixed effects) and the dynamic panel model are (5.7) and (5.8) as below, respectively.

$$\log^*(F)_{it} = \mu_i + \beta_1 \log Y_{it} + \beta_2 I_{it} + \beta_3 FO_{it} + \gamma X_{it} + \delta_t + \varepsilon_{it} \tag{5.7}$$

$$\log^*(F)_{it} = \mu + \rho\log^*(F)_{it-1} + \beta_1\log Y_{it} + \beta_2 I_{it} + \beta_3 FO_{it} + \gamma X_{it} + \varepsilon_{it} \quad (5.8)$$

Panel models (Eqs. 5.7 and 5.8) are estimated including the main variables of interest (i.e., the institutions index, I_{it}; capital account openness, FO_{it}; and economic development, $\log Y_{it}$) and the same standard set of controls (X_{it}) are used for the cross-section analysis.

5.3 Fixed Effects (FE) Model Results

Table 5.1 reports FE estimation results. The institutions index does not completely solve the Lucas paradox, i.e., a significant positive correlation between GDP per capita and capital inflows persists (Model 2) even though country-specific characteristics are controlled for. Moreover, the panel FE estimates show capital account openness is a highly significant determinant of capital inflows and there is no identifiable impact of institutions if capital account openness is controlled for (Model 3). This suggests that more capital flows to the countries with relatively less capital account restrictions. This finding further suggests that foreign investors, and perhaps foreign direct investors in particular, are concerned about the convertibility restrictions of potential investment locations and prefer investment locations that offer relatively generous policies on capital account convertibility.

The Lucas paradox still persists in FE estimation once a standard set of controls (i.e., years of schooling, trade openness, financial development, and macroeconomic stability) are included in the model. Model 4 suggests, if a standard set of controls are added to the model, the results remain the same. Model 5 suggests once we control for common time effects, the significant effect of capital account openness on capital inflows persists whereas the effect of the institutions index remains insignificant. Nevertheless, the Lucas paradox is persistent in the presence of standard controls and even after controlling for common time effects.

Inclusion of common time fixed effects (Model 5) provides results inconsistent with some arguments in the literature (e.g., Fernandez-Arias 1996; Forbes and Warnock 2012) that advocate global common shocks as key determinants of capital inflows and domestic factors less important.[2] More specifically, these studies argue that global factors, such as global investment booms or global risks, primarily determine international flows and domestic factors, such as better financial development or lower levels of restrictions on capital accounts are less important. In contrast,

[2]Forbes and Warnock (2012) examine episodes (sharp increases and sharp decreases) of capital flows and find that domestic factors, such as financial development and capital account openness are far less important and waves of capital flows are primarily determined by global factors, such as global risk and global investment growth. They measure global risk using data from the Volatility Index (VXO), which measures market expectations of volatility and is calculated by the Chicago Board Options Exchanges (CBOE) and global liquidity using data from global money supply growth calculated from the sum of M2 in the US, Euro-zone, and Japan and M4 in the UK.

Table 5.1 Panel fixed effects analysis, N = 98 countries, 1984–2015

Variables	(1)	(2)	(3)	(4)	(5)
Log initial GDP per capita (PPP)	1.504*** (0.135)	1.369*** (0.145)	1.134*** (0.141)	1.318*** (0.157)	0.735*** (0.186)
Index of institutions		0.824** (0.331)	0.110 (0.360)	−0.003 (0.459)	−0.393 (0.480)
Capital account openness			0.201*** (0.030)	0.152*** (0.035)	0.092*** (0.034)
Log years of schooling				0.282* (0.155)	−1.666*** (0.313)
Log trade				0.056 (0.167)	−0.324** (0.159)
Log financial development				−0.049 (0.047)	−0.066 (0.043)
Log inflation				−0.072** (0.035)	−0.017 (0.037)
Observations	675	669	658	544	544
R-squared	0.770	0.775	0.793	0.823	0.855
Country FE	Yes	Yes	Yes	Yes	Yes
Year FE	No	No	No	No	Yes
Normality, *p*-values	0.00	0.00	0.00	0.00	0.00
Hetero, *p*-values	0.00	0.00	0.00	0.00	0.00
Serial correlation, *p*-values	0.00	0.00	0.00	0.00	0.00

Notes Dependent variable is log capital inflows per capita (log*F). With 98 countries and eight time points (computed as four-year averages for each variable over the eight non-overlapping four-year windows from 1984–2017 in 98 countries. To complete this four-year window averages, data years 2016 and 2017 were deleted), the potential number of observations is 98 (countries) × 8 (four-year periods) = 784, which would be the sample size if all country-year observations were non-missing. For the unbalanced panel, the observed sample size varies across estimated models and observations are relatively smaller in Models 4 and 5 due to missing data on years of schooling, inflation rate and financial development. The estimated models were based on using maximum available observations but these models were run on a common sample gives similar results. Robust standard errors are in parentheses. ***$p < 0.01$, **$p < 0.05$, *$p < 0.1$

domestic factors (e.g., capital account openness) are still found highly significant determinants of capital inflows even if global shocks are controlled for (i.e., global shocks are attributed to year dummies in Model 5). Some other studies that share a similar view that global factors are more important than country-specific factors are based on a small sample of countries or on the country samples of a particular region; for example, Fernandez-Arias (1996) examines a sample of 13 middle income countries and Fostel and Kaminsky (2007) use data for 20 Latin American countries. In contrast to these studies, our empirical results suggest domestic factors factors primarily determine international flows and these effects extend beyond the common global shocks in explaining the Lucas paradox. Our results are based on data from 98 countries from all regions.

Overall, the analysis of FE results suggest that, in the presence of capital account restrictions, an improvement in the level of institutional quality is not sufficient to guarantee higher capital inflows and capital account openness is a highly significant determinant. In other words, in the panel FE model the effect of the institutions index on capital inflows is not robust; however, the effect of capital account openness is robust. Therefore, the lack of a statistically significant effect of the institutions index may be due to the use of an aggregate measure of the institutions index, whereas examining the effects of specific aspects of institutional quality on specific types of capital flows may give us a clearer picture of this relationship.[3] Another possible explanation for this insignificant effect is endogeneity of the regressor, which was addressed by using a GMM estimate in Sect. 5.4.

On the other hand, the strong (in terms of statistical significance) effect of capital account openness is persistent across all panel models examined; however, capital account openness is also unable to fully account for the Lucas paradox. An improvement in countries' economic development (GDP per capita) still plays a significant role in attracting capital inflows and the effect of economic development is robust to country-specific effects, common time effects, and inclusion of standard controls. The panel FE findings also suggest capital flows to rich countries, i.e., existence of the Lucas paradox, therefore confirming the cross-section OLS results.

5.3.1 Diagnostic Tests

A formal diagnostic tests of the results are conducted for normality, heteroscedasticity, and serial-correlation.[4] The diagnostic tests for the FE models suggest that the estimated regressions, although using log*-transformed specifications, do not pass any of the tests. The diagnostic tests check whether the untransformed specification of the models used in the literature satisfies any of the diagnostic tests and find the same result.[5] It is observed that there are a few outlier observations (i.e., observations

[3]This issue was considered by analysing individual aspects of institutional quality in Chap. 6.

[4]See details of the diagnostic tests for panel models in Appendix A.

[5]The non-log models and their diagnostic tests are not reported.

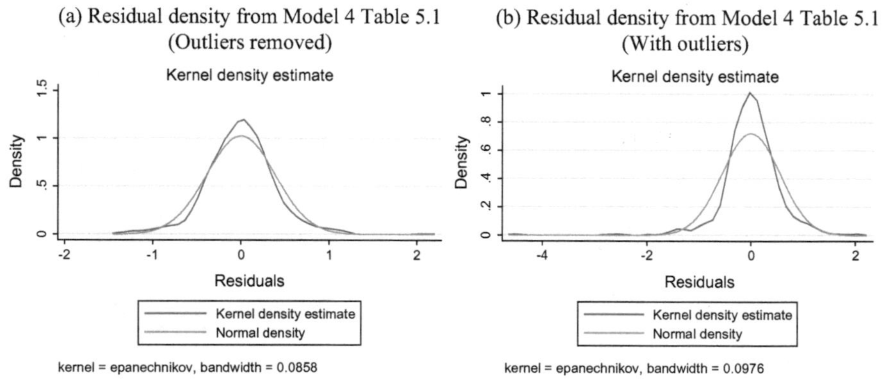

Fig. 5.1 Kernel density and normal density of estimated residuals: 1984–2015

that are substantially different from all other observations) in the sample. It is possible that the failure of the diagnostic tests in the panel FE estimation may be affected by these outliers. Nine outlier observations are found and removed these outliers; however, the estimated regression model excluding these outlier observations does not pass these tests.[6] The residual density plots from the panel model suggest that the log*-transformed model with outliers removed (Fig. 5.1a) is closer to being normally distributed than that with outliers (Fig. 5.1b). However, there is no significant change in the model estimates in Table 5.1 if the outlier observations are removed, which is in contrast to cross-section findings where we found a significant change in model estimates if outlier observations are removed. Based on inspection of the residual density plots, the log* model fits the data better in the panel models and therefore the log model is used for the rest of the panel model analysis.

5.3.2 Decomposition of GDP Per Capita

Similar to cross-section chapter analysis, income per capita is decomposed into total factor productivity (TFP) and capital per worker in this panel data analysis. The panel data analysis goes deeper than the cross-section analysis by examining this decomposition effect for different types of capital inflows (i.e., FDI, portfolio, private debt). A motivation for this extended analysis is to see if the nature of the Lucas paradox changes across types of flows.

Table 5.2 reports empirical results and finds a positive and statistically significant effect of capital stock per worker. This suggests the Lucas paradox extends beyond

[6]Outlier observations are identified by using studentized residuals and we remove all observations that exceed +2.5 and −2.5. For the panel model, the outliers are: Finland, Panama, Japan, Malaysia, Denmark, Hungary, Sweden, Israel, and Korea. The results of the outlier removed models and their diagnostic tests are not reported.

Table 5.2 Panel fixed effects analysis, decomposition of GDP per capita, N = 82 countries, 1984–2015

Variables	Capital inflows (FDI + portfolio)	FDI	Portfolio	Private debt
	(1)	(2)	(3)	(4)
Log initial capital stock per worker	0.419*** (0.113)	0.455*** (0.095)	−0.071 (0.115)	0.023 (0.111)
Log initial TFP	0.751*** (0.138)	0.626*** (0.138)	0.027 (0.155)	0.375*** (0.132)
Institutions index	0.553 (0.492)	0.692* (0.402)	0.224 (0.363)	0.427* (0.227)
Capital account openness	0.180*** (0.036)	0.142*** (0.031)	0.019 (0.031)	0.055** (0.027)
Log trade	0.521*** (0.183)	0.462** (0.180)	0.179 (0.161)	0.026 (0.117)
Log financial development	−0.006 (0.048)	−0.096* (0.050)	0.023 (0.059)	0.039 (0.035)
Log inflation	−0.084** (0.036)	−0.065** (0.032)	−0.097*** (0.037)	−0.016 (0.031)
Observations	509	542	509	344
R-squared	0.809	0.772	0.422	0.441
Country FE	Yes	Yes	Yes	Yes
Year FE	No	No	No	No

Notes The dependent variable in each model is log capital inflows per capita (log*F). All types of capital flows data are not available for all countries in the sample and therefore, the number of observations is changing across models. For the unbalanced panel, observed sample size varies across estimated models using different types of capital inflows. A maximum number of observations (542) is found for FDI inflows and the number of observations (344) is smallest for private debt inflows. The results are checked by using the maximum number of observations on a common sample and similar results are found. Robust standard errors are in parentheses. ***$p < 0.01$, **$p < 0.05$, *$p < 0.1$

the productivity of investment. In particular, capital does not flow downhill in the neoclassical sense even after accounting for variation in TFP differences, capital account imperfections and institutional frictions. The panel model results are consistent with the cross-section results, even though country-specific effects and time-series variation are utilised in the data. The results are robust to standard controls. However, no evidence is found that the institutions index captures the Lucas paradox more precisely than capital account openness in the panel model estimates.[7] The result also suggests that the uphill flows are driven by direct investment (i.e., FDI). In par-

[7]In the cross-section model, inclusion of the institutions index reduces the positive and significant effects of capital stock per worker on capital inflows to a greater extent than the inclusion of capital

ticular, if FDI, portfolio, and private debt are examined separately, then FDI flows are uphill (Model 2); portfolio flows are downhill in the neoclassical sense (Models 3 and 4); however, the effects is not statistically significant. The Lucas paradox does not disappear completely even if the independent effect of capital stock per worker on capital inflows is examined. Accounting for TFP variation across countries or other potential barriers (e.g., capital market imperfections, institutional frictions) is not sufficient to explain why capital tends to flow to capital-abundant rich countries.

5.4 Dynamic Model Analysis

The Lucas paradox is examined in a dynamic model to check whether the failure of the empirical models in the cross-section and panel FE analysis to find an explanation for the Lucas paradox is due to not controlling for the lagged effects of capital flows. In particular, a dynamic model including a lagged dependent variable (LDV), as in Eq. 5.8, is estimated for panel data. However, inclusion of a LDV in the FE model renders the FE estimates biased and inconsistent and therefore a system-GMM estimator addresses endogeneity of the LDV. Two-step GMM is used and the LDV is assumed to be the only endogenous variable. A robust standard errors is obtained from Windmeijer's (2005) methodology that provides a consistent estimator even in the presence of heteroscedasticity and corrects for finite sample biases of the two-step estimator. For the differenced equation, two backward lags of the dependent variable are used to create GMM-type instruments and the differences of all other exogenous explanatory variables are used as standard instruments. For the level equation, lagged differences of the dependent variable are used as GMM-type instruments and constants are used as standard instruments.

Table 5.3 reports system-GMM estimation results and finds that institutional quality and capital account openness are both significant determinants of capital inflows (Model 1). When disaggregated types of flows are examined, FDI, portfolio and private debt flow uphill to rich countries (Models 2–4). The dynamic model findings are also robust to the inclusion of a standard set of controls. When disaggregated types of flows are examined, the effect of capital account openness on FDI inflows is insignificant, in contrast to the FE findings, and is statistically significant in case of capital inflows (sum of FDI and portfolio), suggesting that the evidence is not so strong. However, the specification test (i.e., the Hansen test) suggests that the estimated regression for the FDI model does not pass the specification test. In particular, the Hansen test p-value rejects (at the 5% level) instrument validity for the FDI model (Model 2). Following Roodman's (2009) observation, it is noted that GMM results depend on the assumptions made, such as number of lags used as internal instruments and the choice of variables considered as endogenous or exogenous.

account openness. In the panel model, there is not such a strong change in the effects (results not reported) depending on specific frictions (the institutions index and capital controls).

Table 5.3 Panel GMM, N = 98 countries, 1984–2015

	Capital Inflows (FDI + portfolio)	FDI	Portfolio	Private debt
	(1)	(2)	(3)	(4)
Log initial GDP per capita (PPP)	0.313*** (0.0720)	0.198*** (0.0487)	0.0924** (0.0393)	0.152*** (0.0395)
Institutions index	1.696*** (0.316)	0.967*** (0.207)	1.423*** (0.298)	0.476** (0.205)
Capital account openness	0.0541** (0.0245)	0.0205 (0.0239)	0.00590 (0.0188)	0.0241 (0.0211)
Log trade	0.0532 (0.0922)	0.159* (0.0867)	−0.312*** (0.0746)	−0.0474 (0.0522)
Log financial development	−0.0163 (0.0273)	−0.0368* (0.0223)	0.0646** (0.0304)	−0.0254 (0.0261)
Log inflation	−0.0566* (0.0302)	−0.0180 (0.0258)	−0.0636* (0.0355)	0.00425 (0.0122)
Flows (lagged)	0.323*** (0.109)	0.530*** (0.0992)	0.0678 (0.154)	0.215 (0.192)
Observations	496	575	496	394
Cross-sections	93	94	93	65
No of instruments	27	27	27	27
Hansen J (*p*-values)	0.118	0.0503	0.210	0.245
AR(1) (*p*-values)	0.00192	0.0451	0.0219	0.160
AR(2) (*p*-values)	0.715	0.497	0.849	0.620

Notes The dependent variable in each model is log capital inflows per capita (log*F). For the unbalanced panel, observed sample size varies across estimated models using different types of capital inflows and maximum available observations are utilized in each regression model; however, regression models estimated on a common sample give similar results. Robust standard errors are in parentheses. ***$p < 0.01$, **$p < 0.05$, * $p < 0.1$

5.5 Interaction Effect and Nonlinear Effects of the Determinants of Capital Flows

The empirical exercise in Chap. 4 suggests, when restricting the relationship between capital inflows and institutional quality in a log*-linear model, that the relationship between capital inflows and institutional quality is positive. However, there may be important non-linearity modifying this relationship and institutional quality might have stronger positive effect on capital inflows in the rich countries compared to that in the poor countries. This section examines the non-linearity or non-constant marginal effects of the variables of interest.

It is noteworthy that the determinants of capital inflows across the main categories are closely related and different types of determinants could reasonably interact with each other to have a combined effect on capital inflows both directly and indirectly. For example, a higher level of economic development may have a greater effect on capital inflows if restrictions on the capital account are removed, suggesting a potential interaction effect between capital account openness and economic development on capital inflows. Again, capital account openness may attract more foreign capital if property rights are well defined and contracts are enforced in the liberalized countries, suggesting an interaction effect between capital account openness and institutions on capital inflows. These interaction effects suggest a conditional hypothesis in the sense that the relationships between two variables (in this case, say, capital inflows and the institutions index) depend on the value of one or more other variables (e.g., economic development). A multiplicative model may therefore improve the empirical analysis.

Moreover, anecdotal evidence suggests that it is not unreasonable to expect the relationship between two variables (say, institutional quality and capital inflows) to be nonlinear depending on the value of another variable (say, economic development). From a real-world perspective, there are ample examples of 'sweatshop operations' in developing countries where laws are permissive or weakly enforced and the extent of enforcement is determined by the systematic and deliberate choice of multi-national corporations (MNCs). MNCs in developing countries do not follow the code of business they are obliged to follow if operating in developed countries and capitalize the advantage of low-wage labour and reduce production costs by re-locating investments to developing countries. For example, during the 1990s Nike's supplier factories in developing countries abused labour through long-hours and forced overtime (Litvin 2003). Reebok, Gap, and Walmart were also found to be selling clothes produced by child labour (Spar 1998). These activities of the MNCs were feasible due to the lack of strong institutional standards, such as lack of transparency and less-strict investment rules, in the FDI host developing countries. As the host countries develop, implementation of regulations improves and transparency increases. Investment related rules and regulations and the MNCs activities come under stricter scrutiny, which may encourage MNCs to re-locate their new investments to countries that offer less-strict rules. This suggests that the effects of institutional quality on capital inflows may be non-linear across different stages of economic development of developing countries.

The recent empirical literature on the determinants of capital inflows has emphasized the relevance of nonlinear effect and considers selected interaction effects in empirical model. For example, Reinhardt et al. (2013) focus on the interaction between capital account openness and economic development (GDP per capita relative to the US) and argue that whether capital account openness would increase or decrease capital inflows depends on a country's level of economic development. They show that accounting for an interaction effect between capital account openness and GDP per capita in a panel FE model is sufficient to explain the Lucas paradox. Gourinchas and Jeanne (2013) examine the interaction between capital account openness and productivity and find that capital flows out of countries that are relatively more productive, which they refer to as the 'allocation puzzle'. Okada (2013) investigates an interaction between capital account openness and an index of institutions in a dynamic panel model and finds, in contrast to Alfaro et al. (2008), that the institutions index independently does not solve the Lucas paradox but that the interaction of the institutions index and capital account openness does and significantly determines capital inflows.

The remainder of this section analyses the various interaction effects and examines whether controlling for an interaction term between two determinants, as argued in the literature, provides a solution to the Lucas paradox. In particular, this section examines the robustness of the findings of the interaction effect results in the existing literature and compares the results from different combinations of interaction terms using alternative estimation approaches. Okada's (2013) interaction effect is first examined and then Reinhardt et al. (2013). In addition, on the basis of the arguments and anecdotal evidence presented above, an interaction term is introduced between economic development and the institutions index. The aim of including this new interaction term is to examine whether the marginal effect of the institutions index on capital inflows is a linear function of the interacting variable (i.e., economic development). A margin plot analysis is also completed, which is surprisingly missing in the existing studies that use interaction effects.

5.5.1 *Institutional Quality and Capital Account Openness*

Okada uses five-year average panel data for 112 countries over the period from 1985 to 2009 and uses GMM (Arellano and Bond 1991) to address endogeneity problems (Okada includes a LDV to capture the effects of lagged inflows on current inflows and uses GMM to address the endogeneity resulting from correlation between the LDV and the error term). Okada estimates the following empirical model[8]:

$$F_{it} = \rho F_{it-1} + \beta_2 I_{it} + \beta_3 FO_{it} + \varphi_1 (FO_{it} \Delta I_{it}) + \gamma X_{it} + \mu_i + \delta_t + \varepsilon_{it} \quad (5.9)$$

The interaction term captures the joint effects of capital account openness (FO_{it}) and the institutions index (I_{it}) on per capita inflows (F_{it}). At the margin, the total effect of increasing capital account openness (institutional quality) can be calculated by examining the partial derivatives of per capita inflows (in Eq. 5.9) with respect to capital account openness (the institutions index).

$$\frac{\partial(F_{it})}{\partial(FO_{it})} = \beta_3 + \varphi_1 I_{it} \quad (5.10a)$$

[8]Okada uses a dummy for country-specific fixed effects in his empirical specification but results he reports from the GMM estimates show only time dummies were included in the regression. Time dummies are used only for the Okada replication.

$$\frac{\partial(F_{it})}{\partial(I_{it})} = \beta_2 + \varphi_1 FO_{it} \tag{5.10b}$$

Okada finds that institutions and capital account openness cannot independently determine capital inflows if they are both included separately but their interaction effect has a positive and statistically significant effect on capital inflows. Okada's linear model (i.e., Eq. 5.9), is replicated and then replaced it with preferred log* model (i.e., with a log*-transformed dependent variable) because log* capital inflows per capita is approximately normally distributed compared to the untransformed (i.e., linear) model used by Okada.[9] It is noteworthy that Okada refutes Alfaro et al.'s (2008) findings, arguing that the interaction term can explain the Lucas paradox; however, none of the regression models he reports show the existence of the Lucas paradox, i.e. a strong significant positive effect of GDP per capita on capital inflows.[10]

Table 5.4 reports estimates from Okada's linear model (Eq. 5.9) and also reports estimates from the log* model. The results suggest that Okada's (2013) findings are not robust to an alternative specification (i.e., log* model) and alternative estimator (i.e., panel FE).[11] Model 1 reports Okada's original estimates presented in his paper for his dataset. It is observed that the interaction term is a statistically significant determinant of capital inflows whereas the individual effect of the institutions index is not significant and GDP per capita is insignificant. Models 2 and 3 report empirical findings of our estimation and suggest the interaction term is significant but it no longer makes GDP per capita insignificant regardless of whether the model's dependent variable is linear or log*-transformed (Models 2 and 3, respectively). The results remain the same if Okada's full-model in linear form is used (Model 4). However, the significant effect of Okada's interaction term disappears in the log*-transformed full-model (Model 5). In particular, in a dynamic model if the log* of the dependent variable and logs of the RHS variables are used (i.e., Model 5), Okada's interaction effect is insignificant; however, GDP per capita retains its statistical significance.

FE estimator is also employed to examine whether the results for Okada's interaction effect from GMM estimates are sensitive to alternative estimators and include a LDV to maximize comparability with GMM estimates. The FE estimates with a LDV support the GMM findings and suggest that the specific interaction term proposed by Okada cannot explain the Lucas paradox (Models 6, 7, 8, 9, and 10). It seems Models 7 and 8 with the interaction term can solve the Lucas paradox. However, it was also

[9]This is based on histogram plots, see Fig. C.2 in Appendix C.

[10]See the regression results in Tables 1–3 in Okada (2013, pp. 136–137).

[11]For a replication of Okada's analysis, data were constructed for the variables used in Okada's model from the same sources, for the same number countries, and for the same sample period. So the regression results from Table 5.4 is based on a sample of countries and sample period that are different from our benchmark sample of 98 countries and the benchmark sample period, 1984–2015. The choice of this different sample supports a view that the findings from different empirical chapters are not sensitive to alternative country sample or sample period. Our GMM estimator may not be the same GMM estimator used by Okada as he gives no more details about his GMM estimator. In particular, Okada does not provide information on the number of the instruments used in the GMM, see regression results of Tables 1–3 in Okada (2013, pp. 136–137). Stata's system-GMM was used and the number of instruments are reported in each GMM model.

Table 5.4 Panel GMM and fixed effects (Interaction Model of Okada 2012), N = 110 countries, 1985–2009

Variables	Linear	Linear	Log*	Linear	Log*	Log*	Log*	Log*	Log*	Log*
	GMM					FE				
	(1)	(2)	(3)	(4)	(5)	(6)	(7)	(8)	(9)	(10)
Log initial GDP per capita (PPP)	−0.123 (0.118)	0.183*** (0.030)	1.033*** (0.217)	0.167*** (0.034)	0.966*** (0.347)		0.156 (0.270)	0.303 (0.211)	0.475* (0.266)	0.782*** (0.233)
Index of institutions	0.019 (0.019)	0.319** (0.160)	1.486** (0.751)	0.153 (0.143)	1.345 (0.843)	2.709*** (0.628)	1.477** (0.685)	0.999 (0.688)	1.547** (0.632)	1.537*** (0.592)
Capital account openness	−0.845* (0.468)	−0.132*** (0.040)	−0.555** (0.229)	−0.075** (0.037)	−0.341 (0.245)	−0.422* (0.256)	−0.507** (0.235)	−0.827*** (0.184)	−0.513** (0.240)	−0.959*** (0.193)
(Index of institutions).(Capital account openness)	0.015* (0.008)	0.200*** (0.059)	0.951*** (0.353)	0.117** (0.053)	0.605 (0.369)	0.894** (0.403)	0.865** (0.348)	1.449*** (0.272)	0.885** (0.358)	1.700*** (0.283)
Lagged capital inflows per capita	0.902*** (0.037)	0.446*** (0.043)	0.042 (0.200)	0.403*** (0.039)	0.297 (0.212)		0.301** (0.128)		0.317** (0.123)	
Financial development				0.001*** (0.000)	0.052 (0.111)		0.144 (0.101)	0.163* (0.098)	0.164 (0.100)	0.189* (0.101)
Trade				0.001*** (0.000)	0.017 (0.255)		0.004 (0.183)	−0.042 (0.167)	0.134 (0.189)	0.316* (0.168)

(continued)

Table 5.4 (continued)

Variables	Linear	Linear	Log*	Linear	Log*	Log*	Log*	Log*	Log*	Log*
	GMM					FE				
	(1)	(2)	(3)	(4)	(5)	(6)	(7)	(8)	(9)	(10)
Government consumption				−0.006** (0.003)	−0.334 (0.236)		−0.348* (0.189)	0.061 (0.186)	−0.468** (0.190)	−0.223 (0.173)
Inflation				0.000 (0.000)	0.130* (0.076)		0.101* (0.057)	0.015 (0.022)	0.164*** (0.048)	0.076*** (0.023)
Education	−0.022 (0.182)	0.070** (0.029)	0.069 (0.139)	0.059** (0.024)	−0.168 (0.323)		−0.552** (0.281)	−0.845*** (0.265)	−0.202 (0.238)	−0.039 (0.213)
Observations	375	433	433	412	412	527	412	491	412	491
Number of instruments	Unreported	18	18	22	22					
Number of countries	110	112	112	110	110					
Hansen J (p-value)	0.49	0	0.15	0	0.01					
R-squared						0.638	0.893	0.865	0.887	0.850
Country FE						Yes	Yes	Yes	Yes	Yes
Year FE						No	Yes	Yes	No	No

Model 1 reports Okada's original estimates (See, Okada 2013, Table 3, Model 6, p. 137), Model 2 replicates Okada, Model 3 is Okada but with log* DV, Model 4 replicates Okada's full model (i.e., Okada's untransformed DV and Okada's untransformed RHS), Model 5 to Model 10 use log-models (i.e., log* DV and log RHS variables Model 7 uses FE with LDV, Model 8 uses FE without LDV, Model 9 uses FE excluding common time effects, and Model 10 uses FE excluding LDV and common time effects. Note that this regression result is based on country sample as used in Okada (2013). Robust standard errors are in parentheses, ***$p < 0.01$, **$p < 0.05$, *$p < 0.1$. Initial refers to the first year of each four-year average.). Models estimates use a different scale of institutions index to avoid too small coefficient. Margin plots are drawn based on Model 6. Using (5.10a) coefficient estimates of unscaled institutions index (not reported in the table), the marginal effect of capital account openness start to increase capital inflows from the level of institutional development at 60 ($-0.42(\beta_3) + .009(\varphi_1) * 60 = 0.54$)

examined whether this finding is influenced by the Nickell (1981) bias due to using a LDV or influenced by controlling for common time effects (i.e., year dummies). As common time effects are removed (Model 9) or the LDV is and common time effects are removed (Model 10), GDP per capita is found to retain its strong statistical significant effects on capital inflows. Moreover, the weaker significance of GDP per capita in Model 9 compared to Model 10 is explained by the inclusion of the LDV. The findings therefore remain similar even if an alternative estimation approach (i.e., FE) is employed.

However, the regression estimates do not provide sufficient information on the specific level of institutional quality at which capital account openness starts to increase capital inflows. The marginal effects of capital account openness (institutions index) on capital inflows at different levels of the institutions index (capital account openness) are plotted to answer this question. The margin plots suggest the marginal effect of the institutions index is statistically significant and positive over the observed range capital account openness (Fig. 5.2a) and similar for the capital account openness except for very low values of the institutions index (Fig. 5.2b).[12]

The regression results (Table 5.4) from estimation of Okada's model suggest that if there is a higher degree of property rights and enforcement of contract, capital inflows to a country increase to a greater extent if restrictions on the capital account are reduced. More importantly, the findings from Okada's interaction effect analysis do not suggest a complete solution to the Lucas paradox. Moreover in an empirical specification (i.e., log* model) that better fits the data and with inclusions of standard controls (Model 5), Okada's interaction effect is rather sensitive to the choice of estimators (i.e., insignificant using GMM but significant using FE with a LDV).

5.5.2 Economic Development and Capital Account Openness

Reinhardt et al. (2013) examine the interaction between GDP per capita (relative to the US) and capital account openness and find that capital inflows are higher in poor countries if capital accounts are more open. Reinhardt et al.'s (2013) finding suggests that controlling for capital account restrictions is sufficient to explain the Lucas paradox. More specifically, they argue that the capital account has evolved dramatically over the last 30 years, which has had significant effects on capital inflows. They provide a more careful interpretation of their interaction term than Okada (2013) and the additional information on the total effect (the coefficient sum

[12]Following Brambor et al. (2006), the margin plots are constructed using their Stata code as a basis. Dashed curves around the marginal effect lines (solid lines) show 95% confidence interval, thereby identifying the values of the institutions index (capital account openness) at which the marginal effects are statistically significant at the 5% level. Margin plots are drawn using unscaled institutions index.

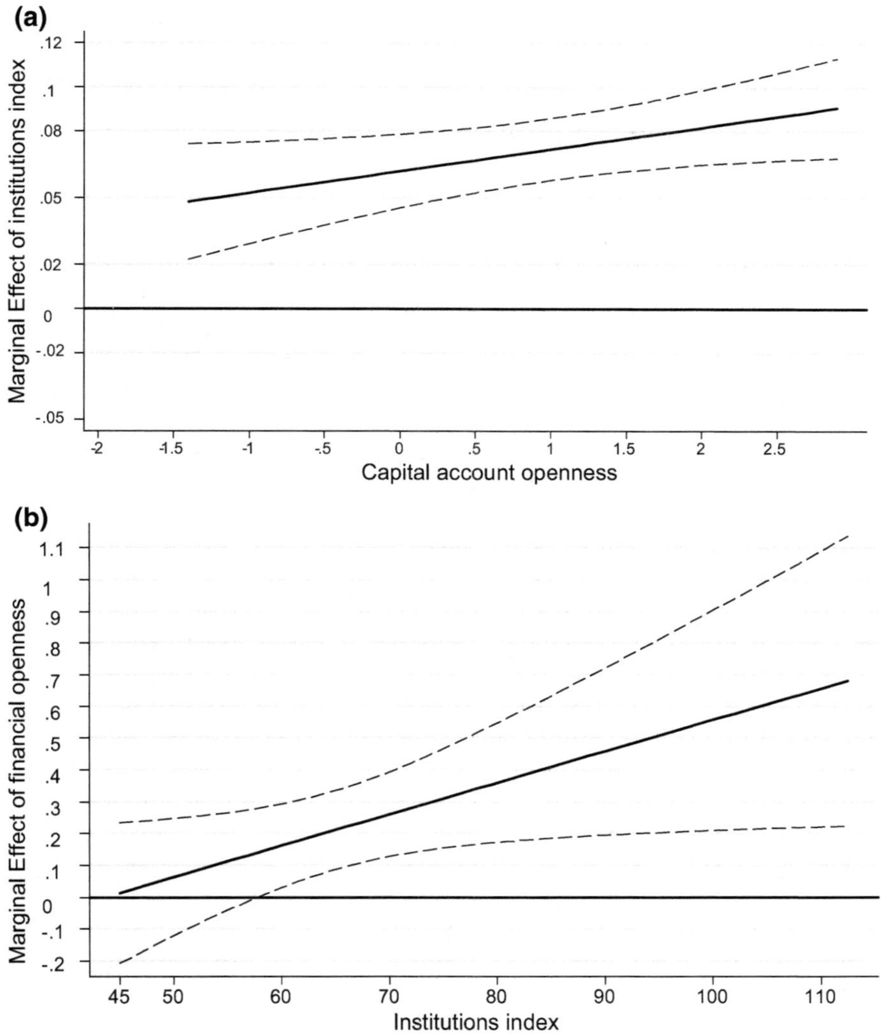

Fig. 5.2 **a** Marginal effects of institutions index at different values of capital account openness. **b** Marginal effects of capital account openness at different values of institution index

of constituent terms and the interaction term).[13] They use the following empirical specification (Eq. 5.11) and examine the dependency of the relationship between capital account openness (FO_{it}) and net capital flows (*Net flows*$_{it}$) on the levels

[13]Reinhardt et al. calculate the total effect of the interaction term between GDP per capita and capital account openness since they normalizing the range of the index of capital account openness to be between 0 and 1.

of economic development (Y_{it}).[14] More specifically, they use the current account balance to GDP ratio (i.e., net capital flows) as the dependent variable. A positive and statistically significant coefficient on the interaction term (φ_2) of their model suggests a current account balance surplus and capital outflows from rich countries if the capital accounts are open.

$$\frac{Netflows_{it}}{GDP_{it}} = \mu_i + \beta_1 \log Y_{it-1} + \beta_3 FO_{it-1} + \varphi_2(\log Y_{it-1} \Delta FO_{it-1}) + \gamma X_{it} + \varepsilon_{it} \quad (5.11)$$

Reinhardt et al.'s interaction term is used to examine the dependency of the relationship between capital account openness and capital inflows on a country's levels of development. This suggests to use gross inflows as the dependent variable to examine Reinhardt et al.'s interaction effect. More specifically, consistent with exercise in previous chapters, the log* of capital inflows per capita (i.e., log* of liabilities of FDI and portfolio equity) is used as the dependent variable, shown in Eq. 5.12. An important difference between the choices of the dependent variables is that the current account is likely an imperfect measure of private capital inflows and, according to balance of payment identity, the current account balance is the counterpart of the sum of the financial account and reserve accumulation.[15] On the other hand, our dependent variable includes only private capital inflows, which is determined by the private rate of return to capital. Therefore, the dependent variable used in this exercise is more relevant for an empirical examination of the implications of Reinhardt et al.'s interaction term for the Lucas paradox.

$$\log^*(F_{it}) = \mu_i + \beta_1 \log Y_{it} + \beta_3 FO_{it} + \varphi_2(\log Y_{it} \Delta FO_{it}) + \gamma X_{it} + \varepsilon_{it} \quad (5.12)$$

Reinhardt et al. interpret a positive and statistically significant coefficient on the interaction term (in Eq. 5.11) as suggesting that capital *outflows* from relatively rich countries if capital accounts are open. In contrast, a positive and statistically significant coefficient on the interaction term (in Eq. 5.12) suggests that capital *inflows* to relatively rich countries if capital accounts are open.

Table 5.5 reports Reinhardt et al.'s interaction effect estimation results using the empirical specification in Eq. 5.12. Model 2 suggests that the marginal effect of capital account openness ($-0.140 + 0.144\log Y$) on capital inflows is positive if countries are rich. Reinhardt et al.'s preferred explanatory variables are included in the model to see whether the main model is robust to other controls and a similar conclusion can be reached (Model 3). Further to that, a robustness check of the significance of

[14]Reinhardt et al. use (t − 1) to refer to initial year which is the year before the respective five-year period window. In contrast, initial year is referred as the first year of each four-year period window. This is consistent with Okada (2013) exercise.

[15]Reinhardt et al. (2013) further refine their dependent variable by netting out reserve accumulation, net official portfolio investment, and other official investment from the current account balance and label it as net private flows (see Table 5.1, p. 245 in Reinhardt et al.). However, the refined dependent variable of net private flows is different from ours in the sense that it still contains private transfers (i.e., remittances) and the net they calculate is inflows minus outflows and we calculate net in the sense of gross inflows net of disinvestment and profit repatriations.

Table 5.5 Panel fixed effects (Interaction Model of Reinhardt et al. 2013): N = 98 countries, 1984–2015

Variables	(1)	(2)	(3)	(4)	(5)	(6)
Log initial GDP pc (PPP) relative to US	0.392*** (0.137)	0.319** (0.131)	0.584*** (0.129)			
Initial capital account openness	0.269*** (0.027)	−0.132*** (0.050)	−0.289*** (0.054)	0.163*** (0.025)	−0.867*** (0.182)	−1.284*** (0.167)
(Log initial GDP pc relative to us). (Initial cap account openness)		0.140*** (0.023)	0.173*** (0.021)			
Log initial GDP per capita				1.160*** (0.140)	1.037*** (0.131)	1.062*** (0.130)
(Log initial GDP pc). (Initial capital account openness)					0.119*** (0.022)	0.164*** (0.020)
Population growth			−0.063 (0.045)			−0.041 (0.047)
Old age dependency ratio			−0.015*** (0.004)			−0.006 (0.004)
Per capita GDP growth			0.019* (0.010)			0.027*** (0.009)
Trade			0.008*** (0.002)			0.004** (0.002)
Observations	654	654	638	655	655	639
R-squared	0.762	0.775	0.811	0.790	0.800	0.829
Country FE	Yes	Yes	Yes	Yes	Yes	Yes
Year FE	No	No	No	No	No	No

Notes The dependent variable in each model is log* capital inflows per capita, more specifically, log* (gross) capital inflows per capita. For the unbalanced panel, observed sample size varies across estimated models and maximum available observations are utilized in each regression model; however, the regression models were estimated on a common sample and found similar results. Robust standard errors are in parentheses, ***$p < 0.01$, **$p < 0.05$, *$p < 0.1$. Initial refers to the first year of each four-year average

Reinhardt et al.'s interaction term was conducted using initial GDP per capita instead of relative GDP per capita to check if the results remain the same (Models 4–6). In other words, controlling for relative income per capita and/or absolute income per capita does not change the overall picture of the findings.

The positive coefficient on the interaction term (e.g., in Model 2 in Table 5.5) suggests that the negative effect of capital account openness changes and eventually increases capital inflows depending on the level of economic development. However, the regression coefficients of the estimated models do not directly inform us of the specific value of economic development (i.e., GDP per capita) at which the marginal effect of capital account openness on capital inflows changes from negative to positive. The margin plot shows the marginal effect of capital account openness on capital inflows at different levels of economic development in Fig. 5.3a. Similarly, Fig. 5.3b shows the marginal effect of GDP per capita at different levels of capital account openness.

Figure 5.3a suggests that the marginal effect of capital account openness on capital inflows changes across different levels of per capita income. In particular, the marginal effect of capital account openness on capital inflows is negative if the country's per capita income is not sufficiently high. More specifically, if a country is poor and log of GDP per capita falls between 6.5 (in dollars $665) and 7 (in dollars $1096) (i.e., the threshold value for this sample), increasing capital account openness significantly reduces capital inflows.

On the other hand, if log of GDP per capita of a country is more than 8 (in dollars $2981), increasing capital account openness significantly increases capital inflows. Based on these results, it can be predicted that if per capita income of a country is at the 25th percentile (equivalent to the values of log GDP per capita at/below 7, such as Ivory Coast or Ghana in the sample we are investigating), increasing capital account openness is predicted to reduce capital inflows. Alternatively, if per capita income of a country is at/above the 50th percentile (equivalent for the values of log GDP per capita at/above 8, such as Belarus or Honduras in the sample we are investigating), increasing capital account openness is predicted to increase capital inflows. However, it is not evident in the sample that the marginal effect of log GDP per capita is negative for any observed range of values for capital account openness (Fig. 5.3b).

Overall, therefore, controlling for the interaction effect between the level of economic development and capital account openness gives us interesting threshold effects of economic development on the relationship between capital inflows and capital account openness. However, controlling for such interaction effect is not sufficient to explain the Lucas paradox. In contrast to Reinhardt et al., the findings of this exercise (gross private) suggests capital inflows are higher in rich countries if capital accounts are open.

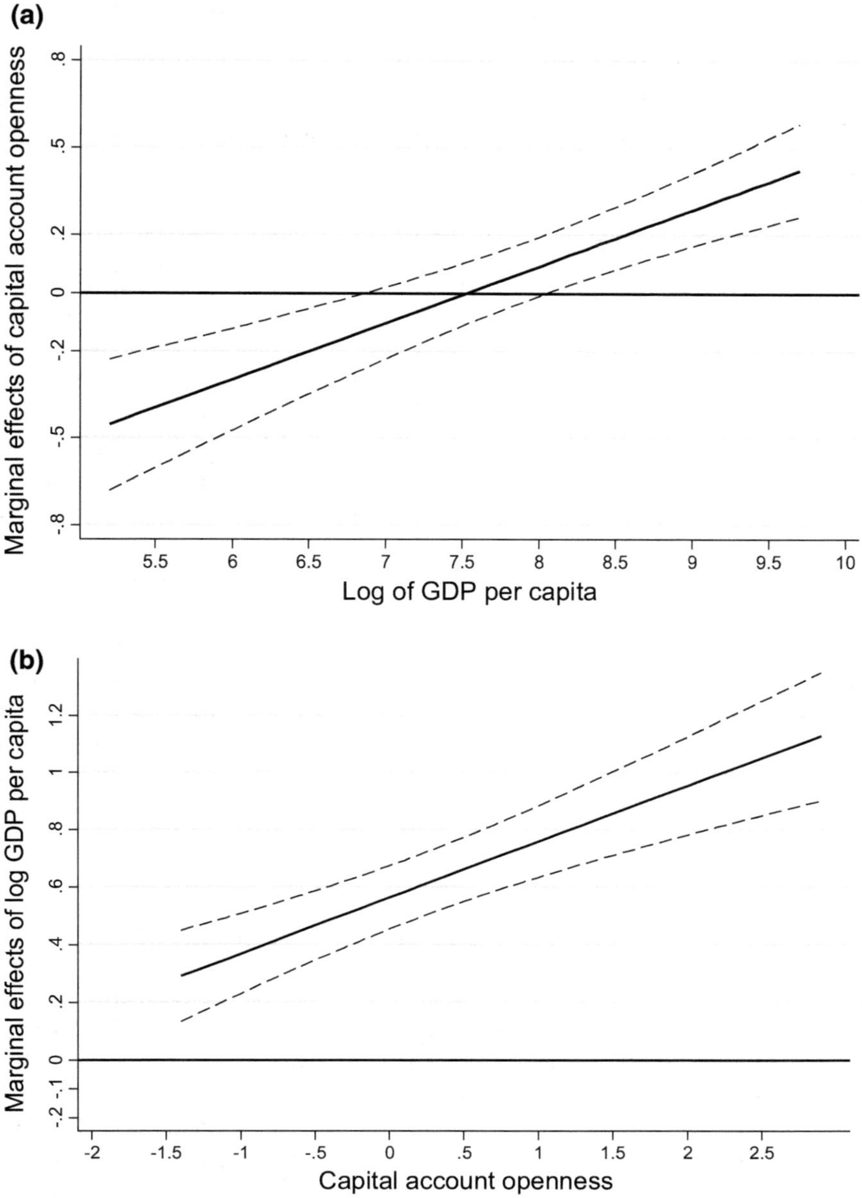

Fig. 5.3 **a** Marginal effects of capital account openness at different values of GDP per capita. **b** Marginal effects of GDP per capita at different values of capital account openness

5.5.3 Economic Development and Institutional Quality

Based on the discussion that the marginal effect of institutional quality on capital inflows may depend on the level of economic development, an interaction effect between economic development and the institutions index is examined on capital inflows. A squared term of the institutions index (and GDP per capita) is also included and considered as a self-interaction, to examine whether the slope of the relationship between the institutions index (GDP per capita) and capital inflows has the same sign and increase monotonically as the quality of institutions (GDP per capita) increases. The empirical model, including squared terms and the interaction term, is as follows.

$$\log^*(F)_{it} = \mu_i + \beta_1 \log Y_{it} + \beta_2 I_{it} + \beta_3 (\log Y_{it})^2 + \beta_4 I_{it}^2 + \varphi_3 (\log Y_{it} \Delta I_{it}) + \gamma X_{it} + \varepsilon_{it} \tag{5.13}$$

where the log* of per capita inflow is assumed to be a function of log GDP per capita ($\log Y$), log of GDP per capita squared $(\log Y_{it})^2$, the institutions index (I), the institutions index squared (I_{it}^2), the interaction between log of GDP per capita and the institutions index ($\log Y \Delta I$), and a set of controls (X). Equation (5.14a) shows the marginal effect of the institutions index when the modifying variable is the log of GDP per capita. In a similar vein, Eq. (5.14b) shows the marginal effect of the log of GDP per capita on capital inflows when the modifying variable is the institutions index:

$$\frac{\partial \log^* F_{it}}{\partial I_{it}} = \beta_2 + 2\beta_4 I_{it} + \varphi_3 \log Y_{it} \tag{5.14a}$$

$$\frac{\partial \log^* F_{it}}{\partial (\log Y_{it})} = \beta_1 + 2\beta_3 \log Y_{it} + \varphi_3 I_{it} \tag{5.14b}$$

Table 5.6 reports the empirical findings for the model including the interaction term and the squared-terms. The coefficient estimate for the interaction term (Model 2) is a positive and statistically significant, which suggests the marginal effect ($-0.111 + 0.015\log Y$) of the institutions index on capital inflows is more positive if the country is sufficiently rich. In particular, the institutions index has a negative marginal effect on capital inflows at lower levels of the GDP per capita and has a positive effect at higher levels. Model 6 suggests that the interaction effect on capital inflows is statistically significant in the presence of the controls (in Model 6) and suggests that the marginal effect of the institutions index on capital inflows is positive if the country is richer.

Examining the margin plot (5.14a)[16] it is found that the marginal effect of the institutions index on capital inflows is negative if the lowest value of log GDP per capita is used from the observed sample ($-0.111 + 0.015(5.62) = -0.03$). However, the marginal effect of the institutions on capital inflows is statistically significantly increase capital inflows for the range of values of log GDP per capita from 8 and

[16]The margin plots are drawn based on Model 2 that excludes the squared terms.

Table 5.6 Panel fixed effects: non-linear effects and new interaction term: N = 98 countries, 1984–2015

Variables	(1)	(2)	(3)	(4)	(5)	(6)
Log initial GDP per capita	1.134*** (0.141)	0.188 (0.237)	1.125*** (0.143)	−3.979*** (0.920)	−3.897*** (0.965)	−5.266*** (0.994)
Log initial GDP per capita squared				0.291*** (0.058)	0.287*** (0.061)	0.302*** (0.068)
Institutions index	0.001 (0.004)	−0.111*** (0.020)	−0.026 (0.019)	0.005 (0.003)	−0.004 (0.019)	−0.068** (0.031)
Institutions index squared			0.021 (0.016)		0.007 (0.016)	−0.032 (0.028)
(Log initial GDP pc) (Institutions index)		0.015*** (0.003)				0.014** (0.006)
Capital account openness	0.201*** (0.030)		0.202*** (0.030)	0.171*** (0.029)	0.172*** (0.029)	0.096*** (0.036)
Log years of schooling						0.413*** (0.151)
Log trade						0.118 (0.151)
Log financial development						−0.047 (0.039)
Log inflation						−0.039 (0.031)
Observations	658	669	658	658	658	535
R-squared	0.793	0.786	0.794	0.805	0.805	0.847
Country FE	Yes	Yes	Yes	Yes	Yes	Yes
Year FE	No	No	No	No	No	No

Notes The dependent variable in each model is log capital inflows per capita (log*F). For the unbalanced panel, observed sample size varies across estimated models and maximum available observations are utilized in each regression model; however, we find the regression models estimated on a common sample give similar results. Robust standard errors are in parentheses, ***$p < 0.01$, **$p < 0.05$, *$p < 0.1$ Initial refers to the first year of each four-year average

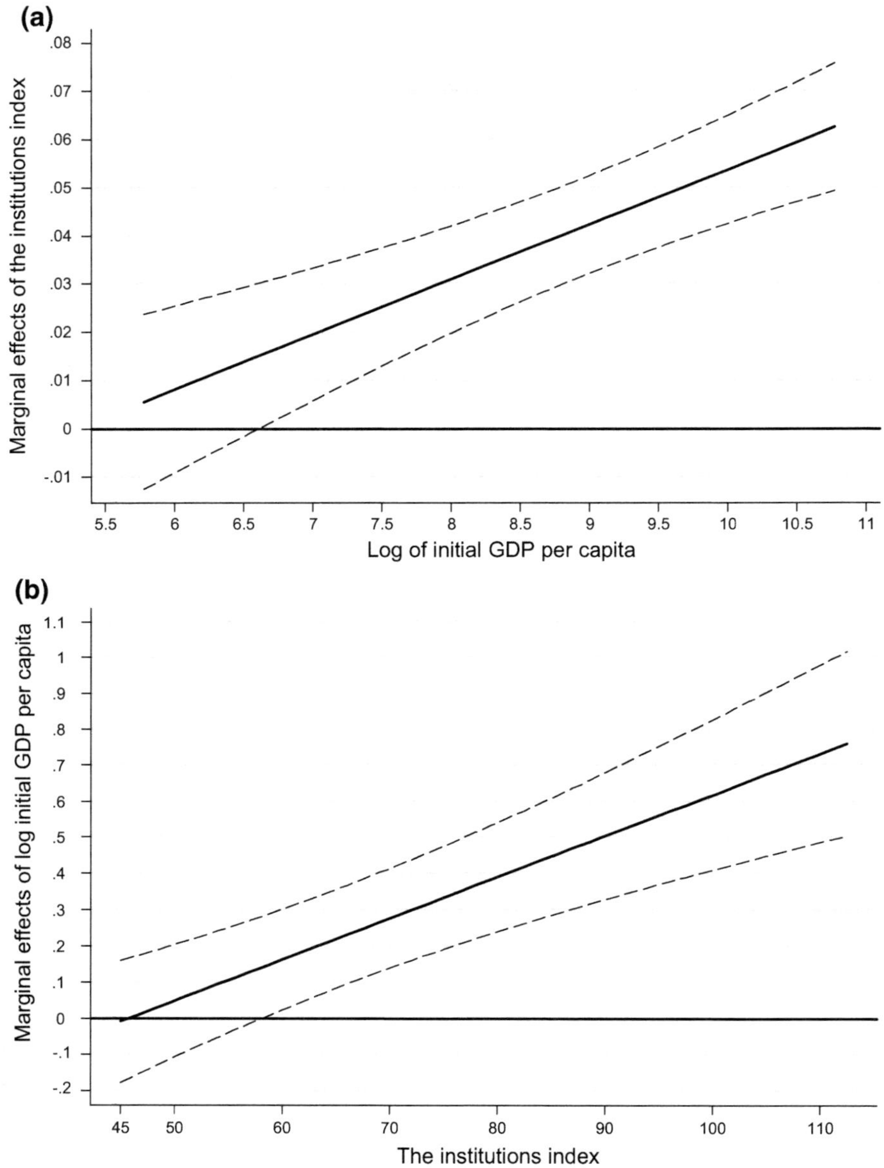

Fig. 5.4 **a** Marginal effects of the institutions index at different values of log GDP per capita. **b** Marginal effects of log GDP per capita at different values of the institutions index

above. Figure 5.4b suggests the marginal effect of log GDP per capita on capital inflows is positive over the observed range of values.

The results from this new interaction effect analysis suggest that the hypothesized relationship is not found in the country sample, which might not be surprising in the sense that an aggregated index for institutional quality was examined for these exercises. In other words, the composite index for institutional quality is unable to examine variation in responses of capital inflows to different aspects of institutional quality. More specifically, an intuitively more plausible argument suggests that, if property rights and contract enforcement are ensured at an early stage of economic development (i.e., a lower-income developing country), then foreign investors prefer these locations from the choice set (i.e., the marginal effect of the institutions index is positive in these locations). As the country reaches a higher stage of economic development (i.e., becomes middle to upper middle income country), other aspects of institutional development, such as stricter environmental rules, investment regulations, and labour standards begin to kick in. The MNCs' cost of doing business in these locations then increases and the MNCs may prefer to relocate their investments (i.e., the marginal effect of the institutions index is then expected to be negative). In Chap. 6, the implications of disaggregated components of the aggregated institutional quality index are examined for FDI flows.

5.6 Summary of Panel Model Analysis

In the panel model analysis, the significant effect of the institutions index disappears and capital account openness is instead a robust determinant of capital inflows in panel FE models. More specifically, this result suggests, once country-specific characteristics are controlled for and time-series effects of the data are utilised, a country's policies relating to capital account convertibility are a highly influential factor for foreign investors in considering investment locations. However, if a dynamic panel model is employed and potential endogeneity is controlled for, then improvement in a country's institutional quality and generous policies to capital account convertibility are both strong determinants of capital inflows. More specifically, strong institutions and removal of restrictions on capital account transactions both have significant positive impacts on decision making when a foreign investor considers a location for a new investment project. However, accounting for policies with respect to capital account convertibility or institutional quality does not fully remove the significant effect of economic development on capital inflows (i.e., the Lucas paradox).

The claims in the panel model literature that the independent effects of the determinants are inadequate to explain the Lucas paradox are examined to check whether an interaction effect helps to provide a satisfactory explanation to the Lucas paradox. More specifically, alternative interaction terms are examined as determinants of capital inflows including interactions between an institutions index and capital account openness, between capital account openness and economic development, and between an institutions index and economic development. The interaction effect results in the existing literature are not robust to alternative model specifications and are sensitive to the choice of estimation methods. Economic development still remains a primary determinant of capital inflows. To sum, the Lucas paradox stands as yet, unresolved. This evidence is based on a reasonably long sample period for a sufficiently large sample of countries.

References

Alfaro L, Kalemli-Ozcan S, Volosovych V (2008) Why doesn't capital flow from rich to poor countries? An empirical investigation. Rev Econ Stat 90(2):347–368

Anderson TW, Hsiao C (1981) Estimation of dynamic models with error components. J Am Stat Assoc 76(375):598–606

Arellano M, Bond S (1991) Some tests of specification for panel data: Monte Carlo evidence and an application to employment equations. Rev Econ Stud 58(2):277–297

Blundell R, Bond S (1998) Initial conditions and moment restrictions in dynamic panel data models. J Econ 87(1):115–143

Brambor T, Clark WR, Golder M (2006) Understanding interaction models: Improving empirical analyses. Polit Anal 14(1):63–82

Chinn MD, Prasad ES (2003) Medium-term determinants of current accounts in industrial and developing countries: an empirical exploration. J Int Econ 59(1):47–76

Fernandez-Arias E (1996) The new wave of private capital inflows: push or pull? J Dev Econ 48(2):389–418

Forbes KJ, Warnock FE (2012) Capital flow waves: surges, stops, flight, and retrenchment. J Int Econ 88(2):235

Fostel A, Kaminsky G (2007) Latin America's access to international capital markets: good behavior or global liquidity? National Bureau of Economic Research, working paper, no. 13194

Gourinchas PO, Jeanne O (2013) Capital flows to developing countries: the allocation puzzle. Rev Econ Stud 0:1–32

Litvin D (2003) Empires of profits. Texere Publishing, Knutsford, Cheshire

Nickell SJ (1981) Biases in dynamic models with fixed effects. Econometrica 49(6):1417–1426

Okada K (2013) The interaction effects of financial openness and institutions on international capital flows. J Macroecon 35:131–143

Papaioannou E (2009) What drives international financial flows? Politics, institutions and other determinants. J Dev Econ 88(2):269

Reinhardt D, Ricci LA, Tressel T (2013) International capital flows and development: financial openness matters. J Int Econ 91(2):235–251

Roodman D (2009) A note on the theme of too many instruments. Oxford Bull Econ Stat 71(1):135–158

Soderbom M (2011) Econometrics II, Lecture 6: Panel data part 1. Retrieved from http://www.soderbom.net/metrix2/lec6_7.pdf

Spar DL (1998) Spotlight and the bottom line—how multinationals export human rights. Foreign Aff 77(7):7–12

Windmeijer F (2005) A finite sample correction for the variance of linear efficient two-step GMM estimators. J Econ 126(1):25–51

Wooldridge JM (2003) Introductory econometrics: a modern approach. South-Western College Pub

Chapter 6
The Effects of Political Risk on Capital Inflows

Abstract The fourth and final empirical study presented in this chapter that examines the relative importance of various political risks (e.g., expropriation risk, corruption, lack of democracy etc.) on different types of capital inflows (i.e., foreign direct investment (FDI), portfolio equity and private debt inflows). The focus of this chapter is on FDI inflows as FDI is the most prominent type of capital inflows and the influence of political risk is most prevalent on FDI inflows. A counterfactual simulation exercise is conducted to evaluate the percentage change in expected FDI inflows associated with improvements (e.g., one-standard-deviation and worst-to-best improvements) in various political risk measures. The results of this empirical analysis find that expropriation risk (i.e., the probability of losing 100% of invested capital) has among the largest effects on FDI, suggesting an intuitively appealing explanation for the lack of FDI flows to many capital-scarce developing countries.

6.1 Introduction

This chapter empirically investigates the individual components of the institutional quality index and their impact on different types of private capital inflows (FDI, portfolio and private debt). However, the empirical literature on political risks and capital inflows is largely dominated by FDI.

FDI and political risk literature has largely focused on the importance of political regimes, such as democracy and autocracy (e.g., Oneal 1994; Jensen 2003; Li 2009) and government corruption (e.g., Wei 2000; Habib and Zurawicki 2002; Méon and Sekkat 2004; Egger and Winner 2005). Other studies have focused on the importance of political stability (e.g., Asiedu 2002), rule of law and bureaucratic quality (e.g., Kinoshita and Campos 2003). Property rights and expropriation are also examined in empirical studies of FDI (e.g., Adam and Filippaios 2007; Asiedu et al. 2009). However, very few studies compare the relative importance of different types of political and institutional risk on FDI (exceptions are Daude and Stein 2007 and Bénassy-Quéré et al. 2007). This chapter empirically examines the relative importance of various forms of political risks on FDI inflow to developing countries.

M. Akhtaruzzaman, *International Capital Flows and the Lucas Paradox*,
https://doi.org/10.1007/978-981-13-9069-2_6

Using data for 83 developing countries covering the 1984–2015 period, the effects of various forms of political risks on FDI are examined using a suite of empirical models that differ according to: dependent variable (net versus gross FDI); specification of the function describing how political risk indexes map into the conditional mean of FDI; the sets of other political risk measures; and estimation technique, reporting each estimate of the effect of a risk index on expected FDI inflows based on cross-sectional averages and dynamic panel data. Following Bénassy-Quéré et al. (2007) and Daude and Stein (2007), an economic interpretation of the empirical evidence regarding which institutions matter most cannot simply rank the effects according to statistical significance. In combination with careful reporting of how precisely the effects of institutional quality on FDI are measured, this chapter shows that different empirical ranges of variation among measures of institutional risk and the magnitudes of their effects on FDI jointly determine the important decision of foreign investors about sending their firm's capital overseas. Specifically, this chapter evaluates the log-approximated percentage change in expected FDI inflows associated with an improvement in institutional quality of one-standard-deviation and another percentage change in expected FDI inflows associated with a worst-to-best improvement (i.e., the product of the estimated coefficient and the political risk variable's empirical range). The motivation is to quantify the perceived differences in various forms of political risks in the decision making process of the foreign investors, which has received surprisingly little attention in the empirical FDI literature.

An important finding from our analysis is that, compared to other institutional political risks to FDI, expropriation risk (i.e., the probability of losing 100% of invested capital) tends to be the most important concern of foreign investors. In particular, our empirical estimates suggest that differences in expropriation risk across countries account for a relatively large proportion of the discrepancies in FDI inflows to developing countries. This finding helps us to understand the decision making process of foreign investors and how they perceive individual political risks in making decision about FDI projects in foreign locations.

Intuitively, this empirical finding should perhaps not be surprising. Contracts between multinationals and sovereign nations are difficult to enforce despite the existence of international tribunals to resolve international investment disputes. The increasing number of incidents involving expropriation of FDI since the mid-1990s suggests that failure of host-country governments and judicial systems to honour contracts with foreign investors could be a growing concern among decision makers responsible for choosing locations for their FDI projects. Expropriation incidents in recent years are concentrated in natural-resource-intensive sectors and are partly explained by sharp increases in oil and other mineral prices over this period (Hajzler 2012; Stroebel and Van Benthem 2013). Countries counted as having expropriated foreign-owned assets in the mining and petroleum sectors over the past decade include Argentina (2012), Algeria (2006), Bolivia (2006, 2007, 2008, 2009, 2010, 2012, 2013), China (2006), Costa Rica (2012), Democratic Republic of Congo (2010), Ecuador (2006, 2008, 2009, 2010), Gambia (2008), Ghana (2011), Guinea (2008, 2013), Kyrgyzstan (2010, 2012, 2013), Pakistan (2011, 2013), Papua New Guinea (2011), Russia (2006, 2007) and Venezuela (2001, 2006, 2007, 2008, 2009, 2012,

2013). The data measuring counts of expropriation also include several incidents in other sectors such as Banking and Insurance, Construction, Food Processing, and Telecommunications.[1]

Despite the anecdotal evidence that expropriation risk matters, the existing literature on the effects of expropriation risk on FDI has delivered mixed results. Ali et al. (2010) and Asiedu et al. (2009) examine the effects of expropriation risk on net FDI flows (inflows minus outflows). Ali et al. (2010) consider a composite index for the strength of property rights (the sum of the Expropriation Risk and Law and Order indexes in ICRG) and find that the strength of property rights significantly increases net FDI. Similarly, Asiedu et al. (2009) find that expropriation risk lowers net FDI flows. They find that this negative relationship is stronger for countries that receive less foreign aid and their finding suggests foreign aid is used as leverage to reduce the threat of expropriation by the host government. Busse and Hefeker (2007) examine the individual effects of each ICRG institutional and political risk variable in both cross-country OLS and a dynamic panel model; however, they do not find robust statistically significant effects of expropriation risk on net FDI inflows. In particular, they find government stability, internal and external conflict, corruption, ethnic tensions, law and order, and democratic accountability are highly significant determinants of FDI, while expropriation risk shows a significant effect only in their panel FE model.

Several other studies report negative effects of expropriation risk on gross FDI inflows. Adam and Filippaios (2007) estimate the effects of expropriation, corruption, bureaucratic quality, and repression of political and civil liberties on gross FDI inflows and find a negative impact of expropriation risk on gross FDI inflows.[2] Harms and Ursprung (2002) examine the effects of expropriation on FDI for developing countries and find a statistically significant relationship in most of their model specifications. Biswas (2002) and Li and Resnick (2003) construct a property rights index based on five ICRG sub-components—Expropriation Risk, Repudiation of Contract, Government Corruption, Quality of Bureaucracy, and Law and Order. Biswas (2002) and Li and Resnick (2003) find that improvements in property rights significantly increase FDI. On the other hand, Jensen (2003) does not find any evidence that expropriation risk has a significant effect on the location of FDI when the degree of democracy and capital controls are controlled for. Naudé and Krugell (2007) fail to find robust evidence that expropriation risk reduces FDI across 19 African economies.

This chapter re-examines the economic significance of property rights and expropriation relative to other institutional and political risks facing foreign investors. It also examines whether methodological differences in this literature, such as differ-

[1]These figures refer to the acts of expropriations in a given year in a given industry (3-digit SIC category), such as ownership transferred to the host country's government or another party) i.e., the host country fails to enforce the foreign owner's claims). See, Kobrin (1984) for a detailed discussion of and justification for this definition.

[2]This significant negative association is robust only for the non-OECD country sample, however, and is relatively strong for countries with high levels of civil rights. Interestingly, they find a positive effect of corruption on FDI inflows.

ences in units of measurement and model specification, help explain the conflicting empirical evidence. The findings of the analysis in this chapter shows that expropriation risk has a robust, statistically and economically significant effect on FDI inflows across countries in an empirical specification that is flexible (in the sense of being neutral with respect to the normalization of the dependent variable) and permits asymmetrical effects of risk on FDI inflows and outflows.

6.2 Literature Review

In addition to the empirical literature on the importance of property rights and expropriation risk on FDI outlined in the introduction, our work is related to an extensive literature on the impact of other forms of political risks on FDI. Asiedu and Lein (2011) find that democracy promotes FDI; however this effect depends on the host country's share of natural resources in total exports. In particular, if a host country's natural resources' share of total exports is below a critical value, then democracy is an important determinant of FDI. Among many others, Jensen (2003) and Busse (2004) find that FDI has a strong positive association with democracy. However, the finding of a positive and significant association between democracies and FDI is not unanimous in the FDI literature. Yang (2007) finds that democracies are not significantly associated with FDI inflows while Resnick (2001) finds a negative relationship between democracies and FDI inflows.

Several studies examine the effect of corruption on FDI and find evidence of a negative impact on FDI (e.g., Wei 2000; Habib and Zurawicki 2002; Mathur and Sing 2013; Asiedu 2006). On the other hand, Egger and Winner's (2005) results suggest corruption may provide a positive stimulus to FDI inflows. The independent effect of political stability and bureaucratic quality have also received attention in the literature and the empirical evidence largely suggests that political instability has no significant effect on FDI (Asiedu 2002) while bureaucratic quality increases FDI inflows to developing countries (Kinoshita and Campos 2003). Table 6.1 lists the key studies specifically outlining differences across studies in the choices of political index variables, dependent variables, sample of countries and sample period, estimation approaches, and main findings.

This literature has largely focused on a narrow set of political risk and institutional determinants of FDI. Few papers have aimed to compare the relative importance of these various risk factors on FDI, with the following exceptions. Daude and Stein (2007) consider the responsiveness of bilateral FDI stocks to property rights using the Rule of Law index from Worldwide Governance Indicators (WGI), which measures confidence in the rules of society, the quality of contract enforcement, property rights, the police, and the courts, including perceived likelihood of crime and violence. The authors do not find any evidence that this measure of property rights increases FDI. However, they do find positive effects on FDI using a more aggregated index, which they refer to as Government Efficiency—comprised of Rule of Law, Control of Corruption, Government Effectiveness, and Regulatory Quality of Government.

Table 6.1 Summary table of empirical literature on individual aspects of institutional quality

Study	Sample	Political index variable	Findings	Dependent variable	Estimation procedure
Ali et al. (2010)	69 developing countries (1981–2005)	Sum of expropriation risk and law and order (ICRG) serves as the institutional quality index	Institutional quality index (Exprop. risk and rule of law) is a significant determinant of FDI	NET FDI/GDP (level)	Random effects (RE)
Adam and Filippaios (2007)	105 developing and developed countries (1989–1997)	Political rights and civil liberties (Freedom House) and expropriation risk, corruption and bureaucratic quality (IRIS)	Expropriation risk is a significant determinant in most specifications, but this finding is somewhat sensitive to the estimator and controls	FDI/GDP	Fixed effects (FE) and random effects
Addison and Heshmati (2003)	110 developing countries (1970–1999)	Democracy (Freedom House)	Democracy increases FDI	Net FDI/GDP	Pooled OLS, fixed effects and GLS
Asiedu (2002)	71 developing countries (1988–1997)	Political instability (Barro and Lee 1993)	Political instability has no significant effect on FDI	NET FDI/GDP (level)	Cross-country and panel FE
Asiedu (2006)	22 African countries (1984–2000)	Corruption, rule of law (ICRG); political risks (Cross-national time series data)	Corruption reduces FDI, while political stability increases FDI	NET FDI/GDP (level)	
Asiedu et al. (2009)	63 developing countries (1983–2004)	Expropriation risk (ICRG)	Expropriation risk has a negative impact on FDI, and foreign aid inflows mitigate this effect	NET FDI/GDP (level)	Difference GMM and system GMM

(continued)

Table 6.1 (continued)

Study	Sample	Political index variable	Findings	Dependent variable	Estimation procedure
Asiedu and Lien (2011)	112 developing countries (1982–2007)	Democracy (Freedom House); corruption, rule of law (ICRG)	Democracy promotes FDI, but to a lesser extent if the host country's total exports are natural resource intensive (i.e., Democracy important when natural resources' share of total exports is below a critical value)	NET FDI/GDP (level)	Difference GMM and system GMM
Bénassy-Quéré, Coupet, and Mayer (2007)	52 origin and destination countries (bilateral FDI stocks) (1985–2000)	75 standardized institutional indices (French Ministry) and 5 indices measuring competitiveness of labour market, credit market regulation and property rights protection (Fraser Institute)	In a ranking of the 75 institutional indicators in terms of a one standard deviation change, contract law ranks 5th of the 25 coefficients reported, and a one standard deviation in this variable for the recipient country increases bilateral FDI by 76%	FDI (log bilateral *stocks*)	OLS and Pooled OLS with time fixed effects
Biswas (2002)	44 developed and developing countries (1983–1990) (FDI is US affiliate investment)	Regime type and duration (IRIS), and sum of Expropriation risk, Repudiation of Contracts, Corruption, Quality of Bureacracy, and Law and Order (ICRG)	Security of property rights increases FDI	FDI/GNI	Fixed effects and pooled OLS

(continued)

Table 6.1 (continued)

Study	Sample	Political index variable	Findings	Dependent variable	Estimation procedure
Busse (2004)	69 developing countries (1972–2001)	Democracy (Freedom House)	Democracy exhibits strong positive association with FDI from 1990s onward, but not during 1970s and 1980s	FDI (log)	Panel (OLS) and Fixed Effects
Busse and Hefeker (2007)	83 countries (1984–2000)	12 subcomponents of ICRG	Corruption, ethnic tensions, law and order, and government stability are negatively associated with FDI; expropriation is not a significant determinant of FDI in cross-sectional and GMM models	NET FDI per capita (log*transform)	OLS, Fixed Effects and GMM
Daude and Stein (2007)	152 hosts from 34 sources of bilateral FDI (1982–2002)	1. Voice and accountability and political stability, rule of law, control of corruption, government effectiveness, and regulatory quality (WGI) 2. Risk of expropriation, government stability, democratic accountability, law and order, and corruption (ICRG)	A one standard deviation improvement in regulatory quality increases FDI by a factor of 2. When the ICRG risk measures are considered, only government stability is significant determinant of FDI, and government stability is not	FDI (log) (bilateral outward *stocks*)	Cross section OLS and IV

(continued)

Table 6.1 (continued)

Study	Sample	Political index variable	Findings	Dependent variable	Estimation procedure
Dutta and Roy (2011)	97 developed and developing countries (1984–2003)	Include all the twelve ICRG political subindexes as interaction terms with financial development	Their interaction model findings suggest after a threshold level of financial development (FD), effects of FD on FDI becomes negative and this relationship depends on political institutions, in particular, higher FD increases FDI if political stability is higher	FDI/GDP	Pooled OLS and FGLS
Egger and Winner (2005)	73 developed and developing countries (1995–1999)	Corruption (Transparency International)	Corruption is a positive stimulus to FDI inflows	FDI (linear) (inward stocks)	Fixed effects and GLS
Gastanaga et al. (1998)	49 developing countries (1970–1995)	Nationalization risk, contract enforcement, and bureacratic quality (BERI: Business Environment Risk Intelligence); corruption (Mauro 1995)	Nationalization risk reduces FDI inflows (findings are based on a small sample of 22 developing countries)	FDI/GDP (level)	Pooled OLS and Fixed Effects
Globerman and Shapiro (2002)	144 Countries (1995–1997)	Governance indices (WGI)	Governance infrastructure has a positive impact on both gross inflows and net inflows	FDI inflows (log), FDI outflows (log), and FDI net (log)	OLS

(continued)

Table 6.1 (continued)

Study	Sample	Political index variable	Findings	Dependent variable	Estimation procedure
Habib and Zurawicki (2002)	89 developing host countries of bilateral FDI from seven source countries (1996–1998)	Corruption (Transperancy International)	Corruption decreases FDI	FDI (log)	OLS and probit
Harms and Ursprung (2002)	62 developing countries (1989–1997)	Freedom House (2000) political rights, extent of civil liberties, and freedom indices and the ICRG political risk index (likelihood of expropriation, exchange controls, and contract repudiation)	Both political rights and freedoms and absence of expropriation risk increase FDI per worker. Effect of expropriation risk on FDI is found to be significant even in the fixed effects estimation, though is somewhat sensitive to the inclusion of outliers	FDI per capita (levels and logs)	OLS and fixed effects
Jensen (2003)	79 countries (1970–1997) for cross-section; 114 countries (1970–1997) for FE	Democracy (polity data); expropriation, corruption, rule of law, bureaucratic quality (Easterly data 1999)	Democracy has a robust positive effect, but other institutional characteristics have no significant effect, on FDI	FDI (linear)	Cross section, FE and RE
Kinoshita and Campos (2003)	25 developing countries (1990–1998)	Rule of law and bureaucratic quality	Both rule of law and bureaucratic quality increase stocks of FDI	FDI stock per capital	GMM

(continued)

Table 6.1 (continued)

Study	Sample	Political index variable	Findings	Dependent variable	Estimation procedure
Kolstad and Tøndel (2002)	61 developing countries (1989–2000)	12 subcomponents of ICRG political institutions sub-indexes	Ethnic tension and internal conflict negatively affect FDI; stability, corruption and bureaucratic quality have no impact; and democracy exhibits a robust positive association with FDI	FDI per capita (log)	
Li (2009)	63 developing countries (1960–1990)	Political regmies (democracy and autocracy) and expropriation risk	Democracies are more likely to expropriate than autocracies if the democratic leaders face little political constraint and frequent leadership changes	Expropriation Acts	OLS
Li and Resnick (2003)	51 developing countries (1982–1995)	Political instability (Banks' index), property rights protection (ICRG), democracy (Polity IV)	Democracy raises FDI through improved property rights protection, but the direct (residual) effect of democracy on FDI may be negative	FDI (level, current dollars)	Poole d OLS
Mathur and Singh (2013)	29 countries, mainly emerging market/developing economies (1980–2000)	Corruption perceptions (transparency international) and democracy	Countries ranking poorly in terms of the Corruption Perceptions index receive low FDI flows. More democratic countries receive less FDI flows than less democratic countries	FDI (log)	Random Effects

(continued)

Table 6.1 (continued)

Study	Sample	Political index variable	Findings	Dependent variable	Estimation procedure
Méon and Sekkat (2004)	107 countries (1990–1999)	Corruption perceptions (transparency international, World Bank and Wei (2000)), government effectiveness, the rule of law (WGI) broad ICRG index	Overall political risk (inverse of ICRG) reduces FDI, with some evidence that corruption lowers FDI (though not robust across corruption indicators)	FDI/GDP (log)	Fixed effects and OLS
Naudé and Krugell (2007)	19 African countries (1970–1990)	Political stability, accountability, regulatory burden, rule of law (WGI) and expropriation risk (instrumented using settler mortality)	Rule of law, accountability, regulatory burden, and expropriation risk (settler mortality) are all significant determinants of FDI, though expropriation is insignificant when all of the controls are added. However, regulatory burden and expropriation risk oddly *increase* FDI, while Accountability decreases FDI—unfortunately the authors do not discuss these results, so the interpretation of their findings is unclear	FDI/GDP	Dynamic difference GMM

(continued)

Table 6.1 (continued)

Study	Sample	Political index variable	Findings	Dependent variable	Estimation procedure
Noorbakhsh et al. (2001)	36 developing countries (1980–1994)	Democracy (Freedom House); instability (Euromoney)	Human capital is the most important determinant of FDI, while democracy and political instability have no significant effects	FDI/GDP	Pooled OLS and Fixed Effects
Schneider and Frey (1985)	80 developing countries (1976, 1979, 1980)	Political instability (Cross-National Data Bank of Political Instability Events: Public Affairs Research Institute; Feierabend and Feierabend 1966)	Political instability reduces FDI inflows	FDI per capita	OLS
Wheeler and Mody (1992)	42 developed and developing countries (1982–1988) (FDI is US affiliate investment in manufacturing and electronics only)	Composite index (based on principal components) that includes bureaucratic red tape, political instability, corruption, attitudes towards foreign investment, and quality of the legal system from Business International Inc. (BI)	Composite risk index does not affect the location of US foreign investment. However, their index of "openness", which includes a measure of expropriation risk, does influence FDI	log FDI relative to benchmark	OLS
Wei (2000)	45 host countries of bilateral FDI from seven source countries (1993)	Corruption (International country risk guide)	Corruption reduces FDI	FDI (log)	OLS (gravity) and Tobit

Daude and Stein find Regulatory Quality has the largest independent effects on FDI and simulate the expected effects on FDI using a standardized unit. In particular, they find a one-standard-deviation improvement in Regulatory Quality increases FDI by a factor of two. The authors also use the ICRG's index to check the robustness of their results. In contrast to Adam and Filippaios (2007) and Harms and Ursprung (2002), Daude and Stein (2007) find that ICRG's Expropriation Risk does not have a significant effect on FDI. Daude and Stein's findings relate bilateral FDI stock data instead of FDI flows.

Bénassy-Quéré et al. (2007) examine bilateral FDI stock data for 52 source countries from 1985 to 2000 and use two different sources for measures of political institutions: the French Ministry of Finance's Institutional Profiles and the Fraser Institute's Property Rights Security. They conduct a simulation of the estimated effects on FDI and also rank the effects. A one-standard-deviation improvement in Contract Law increases bilateral FDI by 76% in the cross-section model. In terms of the one-standard-deviation improvement in a ranking of 75 institutional indicators of Institutional Profiles, they find Contract Law ranks 5th and Formal Property Rights ranks 26th. When they use the Fraser Institute's Property Rights Security in their panel model, they find the significance effect of Property Rights Security on FDI disappears once per capita income is controlled for.

The empirical studies of Daude and Stein (2007) and Bénassy-Quéré et al. (2007) are the closest to ours. A central difference of their findings to ours is that they do not find a robust effect of property rights and expropriation on FDI. In contrast to their studies, our empirical findings are based on FDI flows instead of FDI stock.

6.3 Modelling FDI and Political Risk

This section critically analyses the modelling decisions made in this literature when estimating the effects of political risks on FDI. These modelling decisions include the choice of dependent variable, specification of the conditional mean function, and choice of indexes measuring political risk and institutional quality.[3] Empirical studies often estimate reduced-form relationships that are not based on an explicitly stated structural model of FDI. The conflicting empirical results in the existing literature might be due in part to the variation in specifications of the conditional mean of FDI and these choices are made in the studies without an adequate explanation. An explanation is provided for choosing a specific empirical model from a suite of alternative specifications (see, Sect. 6.4). The mixed results of this literature would also appear to depend on the different estimation procedures adopted (e.g., cross-sectional models based on time-series averages, dynamic fixed effects models, and Blundell-Bond GMM estimation with variation in choices of instruments).

[3]We consider two measure of political risk frequently used in the FDI literature: The Political Risk Group's *International Country Risk Guide* (ICRG) and the World Bank's *Worldwide Governance Indicators* (WGI) risk indexes.

Alternative methodological choices are employed to compare findings from alternative estimation approaches in order to propose a clearer interpretation of which political risks matter in determination of FDI flows. This leads to estimate a suite of empirical models, as described in Sect. 6.4. The estimates from each model are transformed to rankable effect sizes corresponding to the two counterfactuals (one-standard-deviation and worst-to-best institutional improvements, respectively), which are compared in Sect. 6.6.

6.3.1 Net Versus Gross FDI

In Chap. 3, a brief discussion regarding net versus gross was introduced and highlighted the importance of exactly defining the term. This section discusses net FDI versus gross FDI and suggests which of the two is appropriate to use as dependent variable when analysing the effects of political risk (e.g., expropriation risk) on FDI. From a standard, neoclassical growth perspective, it might be argued that net FDI (i.e., the net flow of foreign capital into the host country) is ultimately the variable of interest. It can also be argued, however, that gross inflows from abroad is the more interesting outcome for growth and development, since FDI often involves transfers of technology and know-how that result in positive spillovers to the recipient country, regardless of that country's direct investments flowing to other countries.

Insofar as there are distinct causal mappings from institutional quality into inflows versus outflows, it makes sense to model each of these directional flows with different empirical models. Even if one takes the former view (i.e., that net FDI inflows is the variable of interest), one may learn more by studying the effects of institutional quality on each of the two gross directional flows and then combining them (as in Globerman and Shapiro 2002) rather than estimating a likely misspecified model using net FDI as the dependent variable. Specifically, it is shown that, excluding the very special case in which FDI inflows and negative outflows respond linearly and identically to each of the political risk variables, any attempt to estimate their effects on net FDI using a linear regression model will produce biased estimates due to model misspecification.

To illustrate this point, consider a very simple, dynamic model of FDI in the spirit of Findlay (1978), where foreign investment involves a transfer of capital from the relatively rich to relatively poor region and a transfer of intangible technological knowledge. In Findlay's model, growth in the stock of FDI in country i between periods t and $t+1$, $\dot{K}^f_{it}/K^f_{it}$ is proportional to net profits ρ_{it}:

$$\dot{K}^f_{it}/K^f_{it} = \gamma\rho_{it} \tag{6.1}$$

where $\gamma > 0$ represents a constant fraction of net profits that is re-invested. In Findlay's model, ρ_{it} is an increasing function of the technological gap between the host county and the technological frontier and decreasing in taxes. Using a slightly more general framework, however, ρ_{it} may also be a decreasing function of the economy-wide stock of capital and financial risk. To contrast the effects of expropriation risk on gross and net flows, we first augment the model to express growth in the FDI stock as a function of *ex ante* expected profits, $(1-\pi_{it})\rho_{it}$, where π_{it} is the probability that all profits are expropriated. Further, we can implicitly define an index for the security of investments, s_{it} such that $(1-\pi_{it}) = e^{\beta_1+\beta_2 s_{it}}$, where β_1 and β_2 are parameters to be estimated. FDI inflows per capita, x_{it}, in the augmented model is as follows.

$$x_{it} = \gamma \rho_{it} e^{\beta_1+\beta_2 s_{it}} K_{it}^{f} \tag{6.2}$$

where K_{it}^{f} is the stock of FDI per capita at the beginning of the period and hence FDI inflows per capita are given by $x_{it} = (K_{it+1}^{f} - K_{it}^{f})/pop_{it}$. If the absence of expropriation risk positively influence FDI inflows, then $\beta_1 < 0$ and $\beta_2 > 0$.

Taking the logarithm of both sides of (6.2) yields a simple, log-linear relationship between gross inflows of FDI and the political risk index, s_{it}; i.e., $\partial lnx_{it}/\partial s_{it} = \beta_2$.

However, a simple log-linear relationship between *net* FDI inflows and political risk is not expected. On the contrary, simple model suggests that the marginal effect of an increase in s_{it} on *net* inflows will depend on the magnitudes of both net inflows and gross outflows. To see why, consider the special case in which FDI outflows (new investments representing the controlling interests of residents and firms in country i over productive capital assets abroad) are positively related to s_{it} and negatively related to the domestic productivity gap. FDI outflows per capita, o_{it}, using a functional form similar to that of inflows, is as follows.

$$o_{it} = \gamma (\rho_{it})^{-1} e^{\beta_3-\beta_4 s_{it}} K_{it}^{d} \tag{6.3}$$

where β_3, $\beta_4 > 0$ and K_{it}^{d} is domestically owned capital. If foreign investments are relatively more vulnerable to expropriation (a reasonable assumption in many countries), we would expect $\beta_4 < \beta_2$.

The natural log of *net* inflows per capita, $x_{it}^{net} = x_{it} - o_{it}$, is undefined for $x_{it} < o_{it}$. Burbidge et al. (1988) and Busse and Hefeker (2007) address this issue by first transforming x_{it}^{net} using the monotonic function

$$\log^*(\varphi(x)) = \log^*\left(x + \sqrt{x^2+1}\right) \tag{6.4}$$

It is straightforward to verify that[4]

$$\frac{\partial \log^*(\varphi(x_{it}^{net}))}{\partial s_{it}} = \frac{\varphi'(x_{it}^{net})}{\varphi(x_{it}^{net})}\left(\beta_2 x_{it} + \beta_4 o_{it}\right) = \frac{\beta_2 x_{it} + \beta_4 o_{it}}{\sqrt{(x_{it}^{net})^2+1}}\Bigg) \tag{6.5}$$

[4]See the derivation in Appendix A.

Although the relationship between s_{it} and x_{it}^{net} is strictly positive, it becomes more non-linear as outflows become more positive, provided $\beta_2 \neq \beta_4$.

In particular, if outflows equal zero, then, as inflows increase, the marginal effect of s_{it} on x_{it}^{net} approaches β_2. However, net inflows will be more highly sensitive to risk in countries characterized by large outflows, especially those with relatively low net inflows. Moreover, in the event that the true relationship between country risk and FDI exhibits unequal marginal effects of s_{it} on x_{it} and o_{it}, respectively (i.e., when $\beta_2 \neq \beta_4$), then the estimated effect of risk on net flows from a reduced-form, log-linear model will be biased. Considering that relatively high-risk countries are characterized by low levels of both inflows and outflows, then the estimated effect of risk on net flows will be biased towards zero. A similar conclusion can be drawn under the assumption that outflows are independent of s_{it}, or when estimating the marginal effect of s_{it} on x_{it} in levels rather than logs, and for any monotonic transformation of the dependent variable.

In addition to the econometric advantages of using distinct empirical models for gross inflows and gross outflows, economic theory also supports investigation of the determinants of gross inflows—rather than net flows—as the dependent variable of primary interest. Regardless of the extent to which a developing country's firms choose to invest in foreign projects, inward FDI remains beneficial for further economic development by improving workers' access to intellectual property and physical capital. Inward FDI also remains important for knowledge spillovers and economies of scale, which are important in terms of growth and development, suggesting that estimating marginal effect of s_{it} on gross FDI is more relevant.

6.3.2 Normalization of the Dependent Variable

The existing literature also differs in terms of scaling or normalization of the dependent variable. Some authors choose to model FDI in levels without rescaling the dependent variable, as in Egger and Winner (2005) Jensen (2003) and Li and Resnick (2003), while others model the determinants of FDI in terms of their effect on the log of FDI, as in Busse (2004), Globerman and Shapiro (2002), Mathur and Sing (2013) and Yang (2007), as well as Bénassy-Quéré et al. (2007), Daude and Stein (2007), and Wei (2000) who examine bilateral FDI using gravity models (Wei 2000; and Habib and Zurawicki 2002 also consider, FDI stocks rather than flows). When estimating the determinants of aggregate, unscaled FDI inflows using cross-country data, it is essential to control for country size by including a measure of aggregate economic activity or population (or both) as an explanatory variable. However, even when one controls for country size, a key question is whether a one-unit (or percentage-point) increase in the political risk index of interest will have similar effects on the dollar value of FDI inflows across countries regardless of size, or whether the dollar effects are proportional to market size and the magnitude of FDI. Although this is ultimately an empirical question, it is reasonable to expect that the predicted dollar value effects of a given change in a country's profile of institutional quality should depend on the amount of FDI and overall size of the economy.

Some studies simply normalize the dependent variable by either national income or population size in each country and year. This approach is relatively common in the empirical FDI literature, where net or gross FDI expressed as a share of GDP or GNI is the dependent variable (Ali et al. 2010; Addison and Heshmati 2003; Asiedu 2002, 2006; Asiedu et al. 2009; Asiedu and Lien 2011; Biswas 2002; Gastanaga et al. 1998; Méon and Sekkat 2004; Naudé and Krugell 2007; Noorbakhsh et al. 2001). In other empirical FDI studies, however, the dependent variable is FDI (net or gross) per capita (Schneider and Frey 1985; Chakrabarti 2001; Harms and Ursprung 2002; Kinoshita and Campos 2003; Busse and Hefeker 2007).

Whether to normalize FDI by aggregate economic activity or population should depend on the theoretical linkages being explored and questions being asked. More specifically, if the research question is to identify the relative importance of institutional quality on FDI when FDI is expressed as a share of GDP, it may be difficult to decompose the relative effects of institutional quality on FDI as institutional quality is also directly related to economic activities (i.e., GDP). Although Asiedu (2002, 2006) and Asiedu et al. (2009) used FDI to GDP as the dependent variable, Globerman and Shapiro (2002) rejected this specification because the dependent variable was typically clustered within a narrow range of variation, which produced unreliable parameters estimates with low degrees of explanatory power. It is reasonable to consider that FDI per capita is an appropriate dependent variable to use for this analysis. However, this chapter shows that the estimated political risk effects in preferred model are neutral with respect to the normalization chosen.

Log*-transformation of the dependent variable (i.e., a log* model) is commonly used in the existing FDI literature as this transformation finds support from both theoretical arguments and the statistical properties of the data. For example, Kolstad and Tøndel (2002) and Harms and Ursprung (2002) use log FDI per capita as their dependent variable, while Globerman and Shapiro (2002) and Méon and Sekkat (2004) examine log of FDI as a share of GDP. In addition to considering gross FDI, Globerman and Shapiro (2002) also estimate effects of institutions on log net FDI-to-GDP, and Busse and Hefeker (2007) examine log net FDI per capita as their dependent variable.

Busse and Hefeker's (2007) (hereafter, BH) log* transformation is used, which follows the HIS-transformation, to deal with zero and non-positive values of FDI. The monotonic transformation of dependent variable x employed in BH (2007) is given by Eq. (6.4), which approximates the log function for positive values of x (re-scaled) but linearizes the dependent variable for small and negative values of x. However, negative gross flows are less common in the sample investigated and they are especially rare in cross-sectional analyses based on data averaged over thirty-two years. Net inflows, on the other hand, are much more commonly negative, and some countries are net exporters of capital, having negative net flows on average over time. Globerman and Shapiro (2002) instead transform their dependent variable by separating countries with positive and negative net inflows and assigning a negative value to the latter. A potential drawback of this alternative transformation is that it does not accommodate zero values and is non-monotonic over the range $(-1, 1)$ (and hence the units of measurement of the dependent variable will matter in potentially important ways).

Provided that the conditional mean function is also normally distributed, log* of FDI per capita inflows is closest among the normalizations and transformations (e.g., as a percentage of GDP or GNI) used by other studies to the standard assumptions for OLS and generates the fewest outliers, which provides another motivation for selecting an approximation to the log* transformation as the dependent variable.[5] Moreover, the use of a log*-transformed dependent variable is consistent with the dependent variables used in the previous chapters of this thesis.

6.3.3 Indexes Measuring Political Risk and Institutional Quality

In the analysis of this chapter, several measures of institutional quality and political risk are used and alternative econometric techniques are adopted to verify the robustness of the estimates. Several institutional quality measures are examined in the existing literature. These include indexes of expropriation risk, political instability, government corruption, socioeconomic and ethnic tensions, military conflict and democratic accountability (among others) from the following sources: the Political Risk Group's *International Country Risk Guide* (ICRG), the Freedom House Index, Transparency International's *Corruption Perception Index* (CPI), World Bank's *Country Policy and Institutions Assessments* (CPIA) index, and World Bank's *Worldwide Governance Indicators*. While these indexes capture a wide range of political risk factors, the focus of this chapter is expropriation risk. For this purpose, the sources of information about expropriation risk are taken from the ICRG and WGI indexes, which both include an index measuring the protection of property rights, the likelihood of government theft, non-performance of contractual obligation, bank account bail-ins or freezes, title changes, and many forms of expropriation. The narrowest measures of expropriation risk from these sources are the 'Investment Profile' index in the ICRG data (covering the 1984–2015 periods) and the 'Rule of Law' index in WGI data (covering the 1996–2015 period). The estimated effects are compared to with those corresponding to the other indexes of institutional quality from each source. Detailed descriptions of each institutional quality/political risk index are provided in the Data Appendix B.

[5]This is based on the histogram plots, see Fig. C.3 in Appendix C.

6.3.4 Additional Control Variables

Commonly used controls in the literature on FDI and institutions are GDP or GNI, GNI per capita, GNI per capita growth, openness to international trade, and measures of macroeconomic stability in the host country. GDP or GNI per capita are used to control for the impact of the host country's market size. The FDI literature documents that market size is expected to have a positive impact on FDI, positing that a larger market implies higher demand for goods and services, and this size advantage attracts more market-seeking foreign investment. Absolute GNI instead of GNI per capita is also used in the literature (e.g., Asiedu 2006; Chakrabarti 2001; Root and Ahmed 1979) to capture market size. Openness to international trade is a relevant factor in the decision to invest, as trade influences both access to essential inputs as well as revenues from production in a tradable sector (e.g., Edwards 1992; Wheeler and Mody 1992). Growth in per capita income is also a common control variable (e.g. Schneider and Frey 1985; Busse and Hefeker 2007), interpreted as a signal of potential market performance to foreign investors. Finally, the inflation rate, measured as the annual percentage change in CPI, is used as a proxy for macroeconomic stability that is hypothesized to reduce uncertainty and increase confidence levels in the economy, which attracts higher FDI inflows. Additional details on the controls available in our data and a list of data sources are provided in Data Appendix B.

6.4 Model Specification

A suite of empirical models are examined that differ according to the dependent variable and control variables, motivated by conventions adopted in the related literature.

Specifically, the estimated model is:

$$\log^* FDI_i = \alpha + \beta RISK_i + X_i'\gamma + \varepsilon_i \tag{6.6}$$

where $RISK_i$ represents political risk and X_i is a row vector of control variables. Because variables measuring institutional quality are often correlated, most empirical models in this literature do not include multiple institutional variables in the same equation. Following Bénassy-Quéré et al. (2007), BH (2007), and Daude and Stein (2007), the effects of each political risk variable are estimated individually and then compared. The effect sizes of political risk indexes are ranked according to their role in attracting FDI based on a one-standard-deviation change and a change from worst to best based on the empirical range of each variable measuring political risk. As discussed earlier, the dependent variable is the log of gross inflows per capita, denoted $\log^* FDI_i$ with a monotonic approximation of the log transformation used by Burbidge et al. (1988) and BH (2007) to deal with non-positive values as described in Sect. 6.3.2. For comparison, the model is also estimated with net FDI per capita and unscaled FDI as dependent variables.

Using available cross country data for the 1984–2015 period, each model is estimated by ordinary least squares based on full-period averages. For panel models with fixed effects (FE) and dynamic Arellano-Bond general method of moments (GMM) estimators, four-year panel averages are used. The four different types of models (A, B, C, D) estimated are as follows:

(A) Model A uses log* *net* FDI inflow per capita as the dependent variable to replicate BH (2007) with up-to-date data, and includes two income-related measures as control variables: log of GNI per capita and log of growth in GNI per capita. Common to all model specifications is a set of controls that includes inflation, trade openness and regional dummies.
(B) Model B is identical to Model A except that gross FDI inflows per capita replace net FDI inflows per capita as the dependent variable.
(C) Model C is the same as Model B, but instead of including both of BH's income variables as controls (i.e., log of GNI per capita and log of GNI per capita growth), only log of GNI per capita (PPP, current international dollars) is included. Inclusion of only a single income variable follows the econometric specifications used by others in the empirical FDI literature (e.g., Adam and Filippaios 2007; Asiedu 2002; Asiedu and Lien 2011; Chakrabarti 2001). The drawbacks to using two income variables are: one is a level measure and the other is a growth measure. There are arguments in favour of including both income and income growth as given by BH (2007), Habib and Zurawicki (2002), Jensen (2003), and Schneider and Frey (1985): to independently control for market size and growth potential. However, if the broader goal is to learn which political institutions most influence growth in FDI inflows, then the growth potential as a function of institutional quality is the phenomenon that the political indexes measure. Absorbing some of this growth potential in the local market (which also depends on the political indexes) with a second control variable that is functionally dependent on same-period and last-period realizations of income introduces multiple methodological issues that Model C addresses by removing log of GNI growth per capita from the set of explanatory variables.
(D) Model D provides a more flexible functional form than that of Model C by controlling for both market size and level of development. Model D replaces FDI per capita with gross FDI without any normalization and includes the log of GNI and log of population as explanatory variables. This follows the specification used by Wei (2000). The log-linear specification in Model C can be seen as a restricted version of Model D, which enables the coefficients for log population and log GNI to take on any values. Moreover, the estimated elasticity of FDI with respect to country risk in Model D is independent of how the dependent variable is normalized (i.e., the elasticities with respect to political risks which are of primary interest are invariant to normalization with respect to population, GNI, or no normalization at all). Specifically, the estimated β coefficient in Eq. 6.6 is the same whether the dependent variable is

expressed in per capita terms or as a share of GNI or not normalized at all when both the dependent variable and the explanatory variables are log* transformed.

(E) Model E is the same as Model D except that the six WGI indexes are used in place of each of the corresponding 12 ICRG indexes. It is worthwhile to mention that not all of the WGI indexes are directly comparable to a corresponding ICRG index. From the WGI, only the risk indexes are considered that are broadly consistent with one of the 12 ICRG indexes. One WGI index in particular, Rule of Law, reflects expropriation risk, although it is a more aggregated measure and includes some other forms of risk. See Appendix B for detailed description of these indexes.

6.5 Results

The empirical effects of political institutions on FDI inflows are reported in the following sections and are organised into three parts. Estimates from the cross-sectional data are reported first in Table 6.2, followed by country-fixed-effects models in Table 6.3 and the Blundell-Bond GMM estimates in Table 6.4. Each column reports the estimated risk-index coefficient (and corresponding t-statistics computed using robust standard errors) from the Models A–E. The estimated coefficients for other control variables are omitted for brevity, with full-model estimates from Model D reported in Appendix C. The discussion of Tables 6.2, 6.3 and 6.4 compares information in the data when filtered through different model specifications, focussing on the relative importance of different political institutions. The magnitudes of predicted changes in FDI are simulated in the following thought experiment, presented in Sect. 6.6: if a country with average characteristics in all other respects were to succeed at improving a given political institution from worst to best (i.e., moving from minimum to maximum values across the empirical range of variation), how large would the change in expected FDI be? This is also done for a one-standard-deviation improvement in political risk indexes. The comparison of counterfactual results provides us with evidence on the relative economic significance of different political risk indexes considered.

6.5.1 Cross Section Estimates

Table 6.2 reports OLS estimates for each of the political risk indicators using cross-sectional averages (1984–2015 for the ICRG risk indexes and 1996–2015 for the WGI indexes).[6] Model A presents an attempted replication of Busse and Hefeker (2007) using data extended through to 2015 and suggests that some of the political indexes

[6]For brevity purpose, the coefficient estimates of the political indexes are only presented in Tables 6.2, 6.3 and 6.4. Full Model estimates are reported in the Appendix C.

Table 6.2 Cross section estimates of five empirical models of FDI inflows, 1984–2015

	Models									
	A (Net FDI): BH (2007) Model with 8 more years of data (1984–2015)		B (Gross FDI): Model A with log* Gross FDI per capita instead of log* Net FDI per capita as the dependent variable		C (Gross FDI): Model B with a single income control, log GNI per capita, instead of double-inclusion of growth		D (Gross FDI): Model C with more flexible controls for income and market size (non-per-capita specification)		E (Gross FDI): Model D with WGI instead of ICRG Political Indexes	
Political indexes measuring institutional quality	Coef.	T-stat.	Coef.	T-stat.	Coef.	T-stat.	Coef.	T-stat.	Coef.	T-stat.
Exprop. risk absent (invest. profile in ICRG; rule of law in WGI)	0.00	0.0	0.07	0.5	0.08	0.7	0.09	0.8	0.31*	1.9
Government stability (political stability in WGI)	0.25	0.6	0.16	0.8	0.21	1.2	0.21	1.2	0.11	0.8
Socioecon. stress absent	−0.22	−0.9	0.02	0.1	0.06	0.4	0.04	0.3		
Internal conflict absent	0.13	1.1	0.06	0.8	0.07	0.8	0.04	0.5		
External conflict absent	0.31	1.1	0.04	0.4	0.02	0.2	0.00	0.0		
Corruption absent (corruption absent in WGI)	0.13	1.2	0.08	0.9	0.09	1.2	0.10	1.3	0.33*	2.0
Military absent in politics	0.03	0.4	−0.01	−0.2	0.00	0.0	0.00	0.1		
Religious tensions absent	−0.16	−1.3	−0.06	−1.1	−0.06	−1.1	−0.05	−1.1		
Law and order	0.08	1.0	0.05	0.8	0.08	1.3	0.08	1.3		
Ethnic tensions absent	−0.09	−0.6	0.00	0.0	0.00	0.0	0.00	0.0		
Democratic accountability (voice and accountability in WGI)	0.03	0.3	0.03	0.5	0.04	0.7	0.04	0.7	0.18	1.4

(continued)

Table 6.2 (continued)

		Models									
		A (Net FDI): BH (2007) Model with 8 more years of data (1984–2015)		B (Gross FDI): Model A with log* Gross FDI per capita instead of log* Net FDI per capita as the dependent variable		C (Gross FDI): Model B with a single income control, log GNI per capita, instead of double-inclusion of growth		D (Gross FDI): Model C with more flexible controls for income and market size (non-per-capita specification)		E (Gross FDI): Model D with WGI instead of ICRG Political Indexes	
Political indexes measuring institutional quality		Coef.	T-stat.	Coef.	T-stat.	Coef.	T-stat.	Coef.	T-stat.	Coef.	T-stat.
Bureaucratic quality (government effectiveness in WGI)		0.03	0.3	−0.01	−0.1	0.00	0.0	−0.02	−0.4	0.29	1.5
Normality test: Doornik-Hansen		0.00		0.35		0.51		0.24		0.10	
Heteroscedasticity	White	0.02		0.61		0.65		0.38		0.72	
	Breusch-Pagan	0.51		0.15		0.14		0.10		0.10	
RESET		0.26		0.42		0.47		0.47		0.38	
RMSE		1.31		0.65		0.65		0.65		0.61	

Estimates are computed using the ICRG political indexes from 1984–2015 in Models A, B, C and D; using WGI political indexes from 1996–2015 in Model E (corresponding to the available years of WGI data); and robust standard errors are in parenthesis, $^{***}p \leq 0.01$; $^{**}p \leq 0.05$; $^{*}p \leq 0.1$. Each model includes of regional dummies

Table 6.3 Panel fixed effects estimates of five empirical models of FDI inflows, 1984–2015

	Models									
	A (Net FDI): BH (2007) Model with 8 more years of data (1984–2015)		B (Gross FDI): Model A with log* Gross FDI per capita instead of log* Net FDI per capita as the dependent variable		C (Gross FDI): Model B with a single income control, log GNI per capita, instead of double-inclusion of growth		D (Gross FDI): Model C with more flexible controls for income and market size (non-per-capita specification)		E (Gross FDI): Model D with WGI instead of ICRG Political Indexes	
Political indexes measuring institutional quality	Coef.	T-stat.	Coef.	T-stat.	Coef.	T-stat.	Coef.	T-stat.	Coef.	T-stat.
Exprop. risk absent (invest. profile in ICRG; rule of law in WGI)	0.35***	4.2	0.31***	4.2	0.38***	4.9	0.49***	5.2	0.84*	1.8
Government stability (political stability in WGI)	0.30***	3.8	0.19***	3.3	0.26***	4.2	0.35***	4.1	0.20	0.4
Socioecon. stress absent	−0.12	−1.3	−0.10	−1.4	−0.06	−0.8	0.31**	2.2		
Internal conflict absent	0.15***	2.7	0.14***	3.1	0.14**	2.5	0.22***	2.8		
External conflict absent	0.15**	2.1	0.14**	2.5	0.17***	2.7	0.09	0.9		
Corruption absent (corruption absent in WGI)	−0.04	−0.4	−0.04	−0.6	−0.05	−0.8	0.20**	2.2	1.55***	2.8
Military absent in politics	0.09	1.3	0.04	0.6	0.08	1.2	0.16**	2.1		
Religious tensions absent	0.06	1.1	0.07	1.5	0.17**	2.4	0.31***	3.3		
Law and order	0.07	1.2	0.12**	2.6	0.17***	3.2	0.27***	3.2		
Ethnic tensions absent	0.07	1.1	0.17***	3.0	0.26***	4.0	0.22***	2.7		
Democratic accountability (voice and accountability in WGI)	0.14*	1.8	0.15**	2.3	0.23***	3.3	0.23***	2.7	−0.02	0.0
Bureaucratic quality (government effectiveness in WGI)	−0.02	−0.3	−0.06	−0.9	−0.01	−0.1	0.09	1.0	0.49	0.9

Sample sizes for the unbalanced panels are 420 in Model A; 474 in Model B; 536 in Model C; 536 in Model D; and 390 in Model E; t statistics are computed using robust standard errors, $^{***}p \leq 0.01$; $^{**}p \leq 0.05$; $^{*}p \leq 0.1$. As in Table 6.2, the years of coverage are 1984–2015 in Models A, B, C and D that use the ICRG political indexes and 1996–2015 in Model E that uses the WGI political indexes (corresponding to years in which the WGI data are available). With 83 countries and eight time points (computed as four-year averages for each variable over the seven non-overlapping four-year windows from 1984–2015 in 83 countries), the potential number of observations is 83 (countries) × 8 (four-year periods) = 664, which would be the sample size if all country-year observations were nonmissing. The number of estimates in this table correspond to 12 (ICRG indexes) × 4 (Models A–D) + 5 (WGI Indexes in Model E) = 57 empirical models from which the coefficient and t statistic for the political risk variable in each model is tabled above

Table 6.4 Dynamic panel models (Blundell-bond) of five empirical models of FDI inflows, 1984–2015

	Models:									
	A (Net FDI): BH (2007) Model with 8 more years of data (1984–2015)		B (Gross FDI): Model A with log* Gross FDI per capita instead of log* Net FDI per capita as the dependent variable		C (Gross FDI): Model B with a single income control, log GNI per capita, instead of double-inclusion of growth		D (Gross FDI): Model C with more flexible controls for income and market size (non-per-capita specification)		E (Gross FDI): Model D with WGI instead of ICRG Political Indexes	
Political indexes measuring institutional quality	Coef.	T-stat.	Coef.	T-stat.	Coef.	T-stat.	Coef.	T-stat.	Coef.	T-stat.
Exprop. risk absent (invest. profile in ICRG; rule of law in WGI)	0.27**	2.6	0.07	0.8	0.06	0.7	0.24**	2.5	0.65	1.1
Government stability (political stability in WGI)	0.30***	3.9	0.07	1.2	0.09	1.6	0.18***	2.7	−0.27	−0.9
Socioecon. stress absent	−0.10	−0.7	−0.08	−0.8	0.01	0.1	0.06	0.5		
Internal conflict absent	0.14	1.6	0.10	1.5	0.13**	2.1	0.28***	3.7		
External conflict absent	−0.05	−0.5	0.17**	2.1	0.15**	2.1	0.04	0.4		
Corruption absent (corruption absent in WGI)	−0.04	−0.3	0.05	0.7	0.07	0.9	0.11	1.2	1.05**	2.1
Military absent in politics	0.12	1.2	−0.04	−0.6	−0.02	−0.3	0.20**	2.4		
Religious tensions absent	0.20*	1.8	0.04	0.5	0.03	0.4	0.24**	2.5		
Law and order	−0.03	−0.3	0.10	1.4	0.15**	2.3	0.24***	2.9		
Ethnic tensions absent	0.03	0.3	0.131*	1.9	0.18***	2.9	0.14	1.6		
Democratic accountability (voice and accountability in WGI)	0.02	0.2	0.09	1.4	0.10	1.5	0.08	1.0	0.12	0.3
Bureaucratic quality (government effectiveness in WGI)	−0.01	−0.1	−0.10	−1.3	−0.04	−0.6	0.11	1.3	0.13	0.2

Sample sizes for the unbalanced panels are 393 in Model A; 471 in Model B; 531 in Model C; 531 in Model D; and 390 in Model E; t statistics are computed using robust standard errors, $^{***}p \leq 0.01$; $^{**}p \leq 0.05$; $^{*}p \leq 0.1$. As in Tables 6.2 and 6.3, the years of coverage are 1984–2015 in Models A, B, C and D that use the ICRG political indexes and 1996–2015 in Model E that uses the WGI political indexes (corresponding to years in which the WGI data are available). The number of estimates in this table correspond to 12 (ICRG indexes) × 4 (Models A–D) + 5 (WGI Indexes in Model E) = 53 empirical models from which the coefficient and t statistic for the political risk variable in each GMM model is tabled above

(Internal Conflict Absent, Military in Politics Absent) are statistically significant. This absence of statistical significance is puzzling and, of course, leaves open the possibility that there are indeed economically significant effects that are imprecisely estimated owing to the net measure of the dependent variable or by the double inclusion of two income variables on the right-hand side. Moving to Model B, which examines the effects of political risk indexes on gross FDI flows, and found that none of the political indexes is statistically significant. After refining the specification of the income-FDI relationship in Model C and Model D to eliminate double inclusion of log GNI and GNI growth, still none of the political index variables has a statistically significant effect on FDI. On the other hand, the WGI political indexes (Model E), suggest that both expropriation risk (i.e., Rule of Law) and corruption have statistically significant effects on FDI flows.

Interestingly, the effects of democracy on FDI is not statistically significant for any of our model specifications or political risk variables (i.e., Democratic Accountability in ICRG or Voice and Accountability in WGI), which contrasts with much of the existing literature that finds FDI flows are higher in democratic countries (e.g., in Busse 2004; Jensen 2003; Oneal 1994). The cross-sectional models provide, at best, only a crude indication of the importance of political risks for FDI. They do not account for any dynamic structure in the FDI process and, perhaps most importantly, they are likely to be biased because of correlated regressors and error terms. These potential econometric issues are addressed by making use of the time-series structure of the data and by employing dynamic panel versions of each model.

Before moving to panel model analysis, formal diagnostic checking are of the estimated cross-section models are conducted, a similar exercise to that conducted in Chap. 5. Major diagnostic test results suggest Models B, C, and D are close to satisfying underlying assumptions of statistical adequacy. In particular, the models using gross flows pass normality, homoscedasticity, and functional form tests. The residuals density plots (Fig. 6.1) for Models D and E, which use our preferred empirical specification, are closest to being normally distributed.

6.5.2 Panel Fixed Effects Estimates

Table 6.3 presents the country FE estimates. The balanced panel data are constructed from four-year averages, which provide eight time-series observations for 83 countries. Several political risk indexes become statistically significant across the models in Table 6.3.[7] In particular, Expropriation Risk, Government Stability, Internal Conflict, Law and Order, Ethnic Tensions, and Democratic Accountability are statistically significant in almost all of the ICRG index models (Law and Order and Ethnic Tensions are insignificant in Model A only). Military in Politics and Religious Tensions

[7]Various strategies were employed to look for sensitivity of the estimates to missing country-year observations and check results against those produced by re-running the 53 models using an identical sample of the country-year observations that are non-missing across all models.

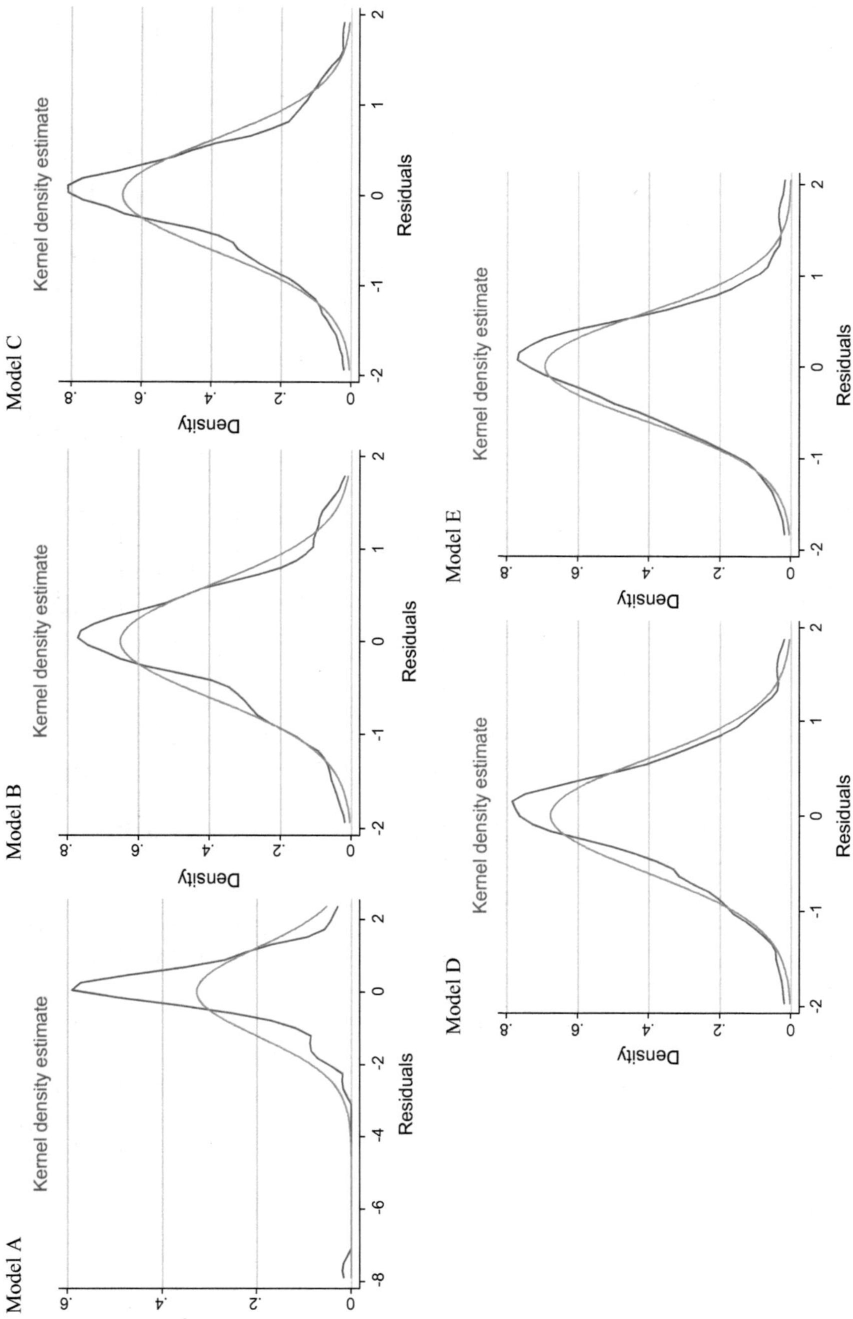

Fig. 6.1 Kernel density and normal density of estimated residuals of Models A–E, 1984–2015

are also statistically significant determinants of FDI flows in preferred specification D. For the WGI data (i.e., Model E), two statistically significant political indexes are: Expropriation Risk and Corruption. It is worthwhile to note the relative magnitudes of the coefficients among the statistically significant political risk indexes across alternative model specifications. Table 6.3 also demonstrates the sensitivity of empirical FDI models to gross versus net FDI inflows as the dependent variable. In models with gross FDI as the dependent variable, the marginal effect of Expropriation Risk is also large relative to other political risk variables, with a relatively high degree of precision in estimation. These results already suggest that Expropriation Risk is important for foreign investment decisions. The expected change in FDI are simulated which take into account the empirical ranges of each political risk index and are reported them in Sect. 6.6.

6.5.3 GMM Dynamic Panel Estimates

Inclusion of a lagged dependent variable (LDV) in the empirical model allows us to control for the dynamics in the underlying process. However, if a linear dynamic panel model is used to capture the own-lagged effect on FDI, then such a model would contain unobserved country-specific effects that are correlated with the LDV; this violates an important assumption of exogeneity of the regressors of the FE estimator, which are therefore biased and inconsistent.[8] The GMM estimator proposed by Arellano and Bond (1991), commonly known as "difference-GMM" uses lagged values of the first difference of the endogenous variables as instruments to provide consistent estimates. One criticism of this standard-GMM approach is that lagged levels are often poor instruments for first differenced variables. Specifically, if the autoregressive process is too persistent, then the lagged-levels are weak instruments. This problem is mitigated by using the system-GMM estimator (Blundell and Bond 1998), which makes use of additional moment conditions.

Table 6.4 reports the results of panel GMM estimation. These results confirm our findings from the panel FE estimator.[9] In particular, Expropriation risk, Government Stability, Internal Conflict, Military in Politics, Religious Tensions, and Law and Order are all statistically significant determinants of gross FDI inflows using the ICRG data, especially when an appropriately specified model is used (i.e., if Model D, our preferred model, is employed). In contrast to the consistently significant effects of expropriation risk on FDI using either ICRG or WGI data when estimated with fixed effects (Models D and E in Tables 6.2 and 6.3), GMM estimates provides a precisely estimated effect of expropriation risk only using ICRG data (i.e., significant in Model D not in Model E).

[8]For details, see Sect. 5.1 in Chap. 5.

[9]Various strategies were employed to look for sensitivity of the estimates to missing country-year observations and check results against those produced by re-running the 53 models using an identical sample of the country-year observations that are non-missing across all models.

In addition to the commonly used controls in the literature (GNI, GNI per capita, trade, macroeconomic stability), the analysis does not include other controls that are found to be significant determinant of FDI flows, such as marginal tax rates (Wei 2000), quality of infrastructure (Asiedu 2002; Asiedu et al. 2009; Ali et al. 2010). These potentially important additional controls are examined to check the robustness of the findings to their inclusion. The additional controls are: number of telephone lines per 1000 persons, paved roads as percentage of total roads, taxes on income, profits, and capital gains as a percentage of total taxes; and they are examined in all three types of estimators. These robustness checks suggest that the overall picture remain largely unchanged across alternative model specifications. In some instances (e.g., FE estimation), the magnitude and precision of the expropriation risk coefficient are higher after controlling for these additional determinants of FDI.

Finally, Table 6.5 reports the estimates of cross-section, panel FE and panel GMM models when capital inflows are portfolio inflows and private debt inflows. It is evident that compared to FDI, these two types of capital inflows are less responsive to most of the political risk variables. Military in Politics and Religious Tension are significant for portfolio inflows and Law and Order is most important for private debt inflows.

6.6 Ranking of Political Risk and Institutional Factors

This section examines the expected percentage change in FDI associated with a ceteris paribus improvement in each of the inverse measures of political risk in the models estimated in the previous section. A higher index value of a political risk index is associated with lower risk and hence would be considered an improvement in that specific dimension of a country's political institutions. The expected change in log FDI is calculated and implied by a relative improvement of one standard deviation from the mean level of political risk, as well as, a worst-to-best improvement that covers the empirical range of each political risk index. Taking the perspective of a decision maker responsible for a high-stakes FDI allocation trying to choose a destination country, these simulations multiply the coefficient estimates in Tables 6.2, 6.3 and 6.4 by changes in the risk variable corresponding to the counterfactuals just described.[10] Holding the controls (X_i) in Eq. 6.6 constant, the expected percentage change in FDI resulting from a given improvement in relative country risk, $\Delta RISK$, is given by:

$$\%\Delta FDI = \left(exp\left[\hat{\beta} \times \Delta RISK\right] - 1\right) \times 100 \qquad (6.7)$$

[10]Because of statistical insignificance of political risk variables in regards to portfolio inflows and private debt inflows, counterfactual simulations are not conducted for portfolio and private debt estimates.

Table 6.5 Estimates of cross-section, panel FE and panel GMM for portfolio inflows and private debt inflows: 1984–2015

Political risk factors	Portfolio inflows						Private debt inflows					
	Cross-section		Panel FE		Panel GMM		Cross-section		Panel FE		Panel GMM	
	Coef.	T-stat.	Coef.	T-stat.	Coef.	T-stat.	Coef.	T-stat.	Coef.	T-stat.	Coef.	T-stat.
Exprop. risk absent (invest. profile in ICRG; rule of law in WGI)	0.15	0.116	−0.53	−0.796	0.87	0.982	2.60	1.181	1.02	1.442	−0.13	−0.143
Government stability (political stability in WGI)	−0.07	−0.037	−0.62	−0.879	0.11	0.127	−0.58	−0.260	0.02	0.022	0.06	0.071
Socioecon. stress absent	0.55	0.373	−0.40	−0.583	0.28	0.273	1.38	0.989	0.49	0.656	0.21	0.186
Internal conflict absent	1.82*	1.801	0.45	0.796	0.42	0.575	0.15	0.162	0.70	1.063	0.01	0.022
External conflict absent	0.93	0.737	0.98	1.491	0.74	0.878	−0.63	−0.492	0.16	0.182	0.64	0.834
Corruption absent (corruption absent in WGI)	0.60	0.508	−0.85	−1.404	−0.17	−0.208	0.97	0.926	−0.17	−0.199	−0.16	−0.199
Military absent in politics	0.67	1.432	1.44***	3.483	1.09*	1.720	1.05**	2.243	0.66	0.995	0.04	0.073
Religious tensions absent	1.25**	2.304	−0.71	−1.440	0.02	0.027	0.75	1.062	0.61	0.890	0.82	1.016
Law and order	1.32*	1.665	0.60	1.037	0.95	1.250	0.93	1.149	2.22***	2.896	2.83***	3.791
Ethnic tensions absent	0.98	1.473	0.04	0.058	−0.44	−0.652	0.29	0.480	0.02	0.026	−1.02	−1.393
Democratic accountability (voice and accountability in WGI)	0.82	1.155	0.74	1.375	0.77	1.306	0.98	1.425	−0.03	−0.069	0.16	0.266
Bureaucratic quality (government effectiveness in WGI)	1.46	1.525	0.82	1.248	1.57	1.617	1.82*	1.701	0.03	0.031	−1.95*	−1.908

Model D is used for portfolio and private debt. 82 observations are found for cross-section model and 68 observations are found for private debt. Sample sizes for unbalanced panels are 435 for panel portfolio
And 406 for panel private debt.***$p < 0.01$, **$p < 0.05$, *$p < 0.1$

where $\hat{\beta}$ is the estimated coefficient corresponding to the associated political risk index and $\Delta RISK$ takes on the values of sample standard deviations and empirical ranges of variation given in Table 6.6. For each of the three estimators, political risk indexes are ranked according to the relative magnitude of the effects, $\hat{\beta} \times \Delta RISK$, limiting our attention to the estimates for Models D and E, which correspond to the preferred model specifications. The mean rank of each risk index across the three estimators are then tabulated.[11]

In the benchmark simulations, the two standardized units of variation in country risk—the standard deviations and the worst-to-best improvements—are based on the full-sample period (1984–2015) for the full country sample (83 countries), which is shown in Table 6.7. The empirical ranges of variation in the political indexes are of course different over different time periods. Assuming that the most recent information about relative institutional quality is important to policy makers and foreign investors considering new investments in developing countries, we therefore also report simulations for the two standardized units over the more recent period (i.e., 2012–2015), which are presented in Table 6.8. Finally, the simulated effects of standardized improvements in risk levels are computed for the subsample of developing countries with sub-median per capita incomes to match the consideration set of FDI investors primarily attracted by low costs of labour. An important consideration of the sub-median developing countries is that poor countries arguably stand to benefit the most from foreign investment and the barriers to foreign investment in these countries are potentially the result of political risks, which may be less prevalent for higher-income developing countries. It is therefore investigate whether the results differ for the sub-median per capita income country sub-sample over the most recent period and presented in Table 6.9.

Turning first to the simulation based on the full country sample and time period, the simulated effects of expropriation risk tend to be larger and economically significant in all cases. A one-standard-deviation improvement in the expropriation risk index is associated with a predicted increase in FDI ranging from 10% (based on the cross-section estimates) to 64% (FE estimates) using the ICRG indexes and from 22 to 71% using the WGI indexes.[12] The effect of a one standard deviation in Expropriation Risk has the second-largest mean rank among both ICRG and WGI indexes. A potential concern with the inclusion of the cross-section estimates in the mean ranking is

[11]It is noted that assigning ranks to simulated effects that are very close in magnitude is potentially problematic because ordinal differences may be assigned to effect sizes that are statistically indistinguishable given the precision of estimation offered by the data. A rule of a threshold difference of one percentage point and assign ranks (and tied ranking otherwise) only to simulated effects that are more than one percentage point different (which is believed to be a reasonable threshold for economic significance).

[12]In the sense of a relatively conservative view on the range of simulated effects of political indexes on FDI, full country sample and the full sample period are considered; however, the estimated range effects are even larger if the recent period sample and the sub-median country sample are considered. For example, for the recent sample period (in Table 6.8), the effects of expropriation risk range from 10 to 127%.

Table 6.6 Empirical ranges of variation used to compute counterfactual improvements in political indexes

Political indexes measuring institutional quality	Cross-sectional summary statistics: full-sample (all years available, 1984–2015)				Full-sample (1984–2015) stdev	2008–2015 subsample stdev	Sub-median-income subsample stdev	Full-sample (1984–2015) empirical range	2008–2015 subsample's empirical range	Sub-median-income subsample's empirical range
	Min	Median	Mean	Max						
ICRG indexes										
Exprop. risk absent	2.88	5.64	5.62	7.98	1.01	1.67	1.38	5.10	8.74	7.08
Government stability	4.64	6.03	6.16	7.67	0.69	1.11	1.13	3.03	4.25	4.25
Socioecon. stress absent	1.06	4.11	4.11	7.01	1.05	1.59	1.14	5.96	7.96	5.36
Internal conflict absent	3.20	6.97	6.86	9.58	1.35	1.10	1.13	6.37	4.96	4.17
External conflict absent	4.21	7.92	7.87	9.85	1.05	0.99	0.94	5.64	4.51	3.89
Corruption absent	1.01	4.44	4.29	6.66	1.11	1.10	1.16	5.65	7.13	5.57
Military absent in politics	0.56	5.03	5.39	10.00	2.41	2.82	2.45	9.44	10.00	8.33
Religious tensions absent	1.81	7.83	7.23	10.00	1.98	2.27	2.47	8.19	8.33	8.33
Law and order	1.65	4.94	5.20	8.66	1.52	1.76	1.62	7.00	6.67	6.67

(continued)

Table 6.6 (continued)

Political indexes measuring institutional quality	Cross-sectional summary statistics: full-sample (all years available, 1984–2015)				Full-sample (1984–2015) stdev	2008–2015 subsample stdev	Sub-median-income subsample stdev	Full-sample (1984–2015) empirical range	2008–2015 subsample's empirical range	Sub-median-income subsample's empirical range
	Min	Median	Mean	Max						
Ethnic tensions absent	1.24	6.32	6.18	10.00	1.96	2.10	2.03	8.76	8.33	6.67
Democratic accountability	1.71	5.79	5.69	9.00	1.72	2.33	1.96	7.29	8.58	8.09
Bureaucratic quality	0.00	4.42	4.37	8.22	1.81	1.99	2.12	8.22	7.50	7.50
WGI indexes										
Rule of law	−1.72	−0.48	−0.43	1.25	0.64	0.64	0.43	2.97	3.08	1.76
Political stability	−2.32	−0.41	−0.45	0.96	0.77	0.83	0.78	3.27	3.68	3.27
Corruption absent	−1.48	−0.53	−0.44	1.43	0.56	0.57	0.33	2.91	2.80	1.41
Voice and accountability	−1.71	−0.32	−0.33	1.04	0.73	0.75	0.55	2.75	2.86	2.18
Government effectiveness	−1.71	−0.36	−0.32	1.19	0.62	0.64	0.43	2.90	2.87	1.68

Table 6.7 Expected percentage changes in FDI and importance rankings from a one-standard-deviation improvements (upper panel) and worst-to-best improvements (lower panel) in institutional quality, full sample (all years with available data used)

	Cross section			Fixed effects			GMM			
Political indexes measuring institutional quality	Expected % change	Rank	Coef. from Table 6.2	Expected % change	Rank	Coef. from Table 6.3	Expected % change	Rank	Coef. from Table 6.4	Mean rank
Simulated one-standard-deviation improvements in institutional quality										
ICRG indexes										
Exprop. risk absent	10%	4.0	0.09	64%	2.0	0.49***	27%	6.0	0.24**	4.0
Government stability	16%	1.0	0.21	27%	9.0	0.35***	13%	8.5	0.18***	6.2
Socioecon. stress absent	4%	7.0	0.04	38%	7.0	0.31**	7%	11.0	0.06	8.3
Internal conflict absent	6%	6.0	0.04	35%	8.0	0.22***	46%	3.0	0.28***	5.7
External conflict absent	0%	9.0	0.00	10%	12.0	0.09	4%	12.0	0.04	11.0
Corruption absent	12%	3.0	0.10	25%	10.0	0.20**	13%	10.0	0.11	7.7
Military absent in politics	0%	9.0	0.00	47%	6.0	0.16**	61%	1.0	0.20**	5.3

(continued)

Table 6.7 (continued)

	Cross section			Fixed effects			GMM			
Political indexes measuring institutional quality	Expected % change	Rank	Coef. from Table 6.2	Expected % change	Rank	Coef. from Table 6.3	Expected % change	Rank	Coef. from Table 6.4	Mean rank
Religious tensions absent	−9%	12.0	−0.05	85%	1.0	0.31***	60%	2.0	0.24**	5.0
Law and order	13%	2.0	0.08	51%	4.0	0.27***	44%	4.0	0.24***	3.3
Ethnic tensions absent	0%	9.0	0.00	54%	3.0	0.22***	30%	5.0	0.14	5.7
Democratic accountability	7%	5.0	0.04	49%	5.0	0.23***	14%	8.5	0.08	6.2
Bureaucratic quality	−4%	11.0	−0.02	18%	11.0	0.09	23%	7.0	0.11	9.7
WGI indexes										
Rule of law	22%	1.0	0.31*	71%	2.0	0.84*	51%	2.0	0.65	1.7
Political stability	9%	5.0	0.11	17%	4.0	0.20	−19%	5.0	−0.27	4.7
Corruption absent	20%	2.5	0.33*	138%	1.0	1.55***	80%	1.0	1.05**	1.5
Voice and accountability	14%	4.0	0.18	−1%	5.0	−0.02	9%	3.0	0.12	4.0
Government effectiveness	20%	2.5	0.29	35%	3.0	0.49	8%	4.0	0.13	3.2

(continued)

Table 6.7 (continued)

	Cross section			Fixed effects			GMM			
Political indexes measuring institutional quality	Expected % change	Rank	Coef. from Table 6.2	Expected % change	Rank	Coef. from Table 6.3	Expected % change	Rank	Coef. from Table 6.4	Mean rank
Simulated worst-to-best improvements in institutional quality										
ICRG indexes										
Exprop. risk absent	58%	4.0	0.09	1116%	2.0	0.49***	233%	5.0	0.24**	3.7
Government stability	89%	1.0	0.21	189%	10.0	0.35***	73%	10.0	0.18***	7.0
Socioecon. stress absent	27%	7.0	0.04	533%	5.0	0.31**	43%	11.0	0.06	7.7
Internal conflict absent	29%	6.0	0.04	306%	8.0	0.22***	495%	4.0	0.28***	6.0
External conflict absent	0%	9.0	0.00	66%	12.0	0.09	23%	12.0	0.04	11.0
Corruption absent	76%	2.5	0.10	209%	9.0	0.20**	88%	8.0	0.11	6.5
Military absent in politics	0%	9.0	0.00	353%	7.0	0.16**	542%	2.0	0.20**	6.0
Religious tensions absent	−34%	12.0	−0.05	1166%	1.0	0.31***	596%	1.0	0.24**	4.7

(continued)

Table 6.7 (continued)

	Cross section			Fixed effects			GMM			
Political indexes measuring institutional quality	Expected % change	Rank	Coef. from Table 6.2	Expected % change	Rank	Coef. from Table 6.3	Expected % change	Rank	Coef. from Table 6.4	Mean rank
Law and order	75%	2.5	0.08	562%	4.0	0.27***	441%	3.0	0.24***	3.2
Ethnic tensions absent	0%	9.0	0.00	587%	3.0	0.22***	226%	6.0	0.14	6.0
Democratic accountability	34%	5.0	0.04	434%	6.0	0.23***	75%	9.0	0.08	6.7
Bureaucratic quality	−15%	11.0	−0.02	110%	11.0	0.09	155%	7.0	0.11	9.7
WGI indexes										
Rule of law	151%	2.0	0.34**	1112%	2.0	0.84*	589%	2.0	0.65	2.0
Political stability	43%	5.0	0.15	92%	4.0	0.20	−59%	5.0	−0.27	4.7
Corruption absent	161%	1.0	0.36**	8940%	1.0	1.55***	2014%	1.0	1.05**	1.0
Voice and accountability	64%	4.0	0.19	−5%	5.0	−0.02	39%	4.0	0.12	4.3
Government effectiveness	132%	3.0	0.29	313%	3.0	0.49	46%	3.0	0.13	3.0

Estimated coefficients used to compute the simulated expected percentage changes in this table are taken from Model D in Tables 6.2, 6.3 and 6.4, repeated here for convenience

Table 6.8 Recent sample (2012–2015) expected percentage changes in FDI and importance rankings from one-standard-deviation improvements (upper panel) and worst-to-best improvements (lower panel) in institutional quality based on full-sample estimated effects and recent-sample ranges of variation

	Cross section			Fixed effects			GMM			
Political indexes measuring institutional quality	Expected % change	Rank	Coef. from Table 6.2	Expected % change	Rank	Coef. from Table 6.3	Expected % change	Rank	Coef. from Table 6.4	Mean rank
Simulated one-standard-deviation improvements in institutional quality										
ICRG indexes										
Exprop. risk absent	16%	2.0	0.09	127%	1.0	0.49***	48%	4.0	0.24**	2.3
Government stability	26%	1.0	0.21	48%	8.0	0.35***	22%	8.0	0.18***	5.7
Socioecon. stress absent	7%	6.0	0.04	63%	4.0	0.31**	10%	11.0	0.06	7.0
Internal conflict absent	5%	7.0	0.04	27%	9.0	0.22***	36%	5.0	0.28***	7.0
External conflict absent	0%	9.0	0.00	9%	12.0	0.09	4%	12.0	0.04	11.0
Corruption absent	12%	4.0	0.10	25%	10.0	0.20**	13%	10.0	0.11	8.0
Military absent in politics	0%	9.0	0.00	57%	7.0	0.16**	74%	1.0	0.20**	5.7

(continued)

Table 6.8 (continued)

	Cross section			Fixed effects			GMM			
Political indexes measuring institutional quality	Expected % change	Rank	Coef. from Table 6.2	Expected % change	Rank	Coef. from Table 6.3	Expected % change	Rank	Coef. from Table 6.4	Mean rank
Religious tensions absent	−11%	12.0	−0.05	102%	2.0	0.31***	71%	2.0	0.24**	5.3
Law and order	15%	3.0	0.08	61%	5.0	0.27***	53%	3.0	0.24***	3.7
Ethnic tensions absent	0%	9.0	0.00	59%	6.0	0.22***	33%	6.0	0.14	7.0
Democratic accountability	10%	5.0	0.04	71%	3.0	0.23***	20%	9.0	0.08	5.7
Bureaucratic quality	−4%	11.0	−0.02	20%	11.0	0.09	25%	7.0	0.11	9.7
WGI indexes										
Rule of law	22%	1.0	0.31*	71%	2.0	0.84*	51%	2.0	0.65	1.7
Political stability	10%	5.0	0.11	18%	4.0	0.20	−20%	5.0	−0.27	4.7
Corruption absent	21%	2.0	0.33*	141%	1.0	1.55***	82%	1.0	1.05**	1.3
Voice and accountability	15%	4.0	0.18	−1%	5.0	−0.02	9%	3.0	0.12	4.0
Government effectiveness	20%	3.0	0.29	37%	3.0	0.49	9%	4.0	0.13	3.3

(continued)

Table 6.8 (continued)

	Cross section			Fixed effects			GMM			
Political indexes measuring institutional quality	Expected % change	Rank	Coef. from Table 6.2	Expected % change	Rank	Coef. from Table 6.3	Expected % change	Rank	Coef. from Table 6.4	Mean rank
Simulated worst-to-best improvements in institutional quality										
ICRG indexes										
Exprop. risk absent	120%	2.0	0.09	7149%	1.0	0.49***	687%	1.0	0.24**	1.3
Government stability	144%	1.0	0.21	343%	8.0	0.35***	117%	9.0	0.18***	6.0
Socioecon. stress absent	37%	6.0	0.04	1080%	3.0	0.31**	62%	11.0	0.06	6.7
Internal conflict absent	22%	7.0	0.04	198%	10.0	0.22***	301%	5.0	0.28***	7.3
External conflict absent	0%	9.0	0.00	50%	12.0	0.09	18%	12.0	0.04	11.0
Corruption absent	104%	3.0	0.10	316%	9.0	0.20**	122%	8.0	0.11	6.7
Military absent in politics	0%	9.0	0.00	395%	7.0	0.16**	617%	2.5	0.20**	6.2
Religious tensions absent	−34%	12.0	−0.05	1224%	2.0	0.31***	621%	2.5	0.24**	5.5

(continued)

Table 6.8 (continued)

	Cross section			Fixed effects			GMM			
Political indexes measuring institutional quality	Expected % change	Rank	Coef. from Table 6.2	Expected % change	Rank	Coef. from Table 6.3	Expected % change	Rank	Coef. from Table 6.4	Mean rank
Law and order	70%	4.0	0.08	505%	6.0	0.27***	399%	4.0	0.24***	4.7
Ethnic tensions absent	0%	9.0	0.00	525%	5.0	0.22***	208%	6.0	0.14	6.7
Democratic accountability	41%	5.0	0.04	619%	4.0	0.23***	94%	10.0	0.08	6.3
Bureaucratic quality	−14%	11.0	−0.02	96%	11.0	0.09	135%	7.0	0.11	9.7
WGI indexes										
Rule of law	160%	1.0	0.34**	1227%	2.0	0.84*	639%	2.0	0.65	1.7
Political stability	50%	5.0	0.15	109%	4.0	0.20	−63%	5.0	−0.27	4.7
Corruption absent	152%	2.0	0.36**	7597%	1.0	1.55***	1796%	1.0	1.05**	1.3
Voice and accountability	67%	4.0	0.19	−6%	5.0	−0.02	41%	4.0	0.12	4.3
Government effectiveness	130%	3.0	0.29	307%	3.0	0.49	45%	3.0	0.13	3.0

Table 6.9 Recent sample (2012–2015) sub-median-income countries' expected percentage changes in FDI and importance rankings from one-standard-deviation improvements (upper panel) and worst-to-best improvements (lower panel) in Institutional quality based on full-sample estimated effects and recent-sample ranges of variation computed among sub-median-income countries

	Cross section			Fixed effects			GMM			
Political indexes measuring institutional quality	Expected % change	Rank	Coef. from Table 6.2	Expected % change	Rank	Coef. from Table 6.3	Expected % change	Rank	Coef. from Table 6.4	Mean rank
ICRG indexes										
Exprop. risk absent	13%	3.5	0.09	97%	2.0	0.49***	39%	4.0	0.24**	3.2
Government stability	27%	1.0	0.21	49%	6.0	0.35***	23%	8.0	0.18***	5.0
Socioecon. stress absent	5%	6.5	0.04	42%	8.0	0.31**	7%	11.0	0.06	8.5
Internal conflict absent	5%	6.5	0.04	28%	9.0	0.22***	37%	5.0	0.28***	6.8
External conflict absent	0%	9.0	0.00	9%	12.0	0.09	3%	12.0	0.04	11.0
Corruption absent	12%	3.5	0.10	26%	10.0	0.20**	14%	10.0	0.11	7.8
Military absent in politics	0%	9.0	0.00	48%	7.0	0.16**	62%	2.0	0.20**	6.0

(continued)

Table 6.9 (continued)

	Cross section			Fixed effects			GMM			
Political indexes measuring institutional quality	Expected % change	Rank	Coef. from Table 6.2	Expected % change	Rank	Coef. from Table 6.3	Expected % change	Rank	Coef. from Table 6.4	Mean rank
Religious tensions absent	−12%	12.0	−0.05	115%	1.0	0.31***	80%	1.0	0.24**	4.7
Law and order	14%	2.0	0.08	55%	5.0	0.27***	48%	3.0	0.24***	3.3
Ethnic tensions absent	0%	9.0	0.00	56%	3.5	0.22***	32%	6.0	0.14	6.2
Democratic accountability	8%	5.0	0.04	57%	3.5	0.23***	16%	9.0	0.08	5.8
Bureaucratic quality	−4%	11.0	−0.02	21%	11.0	0.09	27%	7.0	0.11	9.7
WGI indexes										
Rule of law	14%	1.0	0.31*	44%	2.0	0.84*	33%	2.0	0.65	1.7
Political stability	9%	5.0	0.11	17%	4.0	0.20	−19%	5.0	−0.27	4.7
Corruption absent	11%	3.0	0.33*	66%	1.0	1.55***	41%	1.0	1.05**	1.7
Voice and accountability	10%	4.0	0.18	−1%	5.0	−0.02	7%	3.0	0.12	4.0
Government effectiveness	13%	2.0	0.29	23%	3.0	0.49	6%	4.0	0.13	3.0

(continued)

Table 6.9 (continued)

	Cross section			Fixed effects			GMM			
Political indexes measuring institutional quality	Expected % change	Rank	Coef. from Table 6.2	Expected % change	Rank	Coef. from Table 6.3	Expected % change	Rank	Coef. from Table 6.4	Mean rank
ICRG indexes										
Exprop. risk absent	64%	2.0	0.09	347%	1.0	0.49***	167%	2.0	0.24**	1.7
Government stability	89%	1.0	0.21	149%	6.0	0.35***	77%	8.0	0.18***	5.0
Socioecon. stress absent	21%	6.0	0.04	166%	5.0	0.31**	32%	11.0	0.06	7.3
Internal conflict absent	17%	7.0	0.04	92%	10.0	0.22***	117%	5.0	0.28***	7.3
External conflict absent	0%	9.0	0.00	35%	12.0	0.09	14%	12.0	0.04	11.0
Corruption absent	56%	3.0	0.10	111%	9.0	0.20**	62%	9.5	0.11	7.2
Military absent in politics	0%	9.0	0.00	133%	8.0	0.16**	164%	3.0	0.20**	6.7
Religious tensions absent	−42%	12.0	−0.05	258%	2.0	0.31***	197%	1.0	0.24**	5.0

(continued)

Table 6.9 (continued)

Political indexes measuring institutional quality	Cross section			Fixed effects			GMM			
	Expected % change	Rank	Coef. from Table 6.2	Expected % change	Rank	Coef. from Table 6.3	Expected % change	Rank	Coef. from Table 6.4	Mean rank
Law and order	53%	4.0	0.08	180%	4.0	0.27***	161%	4.0	0.24***	4.0
Ethnic tensions absent	0%	9.0	0.00	147%	7.0	0.22***	90%	6.0	0.14	7.3
Democratic accountability	32%	5.0	0.04	186%	3.0	0.23***	62%	9.5	0.08	5.8
Bureaucratic quality	−15%	11.0	−0.02	68%	11.0	0.09	86%	7.0	0.11	9.7
WGI indexes										
Rule of law	55%	1.0	0.34**	148%	2.0	0.84*	115%	2.0	0.65	1.7
Political stability	36%	5.0	0.15	65%	4.0	0.20	−88%	5.0	−0.27	4.7
Corruption absent	46%	3.0	0.36**	218%	1.0	1.55***	148%	1.0	1.05**	1.7
Voice and accountability	39%	4.0	0.19	−4%	5.0	−0.02	26%	3.0	0.12	4.0
Government effectiveness	49%	2.0	0.29	82%	3.0	0.49	22%	4.0	0.13	3.0

Estimated coefficients used to compute the simulated expected percentage changes in this table are taken from Model D in Tables 6.2, 6.3 and 6.4, repeated here for convenience that all of these cross-section effects are statistically indistinguishable from zero at conventional levels.

If the FE and GMM estimates are included in the average ranking, where many of the political indexes are statistically significant, a very similar result is obtained. In particular, Religious Tensions and Military in Politics are ranked highest in importance of mean ranking followed by Expropriation Risk, Law and Order, and Ethnic Tensions (which tie for the third highest ranking). It is notable that these categories of political risks—Expropriation risk, Law and Order, Internal Conflict, Military in Politics, and Religious Tensions—likely pose similar threats to foreign investors. An effective and impartial legal system is a key feature of contract enforcement; and investors are likely to be concerned about the risks to their property rights in a country with ineffective legal system. Internal Conflicts, and Ethnic and Religious Tensions may result in disruptions to the normal operations of foreign-owned enterprises and create uncertainty about normal operation in the future. When acute tensions arise between political, ethnic or religious groups, the institutions that enforce contracts and safeguard the property rights of foreign investors tend to become more fragile. This is particularly the case when foreign investments themselves are perceived as having political ties to a particular group involved in the conflict, which raises the risk that incumbent political leaders will be replaced and thereby lowers the expected cost of confiscating foreign investors' assets (Ali et al. 2010). Similarly in situations of civil conflict and unrest, production and trade may become severely restricted, potentially rendering the value of foreigners' assets worthless. These findings can be interpreted that risk of total asset loss or expropriation risk has the largest weight on foreign investors' decisions relating to other institutional factors.

Ranking the simulated effects based on the five WGI indexes, a one-standard-deviation improvement in the index representing expropriation risk—Rule of Law—has the second largest effect on FDI, with Corruption ranking the first. Interestingly, corruption's average rank among the ICRG indexes is relatively low (ranking 9th); however, corruption becomes more important among the ICRG indexes when considering worst-to-best improvements, since its empirical range is relatively large.

The lower panel of Table 6.7 shows the simulated effects of worst-to-best improvements in the political indexes. Law and Order ranks first among the ICRG indexes, with Expropriation Risk ranking second. Religious Tensions ranks 3rd, followed by a three-way tie between Internal Conflict, Ethnic Tensions and Military in Politics. In contrast to the one-standard-deviation changes, however, Corruption ranks 7th on average, above Government Stability and Democratic Accountability. The ordering of mean rank among the effects of worst-to-best improvements in the WGI indexes are the same as for one-standard-deviation changes in the upper panel.

Table 6.8 calculates the simulated effects using standard deviations and empirical ranges of variation in each political risk index from the most recent four-year period (i.e., 2012–2015). However, we use the same estimated coefficients based on all available years of data as reported in Tables 6.2, 6.3 and 6.4. The motivation for the simulation in this table is to learn something about the point of view of a prospective FDI investor who considers the most recent information on the improvement of political indexes between candidate countries for new FDI projects. The relative importance of Expropriation Risk becomes more pronounced in the ICRG mean rankings when using the recent-year empirical variation across countries' institutional profiles. In particular, Expropriation Risk has the largest simulated effect on FDI among the ICRG indexes (based on the mean ranking of simulated effects of political indexes) for both the one-standard-deviation and worst-to-best improvements in political risk, followed by Law and Order. Based on the recent four-year period among the WGI indexes, Expropriation Risk (i.e., Rule of Law) has the second largest impacts on FDI following Corruption which ranks first, by average ranking.

Table 6.9 calculates the simulated effects of a one-standard-deviation improvement and empirical ranges of variation among only sub-median-income countries in the recent four-year period, 2012–2015. Again, the estimated coefficients used are based on all available years as reported in Tables 6.2, 6.3 and 6.4. The motivation of this third and final simulation is to learn something about the point of view of a prospective FDI investor who is primarily interested in low labour costs and therefore considers only the low-wage developing countries as a potential destination for investment projects. The simulated effects from this table suggest that Expropriation Risk has the largest effects on FDI among countries with sub-median income. In particular, Expropriation Risk has the largest mean rank (in terms of effect size on FDI) for the two standardized units (i.e., worst-to-best improvement and one-standard-deviation improvement) across the three estimators for the ICRG indexes, followed by Law and Order. Among the WGI indexes, Expropriation Risk (i.e., Rule of Law) and Corruption tie for first place by the criterion of mean rank in the both standardized units.

Taken together, the simulated effects of political indexes on FDI suggest that expropriation risk is among the most important, if not the most important, political risk factor influencing the allocation of FDI across developing countries. Other relatively important risk factors include the strength and impartiality of the legal system and judiciary (i.e., ICRG's Law and Order), as well as political conflicts that may also be associated with risk of abrupt asset destruction or seizure (e.g., the ICRG's Internal Conflict, Military in Politics, Ethnic and Religious Tensions). This empirical finding suggests a rather coarse but nonetheless informative two-category taxonomy of risks: risks that affect the probability of abruptly losing 100% of invested capital; and risks that lower expected return or increase volatility of returns on investment conditional on the value of that investment remaining strictly positive. The evidence is consistent with the hypothesis that Expropriation Risk is a primarily important concern to foreign investors.

One limitation of the analysis so far is that the estimates do not identify the direct effects of each individual risk index holding other risk indexes constant. The political risk indexes overlap conceptually, suggesting that these variables are highly collinear. Estimating the effect of each risk index one by one may yield more informative information about the marginal effects in the presence of multicolinearity. Nevertheless, this strategy may also introduce omitted variable bias. This concern is addressed by comparing joint estimation using principal components of statistically related indexes in the following section.

6.7 Effects of Composite Risk Measures

Including all political risk factors simultaneously to estimate the joint effects could lead to a serious problem of multicolinearity and limit the extent to which the relevance of each institutional dimension can be identified (Bénassy-Quéré et al. 2007; Daude and Stein 2007). One solution is to group these variables into an aggregated index, or a small number of aggregated indexes that capture similar dimensions (See, for example, Daude and Stein 2007). Since our primary interest is to understand the relative importance of political risk indexes in determining FDI, our approach is to use principal components to: (i) extract information while reducing the dimensionality of the political risk variables using data driven criteria; (ii) estimate the simultaneous effects of component factors that satisfy the (perhaps overly inclusive) criterion of having an associated eigenvalue strictly greater than 1; and (iii) examine the weights of different political risk indexes in any principal components that show up as statistically and economically significant in the FDI model (See also Globerman and Shapiro 2002; Wheeler and Mody 1992).

The principal components analysis (PCA) is applied to reduce the dimensionality of the 12 ICRG indexes and 5 WGI indexes and to estimate an empirical FDI model that better captures the information contained in their joint distribution. The first three principal components are sued for the estimated regression applying the admittedly ad hoc factor-inclusion criterion of having an associated eigenvalue greater than 1.[13] Model D is estimated using those three factors $(\beta_{F1} F1_i + \beta_{F2} F2_i + \beta_{F3} F3_i)$ in place of the single risk index $(\beta RISK_i)$ in the conditional mean of log* FDI (Eq. 6.6).[14] For the WGI indexes, the first principal component was used applying the same inclusion criterion of an associated eigenvalue greater than 1.

Table 6.10a reports the factor loadings of the political indexes and the principal factors that exceed eigenvalues greater than 1. The cross-section regression results using the original model (Eq. 6.6) but with the principal components (Factors 1, 2, and 3) replacing the individual risk factor are presented in Table 6.10b. The sample size for the ICRG was reduced to 1996–2015 to compare the results with that of the WGI. The largest factor loadings from all years (1984–2015) of the individual political indexes (Table 6.10a) on the first principal component, in order, are Internal Conflict (loading = 0.83), Military in Politics (loading = 0.82), and Expropriation Risk (loading = 0.81). The ranking of the Expropriation Risk in the factor loading is the same in the reduced sample of the ICRG (1996–2015). The result suggests that the factor that contains the Expropriation Risk or risk related to expropriation measure is statistically significant in the regression. In the WGI, the factor loadings of Corruption and Expropriation Risk are equal to each other in the first principal component. Similarly, for the WGI indexes, the single factor included in the model (with eigenvalue exceeding one) contains Rule of Law and is statistically significant.

---

[13]It is plausible that other extraction criterion can also be used, such as Scree test, Cumulative total percent of variance, Interpretability criteria.

[14]The β coefficients are the relative weights of the principal factors in the total variance.

Table 6.10 a Factor loadings in the cross-sectional samples. b Cross-sectional estimates of Model D using principal factors with eigenvalues greater than 1

a

Political indexes measuring institutional quality	1984–2015			1996–2015		
	Factor 1	Factor 2	Factor 3	Factor 1	Factor 2	Factor 3
ICRG indexes						
Expropriation risk absent	0.81	−0.11	−0.19	0.79	0.01	−0.18
Government stability	0.46	−0.72	0.20	0.03	0.84	0.09
Socioecon stress absent	0.78	−0.34	−0.11	0.75	0.27	−0.33
Internal conflict absent	0.83	0.02	0.34	0.83	0.18	0.32
External conflict absent	0.62	0.36	0.03	0.59	−0.22	0.28
Corruption absent	0.72	0.06	−0.12	0.69	−0.06	−0.01
Military not in politics	0.82	0.19	−0.13	0.86	−0.09	−0.03
Religious tensions absent	0.40	0.56	0.49	0.48	−0.21	0.66
Law and order	0.73	−0.39	0.13	0.56	0.58	−0.17
Ethnic tensions absent	0.57	0.08	0.55	0.60	0.18	0.33
Democratic accountability	0.61	0.54	−0.38	0.56	−0.66	−0.18
Bureaucratic quality	0.74	−0.09	−0.45	0.69	−0.16	−0.48
Eigenvalues	5.70	1.58	1.16	5.12	1.76	1.18
WGI Indexes (1996–2015)						
Rule of law				0.95		
Political stability				0.82		
Corruption absent				0.95		
Voice and accountability				0.79		
Government effectiveness				0.93		
Eigenvalue				3.97		

Three factors have eigenvalues greater than 1 among the ICRG political risk variables in both the 1984–2015 and 1996–2015 cross-sectional samples. Only one factor has an eigenvalue greater than 1 among the WGI political risk variables in the 1996–2015 cross-sectional sample (i.e., years for which WGI data are available)

b

	ICRG, 1984–2015		ICRG, 1996–2015		WGI, 1996–2015	
	Coef.	T-stat.	Coef.	T-stat.	Coef.	T-stat.
Factor 1	0.15	1.2	0.22*	1.8	0.22**	2.1
Factor 2	0.04	0.5	0.06	0.9		
Factor 3	0.06	0.7	0.04	0.4		
Log GNI	1.01***	8.8	0.98***	9.7	0.97***	9.6
Log trade	0.45*	2.0	0.24	1.0	0.31	1.4
Log inflation	−0.10	−1.0	0.01	0.1	0.00	0.0
Log pop	−0.13	−0.9	−0.16	−1.2	−0.15	−1.2
Obs.	81		81		81	
R-squared	0.87		0.86		0.86	

The factor loadings of the political indexes show a similar pattern when we use 4-year panel averages; however a total of four principal components have eigenvalues greater than 1 (Table 6.11a). The first four principal components are used and found that the first principal component has statistically significant effects on FDI in FE estimator and panel GMM estimator. Again, Expropriation Risk or risk related to expropriation risk has a relatively larger, if not the largest, weight on the first principal component and the first component is statistically significant in the panel models. More relevant to the general findings, the second and third or fourth principal components are not significant in any of the models estimated. Taken together, the findings from this composite risk measures analysis also support previous findings and suggest that Expropriation Risk or risks that are highly related with abrupt destruction of assets or seizure are among the most important political risk factors determining FDI inflows to developing countries.

6.8 Summary of Expropriation Risk Analysis

Absence of expropriation risk has large effects on FDI and this finding contrasts with the mixed results reported in previous studies. The result propose an intuitive interpretation for the special importance of expropriation risk and other institutional qualities related to the risk of abrupt and 100% loss of invested capital. The empirical evidence in this chapter is consistent with the theory that there exists a threshold effect for a significant number of foreign investors: if perceived risks of expropriation are sufficiently large, then other institutional risks that affect expected returns and volatility of returns become less important because they cannot compensate for the losses of 100% principal. An important question is then why were the previous empirical studies unable to identify the effects of expropriation risk on FDI? One possible reason is model misspecification that have been discussed and argued in Sects. 6.3–6.4, which raises concerns over alternative choices of dependent variables and ad hoc choices of conditional mean functions. The empirical model of the analysis is based on theoretical arguments and finds that absence of expropriation risk has a robust, statistically and economically significant effect on FDI.

The empirical results in this chapter echo the results from a recent survey conducted by the World Bank's Multilateral Guarantee Agency (MIGA), which suggests that the most important factor among a set of risk factors thought to affect MNE's choices of location is expropriation risk (MIGA-EIU, Political Risk Survey 2011). Specifically, this survey study indicates that the three most worrisome political risks in emerging economies are breaches of contract, sudden regulatory changes, and transfer and convertibility restrictions. The investment profile of the ICRG used as a measure of expropriation risk is constructed based on precisely these three indexes.

Finally, two examples are presented here to demonstrate the importance of why foreign investors have good reasons to prioritize the risk of expropriation when considering new FDI projects in foreign countries. Ecuador ranks at the top of lists comparing the risks of expropriation in different countries. One reason is that Ecuador

Table 6.11 a Factor loadings in four-year averaged panel samples. b Fixed-effects and GMM estimates of Model D using principal factors with eigenvalues greater than 1

a

Political indexes measuring institutional quality	Factor 1	Factor 2	Factor 3	Factor 4
ICRG indexes (1984–2015)				
Expropriation risk absent	0.68	−0.36	−0.39	−0.16
Government stability	0.49	−0.68	−0.26	0.19
Socioecon stress absent	0.53	0.42	−0.25	0.30
Internal conflict absent	0.82	−0.23	0.19	0.12
External conflict absent	0.63	−0.31	0.19	−0.22
Corruption absent	0.46	0.60	0.13	0.18
Military not in politics	0.74	0.28	−0.01	−0.21
Religious tensions absent	0.45	0.03	0.66	−0.23
Law and order	0.72	−0.01	−0.04	0.45
Ethnic tensions absent	0.61	−0.10	0.42	0.28
Democratic accountability	0.60	0.13	−0.12	−0.61
Bureaucratic quality	0.65	0.34	−0.40	−0.08
Eigenvalues	4.68	1.51	1.15	1.00
WGI indexes (1996–2015)				
Rule of law	0.94			
Political stability	0.81			
Corruption absent	0.94			
Voice and accountability	0.79			
Government effectiveness	0.92			
Eigenvalue	3.90			

Four factors have eigenvalues greater than 1 among the ICRG political risk variables. Only the first factor has an eigenvalue greater than 1 among the WGI political risk variables

b

	Fixed effects				GMM			
	ICRG, 1984–2015		WGI, 1996–2015		ICRG, 1984–2015		WGI, 1996–2015	
	Coef.	T-stat.	Coef.	T-stat.	Coef.	T-stat.	Coef.	T-stat.
Factor 1	0.97***	4.8	0.66	1.6	0.65***	7.9	0.38*	1.9
Factor 2	−0.19	−1.1			−0.03	−0.4		
Factor 3	−0.27	−1.2			0.06	0.4		
Factor 4	−0.03	−0.2			0.10	1.2		
FDI (lagged)					0.29***	5.9	0.41***	6.6
Log GNI	0.27	0.5	1.11	1.5	0.43**	2.3	0.65***	3.8
Log trade	1.79**	2.5	1.92*	1.7	1.49***	4.9	0.84**	2.3
Log inflation	0.00	0.0	−0.51	−0.8	0.07	2.0	−0.05	−0.6

(continued)

Table 6.11 (continued)

b

	Fixed effects				GMM			
	ICRG, 1984–2015		WGI, 1996–2015		ICRG, 1984–2015		WGI, 1996–2015	
	Coef.	T-stat.	Coef.	T-stat.	Coef.	T-stat.	Coef.	T-stat.
Log pop	3.76***	3.0	3.44*	1.8	2.00	4.5	0.52	1.5
Obs.	471			318	466		317	
# of countries	81			81	81		81	
R-squared	0.65			0.69				
Country FE	No			No				
Year FE	No			No				
#of instru-ments					29		22	

introduced a new law in 2007 requiring private oil companies to re-negotiate their production and sharing contracts with the government. Companies that choose not to comply face the following threat as stated by President Rafael Correa: "With this new law, petroleum companies that do not abide by the policies of the state will have their fields nationalized and they will leave the country" (*Expropriation News*, July 30, 2010).

Another example is Venezuela, where relatively recent nationalizations of foreign owned assets moved the country to one of the highest rankings by expropriation risk. Hugo Chavez ordered an abrupt nationalization of the cement producer, Cemex, on August 19, 2008. All rice processing and packaging plants were nationalized in an announcement made on February 28, 2009. US energy exploration firm, Helmerich and Payne, had its Venezuela assets nationalized on June 24, 2010. In addition, two glass manufacturing plants in Venezuela were nationalized on October 25, 2010 (US Department of State, online data). These examples, combined with the information revealed by filtering the available panel data through the empirical models compared in this chapter, provide a relatively sharp evidential base that matches a nearly obvious intuition: If a country's institutional quality cannot credibly deliver a high probability of avoiding expropriation, then other institutional differences have little chance to compensate and attract new foreign investors.

References

Adam A, Filippaios F (2007) Foreign direct investment and civil liberties: a new perspective. Eur J Polit Econ 23(4):1038–1052

Addison T, Heshmati A (2003) The new global determinants of FDI flows to developing countries: the importance of ICT and democratization. WIDER discussion paper, no. 45

Ali FA, Fiess N, MacDonald R (2010) Do institutions matter for foreign direct investment? Open Econ Rev 21(2):201–219

Arellano M, Bond S (1991) Some tests of specification for panel data: Monte Carlo evidence and an application to employment equations. Rev Econ Stud 58(2):277–297

Asiedu E (2002) On the determinants of foreign direct investment to developing countries: Is Africa different? World Dev 30(1):107–119

Asiedu E (2006) Foreign direct investment in Africa: the role of natural resources, market size, government policy, institutions and political instability. World Econ 29(1):63–77

Asiedu E, Lien D (2011) Democracy, foreign direct investment and natural resources. J Int Econ 84(1):99–111

Asiedu E, Jin Y, Nandwa B (2009) Does foreign aid mitigate the adverse effect of expropriation risk on foreign direct investment? J Int Econ 78(2):268–275

Barro RJ, Lee JW (1993) International comparisons of educational attainment. J Monet Econ 32(3):363–394

Bénassy-Quéré A, Coupet M, Mayer T (2007) Institutional determinants of foreign direct investment. World Econ 30(5):764–782

Biswas R (2002) Determinants of foreign direct investment. Rev Dev Econ 6(3):492–504

Blundell R, Bond S (1998) Initial conditions and moment restrictions in dynamic panel data models. J Econ 87(1):115–143

Burbidge JB, Magee L, Robb AL (1988) Alternative transformations to handle extreme values of the dependent variable. J Am Stat Assoc 83(401):123–127

Busse M (2004) Transnational corporations and repression of political rights and civil liberties: an empirical analysis. Kyklos 57(1):45–65

Busse M, Hefeker C (2004) Political risk, institutions and foreign direct investment. Eur J Polit Econ 23(1):397–415

Chakrabarti A (2001) The determinants of foreign direct investments: sensitivity analyses of cross-country regressions. Kyklos 54(1):89–114

Daude C, Stein E (2007) The quality of institutions and foreign direct investment. Econ Polit 19(3):317–344

Dutta N, Roy S (2011) Foreign direct investment, financial development and political risks. J Dev Areas 303–327

Edwards S (1992) Capital flows, foreign direct investment, and debt-equity swaps in developing countries. National Bureau of Economic Research, working paper, no. 3497

Egger P, Winner H (2005) Evidence on corruption as an incentive for foreign direct investment. Eur J Polit Econ 21(4):932–952

Feierabend IK, Feierabend RL (1966) Aggressive behaviors within polities, 1948–1962: a cross-national study. J Conflict Resolut 10(3):249–271

Findlay R (1978) Relative backwardness, direct foreign investment, and the transfer of technology: a simple dynamic model. Q J Econ 92(1):1–16

Gastanaga VM, Nugent JB, Pashamova B (1998) Host country reforms and FDI inflows: how much difference do they make? World Dev 26(7):1299–1314

Globerman S, Shapiro D (2002) Global foreign direct investment flows: the role of governance infrastructure. World Dev 30(11):1899–1919

Habib M, Zurawicki L (2002) Corruption and foreign direct investment. J Int Bus Stud 33(2):291–307

Hajzler C (2012) Expropriation of foreign direct investments: sectoral patterns from 1993 to 2006. Rev World Econ 148(1):119–149

Harms P, Ursprung HW (2002) Do civil and political repression really boost foreign direct investments? Econ Inq 40(4):651–663

Jensen NM (2003) Democratic governance and multinational corporations: political regimes and inflows of foreign direct investment. Int Org 57(03):587–616

Kinoshita Y, Campos NF (2003) Why does FDI go where it goes? New evidence from the transition economies. William Davidson Institute, working paper, no. 573

Kobrin SJ (1984) Expropriation as an attempt to control foreign firms in LDCs: trends from 1960 to 1979. Int Stud Q 28(3):329–348

Kolstad I, Tøndel L (2002) Social development and foreign direct investments in developing countries. Chr. Michelsen Institute, working paper, no. 11

Li Q (2009) Democracy, autocracy, and expropriation of foreign direct investment. Comp Polit Stud 42(8):1098–1127

Li Q, Resnick A (2003) Reversal of fortunes: democratic institutions and foreign direct investment inflows to developing countries. Int Org 57(1):175–211

Mathur A, Singh K (2013) Foreign direct investment, corruption and democracy. Appl Econ 45(8):991–1002

Mauro P (1995) Corruption and growth. Q J Econ 110(3):681–712

Méon PG, Sekkat K (2004) Does the quality of institutions limit the MENA's integration in the world economy? World Econ 27(9):1475–1498

MIGA (2011) Political risk and developing countries. Multilateral Investment Agency, World Bank Group, Washington, DC

Naudé WA, Krugell WF (2007) Investigating geography and institutions as determinants of foreign direct investment in Africa using panel data. Appl Econ 39(10):1223–1233

Noorbakhsh F, Paloni A, Youssef A (2001) Human capital and FDI inflows to developing countries: new empirical evidence. World Dev 29(9):1593–1610

Oil firms face Ecuador asset grab (30 July 2010). Expropriation news. Retrieved from http://expropriationnews.com/2010/07/30/oil-firms-face-ecuador-asset-grab/

Oneal JR (1994) The affinity of foreign investors for authoritarian regimes. Polit Res Q 47(3):565–588

Resnick AL (2001) Investors, turbulence, and transition: democratic transition and foreign direct investment in nineteen developing countries. Int Interact 27(4):381–398

Root FR, Ahmed AA (1979) Empirical determinants of manufacturing direct foreign investment in developing countries. Econ Dev Cult Change 27(4):751–767

Schneider F, Frey BS (1985) Economic and political determinants of foreign direct investment. World Dev 13(2):161–175

Stroebel J, Van Benthem A (2013) Resource extraction contracts under threat of expropriation: theory and evidence. Rev Econ Stat 95(5):1622–1639

Wei SJ (2000) How taxing is corruption on international investors? Rev Econ Stat 82(1):1–11

Wheeler D, Mody A (1992) International investment location decisions: the case of US firms. J Int Econ 33(1):57–76

Yang B (2007) Autocracy, democracy, and FDI inflows to the developing countries. Int Econ J 21(3):419–439

Chapter 7
The Future of the Lucas Paradox

7.1 Introduction

This chapter highlights some of the developments in geopolitics, forecasts made about future capital flows by academics and makes prediction about the direction of future global capital flows based on these highlights and on the basis of the findings of empirical chapters of this book as well that would help us understanding about the future of the Lucas Paradox, uphill flows of capital.

7.2 Predictions About Capital Flows, Geopolitics and Possible Impacts

Bank of England makes a projection, based on Haldane's (2010) simulation, about the G20 countries' capital flows and external balance sheets over the next 40 years. The key results in the report suggest that the overall size of external balance relative to GDP across the entire G20 would increase a ratio of around 1.3–2.2. Interestingly, more than 40% of all external assets will be held by the BRICs (Brazil, Russia, India, China) by 2050, which is up from the current 10%, the report predicts. Global current account imbalances (the sum of deficits and surpluses) would rise from around 4% of world GDP to around 8% at their peak.

Capital flows to developing countries took a sharp reversal since 2015 and net capital outflows of developing countries exceeded $600 billion, which is more than a quarter of total inflows to developing countries received over the six years from 2008–2014 (Stiglitz and Rashid 2016). The large amount of capital outflows from developing counties will have substantial negative impacts on the growth and development of developing countries. Developing countries might consider to increase interest rate to attract more capital inflows; however, increase in interest rate might be counterproductive as the increase in interest rate is more likely to hurt the growth of developing economies. Increase in interest rate also adversely affect big businesses

M. Akhtaruzzaman, *International Capital Flows and the Lucas Paradox*,
https://doi.org/10.1007/978-981-13-9069-2_7

in developing countries as large capital outflows affect the equity prices negatively. Higher interest rate could cause in loss in equity prices and increase in the costs of borrowing that are likely to adversely affect the growth in developing countries.

Monetary policy in advanced economies and particularly in the US could affect the capital flows to the emerging market economies (EMEs). As the interest rate gaps between US and emerging markets are narrowing, the capital flows from the US to the EMEs will be lowering. The Fed has made its eighth raise in interest rate since 2015 and is targeted to raise the interest rate to 2–2.25% (Effective Federal Funds Rate: Federal Reserve). The Fed also predicted to raise the rate in 2019 and to reach federal funds rate to about 3.4% by 2020. Recent upward trend in the interest rate in developed countries as such in the US could reduce the downstream flows of capital from developed to developing countries. A co-movement is observed between EMEs local currency yields and Federal Funds rate. Clark et al. (2016) found that the decline in net capital flows to EMEs is due to fall in commodity prices and decline in EMEs growth. Commodity prices and domestic investment in commodity co-move and high commodity prices make commodity sector more attractive and more capital inflows.

China–US trade war and the recent changes in the US policies are more likely to affect the global capital flows. The China–US trade war has already changed Chinese FDI into the US and, by the first half of 2018, Chinese FDI into the US is down by 90% totalling to only $1.8 billion, the lowest amount of the last seven years (Putz et al., n.d.). If this trend continues, the volume of total uphill capital flows (i.e., the Lucas Paradox) will substantially be reduced unless there is a change in ongoing tension between China and the US. The US introduced new tariffs and imposed on her major trading partners such as China, Mexico, Canada and the EU. The changes in goods trade due to the new tariffs are likely to affect capital trade adversely. Capital flows would then be reduced not only from developing countries to developed countries but also between the developed countries.

If other developed countries embrace similar protectionist policies and the changes are likely to happen in those countries where far right political forces are rising (e.g., centre-right in Sweden, conservative and populists in Norway). The tie between those developed countries could further be tightened and more capital will flow between them. As a result, the world might observe lower level of capital flows from developed to developing countries and more capital flows between developed countries.

A potential scenario of protectionist policies of the US could eventually isolate the world's largest economy from rest of the world. And, if other developed countries (e.g., Germany, Canada, UK) or the developing countries (e.g., China, India, Brazil) do not follow the suit of the US, a new global financial order might emerge leaving the US aside. Another likely scenario is that more capital will flow from China or similar developing countries to developed countries excluding the US. There is another possibility of stronger tie between China and neighbouring countries or the like-minded countries that could further strengthen China's leading position in global trade of goods and capital.

The findings of empirical chapters of this book suggest that better institutional quality is an important determinant but not as strong determinant as capital account openness policies are in determining capital flows, in particular for downhill capital flows. Relative importance of expropriation risk compared to other political risks (measured by institutional quality) would determine which particular location is more attractive to foreign investors. And, the geopolitical tension in the recent past could further magnify the risk of expropriation and thus could change the direction and volume of global capital flows.

7.3 Conclusion

The future of capital flows would largely depend on the development of geopolitics, future polarization of economic superpowers, and changes in macroeconomic policies in both developed and developing countries. In addition to the current clusters of countries like BRICs, G7 we might see more homogenous group of economic and political power clusters and future capital flows will follow the lead of those clusters. It could be challenging for developing countries to attract more capital inflows as they were able to attract in the past if they can't improve further institutional environment and maintain stable economic policies including financial development and capital account openness. Capital account openness played an important role in the historical flows and would play a similar effective role in future capital flows. The capital flows could further be strengthened between the developed countries, as discussed in this chapter. The multilateral bodies, WTO, WB, IMF are also important in determining future capital flows around the world. The terms and conditions stick to these organizations might change and might also shape the future capital flows.

References

Clark J, Converse N, Coulibaly B, Kamin S (18 Oct 2016) Emerging market capital flows and U.S. Monetary Policy. Board of Governors of the Federal Reserve System. Retrieved from https://www.federalreserve.gov/econresdata/notes/ifdp-notes/2016/emerging-market-capital-flows-and-us-monetary-policy-20161018.html

Effective Federal Funds Rate (2019) Federal reserve. Retrieved from: https://fred.stlouisfed.org/series/FEDFUNDS

Haldane AG (2010) Global imbalances in retrospect and prospect. In: Speech in November

Putz A, Mirhaydari A, Clark K (n.d.) How Trump's trade war with china will affect U.S. investment markets. Seattle Business. Retrieved from https://www.seattlebusinessmag.com/finance/how-trumps-trade-war-china-will-affect-us-investment-markets

Stiglitz JE, Rashid H (16 Feb 2016). How can developing countries stop their capital draining away? World Economic Forum. Retrieved from https://www.weforum.org/agenda/2016/02/how-can-developing-countries-stop-their-capital-draining-away

Chapter 8
Conclusion

This book empirically investigates the determinants of international capital flows and searches for a solution to the Lucas paradox. It considers the claims in the existing literature that specific factors (e.g., institutional quality or capital account openness) explains why capital does not flow from rich to poor countries, replicating several closely related empirical studies using updated data. The finding suggests that explanations for the Lucas paradox in existing studies are not robust to alternative model specifications and econometric approaches.

Various empirical exercises are conducted to find a solution to the Lucas paradox. Revised estimates of the marginal product of capital (MPK) are examined in order to understand the pattern of international capital flows. Using a bivariate scatter plot analysis, it is found that the revisions of MPK estimates are not sufficient to predict the pattern of international capital flows. Specifically, if these revised estimates are used, capital tends to flow to relatively low-return countries, which does not solve the Lucas paradox and rather runs opposite to the prediction of standard theory.

Cross-sectional and panel data regression analysis are conducted to explore alternative empirical specifications for modelling international capital flows. These analyses lead to the conclusion that, if more appropriately specified empirical models are used, the Lucas paradox still persists. In other words, the initial level of economic development is still positively correlated with international flows. Differences in institutional quality between rich and poor countries are a significant determinant of international capital flows; however, controlling for differences in institutional quality does not alone explain the Lucas paradox. More specifically, in cross-section analysis, a country's level of economic development is a significant determinant of capital inflows even if a country's institutional quality is controlled for. The same conclusion is reached using a dataset covering the most recent decade of international capital flow data.

The institutional quality does not solve the Lucas paradox even if we control for country-specific characteristics and examine time-series variation in the data. More specifically, in panel data analysis, a country's policies relating to capital account convertibility have relatively robust effects on international capital inflows compared to a country's institutional qualities, such as property rights or contract

M. Akhtaruzzaman, *International Capital Flows and the Lucas Paradox*,
https://doi.org/10.1007/978-981-13-9069-2_8

enforcements. However, accounting for differences in policies on capital account restriction or institutional quality does not fully capture the effect of differences in economic development. Further to the independent effect of the determinants of capital flows, interaction effects (i.e., multiplicative terms between two determinants) are considered to check if a solution to the Lucas paradox is found. In contrast to the claims in the existing literature, none of the interaction effects provides a complete explanation for why not much capital flows to poor countries. The Lucas paradox therefore remains unresolved in panel data analysis as well.

The regression-based analysis goes deeper and attempts to find a solution of the Lucas paradox by examining differences between rich and poor countries in their levels of capital stock per worker and in productivity. The results suggest even when accounting for productivity differences between rich and poor countries in addition to the differences in institutional quality and capital account restrictions, capital does not flow to poor countries. The Lucas paradox extends beyond country productivity differences and capital flows to countries that are already relatively capital abundant.

Therefore, initial level of economic development (i.e., initial GDP per capita) of a country is found to be the main driving force and a robust determinant of capital inflows. There is evidence that capital market imperfections or institutional frictions or a measure of fundamentals (e.g., stock of human capital) or other potential factors (e.g., financial development, trade openness) or a combination of any two factors are statistically significant determinants of capital inflows, depending on the empirical model specifications and estimation approaches. However, none of these determinants, either individually or jointly, can fully capture the effects of economic development. In other words, the Lucas paradox stands, as yet, unresolved.

The last empirical chapter of this book examines the relative importance of specific aspects of institutional quality (e.g., expropriation risk, corruption, lack of democracy etc.) and maps perceived effects of each type of political risk for capital flows to developing countries. Expropriation risk is found to have the largest effect in explaining the lack of FDI flows to developing countries. When the perceived risks of expropriation (i.e., the probability of losing 100 percent of invested capital) are large, a developing country has little chance of attracting new foreign investors. More specifically, a one-standard-deviation deterioration in expropriation risk measures is associated with an expected loss of 64 percent of FDI flows to developing countries.

This book strives for a solution to the Lucas paradox examining empirically various potential explanations of the Lucas paradox in the context of neoclassical model. Given the persistence of the Lucas paradox in the empirical exercise of this book, a potentially fruitful line of inquiry may be to look beyond the standard neoclassical framework. Considering such perspectives may potentially account for why capital still flows to capital abundant high income countries. Capital flow data in the future might also be influenced significantly by the recent developments in geopolitics that is highlighted briefly in Chap. 7.

New growth theory aspects (e.g., spillover effects, economies of scale effects) might suggest a possible solution to the Lucas paradox. A large volume of capital flows between similar developed countries and FDI-type investments seem to be horizontal suggesting that FDI primarily serves the foreign host country instead of exporting (Markusen and Venables 1998). In the spirit of new trade theory, FDI-firms can internalize economies of scale (Krugman 1979). This suggests that FDI-type investments involve large fixed costs/sunk costs (factories, intellectual property protection, government approval) and it is natural for a producer to gain from market concentration by spreading out the costs over a larger production base.

From this point of view, economies of scale might suggest a direction for future research and a potential solution to the Lucas paradox. GDP was considered independently to capture the market size effect; however, there must be a high correlation between GDP and GDP per capita. It is also difficult to identify separate effects of GDP and population from GDP per capita suggesting that identifying the importance of economies of scale is difficult at aggregate country level data and examining the decisions of foreign investors at firm-level data is a promising avenue for future research.

References

Krugman PR (1979) Increasing returns, monopolistic competition, and international trade. J Int Econ 9(4):469–479

Markusen JR, Venables AJ (1998) Multinational firms and the new trade theory. J Int Econ 46(2):183–203

Appendix A
Further Explanation to the Footnotes

Inverse Hyperbolic Sine (IHS) Transformation

We follow a log-transformation method used by Burbidge et al.'s (1988) and Busse and Hefeker (2007): y $= \log^*\left(x + \sqrt{x^2+1}\right)$ The first derivative of the term inside the bracket is $\left(1 + \frac{x}{\sqrt{x^2+1)}}\right)$ where the term $\left(\frac{x}{\sqrt{x^2+1)}}\right)$ should be less than 1 in absolute value for all x but nevertheless strictly increasing for all x. This monotonic function deals with zero and negative values of capital inflows transforming them into positive values, which is similar to the problem of zero-valued trade flows in Gravity models (e.g., Linders and de Groot 2014; Helpman et al. 2008). BH argue that this transformation maintains the sign of the variable of interest, does not reduce the number of observations, and the values of the variable pass from a linear scale at small absolute values to a logarithmic scale at large values. However, adding a small positive number is arbitrary and different positive numbers can give different values of the log-transformed variable. However, this problem is not unique to this transformation and instead plagues all log models. In other words, no transformation is neutral.

Flowerdew and Aitkin (1982) showed that small differences in the selected constant can distort the result seriously. Moreover, the log-model generates estimates of the log of capital inflows not of capital inflows and the antilogarithms of these estimates tend to be biased (Haworth and Vincent 1979). The concavity of the log function should create a downward bias when using OLS and Jensen's inequality implies that E (ln(y)) $\neq$ lnE(y).

There are other potential transformations, such as Box–Cox (1964) transformation $(\frac{x^\lambda - 1}{\lambda})$. Box–Cox transformation works with negative values if $\lambda < 0$; however transformation is then non-monotonic. Out of total 2744 (98×28) observations in the sample we are investigating, we have 477 (17.38% of total) observations of per capita inflows, the dependent variable, with zero (333) and

M. Akhtaruzzaman, *International Capital Flows and the Lucas Paradox*,
https://doi.org/10.1007/978-981-13-9069-2

negative (144) values. The IHS-transformation maps zero and negative values into positive values that are then log-transformed.

The IHS-transformation or Busse and Hefeker's log transformation:

$$log^*(\varphi(x)) = log^*\left(x + \sqrt{x^2+1}\right)$$

For simplicity, assume$y = \log(u)$. By the chain rule,

$$\frac{dy}{du} = \frac{1}{u}\frac{du}{dx} = \frac{u'}{u} = \frac{1+\frac{x}{\sqrt{x^2+1}}}{\left(x+\sqrt{x^2+1}\right)} = \frac{1}{\sqrt{x^2+1}}$$

Therefore (the notations are defined in Section 6.3.1),

$$x_{it}^{net} = x_{it} - o_{it} = \gamma\rho_{it}e^{\beta_1+\beta_2 s_{it}}K_{it}^f - \gamma(\rho_{it})^{-1}e^{\beta_3-\beta_4 s_{it}}K_{it}^d$$

$$\frac{\partial(x_{it}^{net})}{\partial s_{it}} = \beta_2 x_{it} + \beta_4 o_{it}$$

$$\frac{\partial \ln(\varphi(x_{it}^{net}))}{\partial s_{it}} = \frac{\varphi'(x_{it}^{net})}{\varphi(x_{it}^{net})}(\beta_2 x_{it} + \beta_4 o_{it}) = \frac{\beta_2 x_{it} + \beta_4 o_{it}}{\sqrt{(x_{it}^{net})^2+1}}$$

Diagnostic tests for cross-section models

Normality: The Stata routine *omninorm* is used for testing residual normality, which performs an omnibus test (to test whether the explained variance is significantly greater than the unexplained variance), proposed by Doornik and Hansen (2008). The test statistics is based on the skewness and kurtosis of the OLS residuals and is asymptotically distributed as chi-square (2) under the null of normality. Based on simulation results, Doornik and Hansen suggest this test has better size and power than other test of normality such as multivariate Shapiro-Wilk test by Royston (1983). We also use the Shapiro-Wilk W test where the p-value is based on the assumption that the distribution is normal.

Homoscedasticity: Homoscedasticity describes a situation in which the variance of errors is the same for all values of the independent variables. In the absence of homoscedasticity, it is difficult to gauge the true standard deviation of the forecast errors. In particular, if the variance of the errors is increasing over time, then confidence intervals for out-of-sample predictions will tend to be unrealistically narrow. We employ two tests for homoscedasticity: the Breusch–Pagan (1980) test and White's (1980) test (a special case of the Breusch–Pagan test). The p-value of the null hypothesis is based on the assumption that the variance of the errors is constant.

Functional form: A model specification error can occur when one or more relevant variables are omitted or one or more irrelevant variables are included in the model. We use Ramsey's RESET (1969) test (Stata's *ovtest*) that creates two new variables: the squared and cubed predicted values of the dependent variable.

For example, a regression model is:

$$y = \beta_0 + \beta_1 x + \cdots + \beta_3 x_k + u$$

In regards to the specific example we are investigating, y is capital inflows per capita and the x's are the explanatory variables. The RESET test examines whether non-linear functions of the independent variables are significant. First, estimate the original regression model and then augment the model with fitted values (usually, squares and cubes are added) as follows:

$$y = \beta_0 + \beta_1 x + \cdots + \beta_3 x_k + \delta_1 \hat{y}^2 + \delta_2 \hat{y}^3 + e$$

where $\hat{y}^2$ and $\hat{y}^3$ are nonlinear functions of the x's. RESET is testing a null: $H_0 = \delta_1 = \delta_2 = 0$. A significant F (i.e. a rejection of the null) suggests that there is some evidence of omitted non-linearity.

RMSE (root mean square error): RMSE is frequently used as a measure of the difference between values predicted by a model or an estimator and the values actually observed. In other words, it is the standard deviation of the errors and measures the spread of the data around the regression line. The smaller the value of RMSE, the better the fitted line in terms of prediction.

Diagnostic tests for Panel models

Normality: The Stata routine *omninorm* test is a chi-squared test for normality is based on skewness and kurtosis, combining two tests into one overall test statistic. See the details of Normality test in the discussion of diagnostic tests for the cross-sectional models.

Heteroscedasticity: Stata's *xttest3* calculates a modified Wald statistic for group-wise hetersoscedasticity in the residuals of a FE regression model. It is likely that the variances across the cross-sectional units are not homosckedastic. The Modified Wald test for group-wise heteroscedasticity assumes a null of constant variances. The modified Wald test is valid even if the assumption of normality is violated.

Serial correlation: Stata's *xtserial*, developed by Drukker (2003), is based on Wooldridge's (2002) test for serial correlation and is applied to the idiosyncratic errors. In a panel model, FE and RE both assume that the errors are serially uncorrelated and in the presence of serial correlation the standard errors of the coefficients are smaller than they actually are and the estimates are then less efficient. If the errors are not serially correlated, then the correlation coefficient of the lagged residuals on current residuals from a regression in first-differences should be −0.5. Under the null hypothesis, *xtserial* tests no first order autocorrelation [i.e., no AR (1)].

References

Box GE, Cox DR (1964) An analysis of transformations. J R Stat Soc Ser B (Methodological) 26 (2):211–252

Breusch T, Pagan AR (1979) A simple test for heteroscedasticity and random coefficient variation. Econometrica 47(5):1287–1294

Busse M, Hefeker C (2007) Political risk, institutions and foreign direct investment. Eur J Political Econ 23(2):397–415

Doornik JA, Hansen H (2008) An omnibus test for univariate and multivariate normality. Oxford Bull Econ Stat 70(s1):927–939

Drukker DM (2003) Testing for serial correlation in linear panel-data models. Stata J 3(2):168–177

Flowerdew R, Aitkin M (1982) A method of fitting the gravity model based on the poisson distribution. J Reg Sci 22(2):191–202

Haworth JM, Vincent PJ (1979) The stochastic disturbance specification and its implications for log-linear regression. Environ Plan A 11(7):781–790

Helpman E, Melitz M, Rubinstein Y (2008) Estimating trade flows: trading partners and trading volumes. Q J Econ 123(2):441–487

Linders GJM, de Groot HL (2014) Estimation of the gravity equation in the presence of zero flows. Econometrica 82(2):705–730.

Ramsey JB (1969) Tests for specification errors in classical linear least-squares regression analysis. J R Stat Soc Ser B (Methodological) 31(2):350–371

Royston JP (1983) Some techniques for assessing multivarate normality based on the Shapiro-Wilk W. Appl Stat 32(2):121–133

Wooldridge JM (2002) Econometric analysis of cross section and panel data. MIT Press, Cambridge, Massachusetts

Appendix B
Data Descriptions, Constructions, and Sources (Sample Period is from 1984–2015, if not Mentioned Otherwise) and Summary Statistics of Main Variables of Interest

Capital inflows per Capita	Sum of FDI (IFS line: BFDIA) and portfolio (IFS line: BFPLE) inflows (2017). The data are in current US dollars, deflated by US CPI with base year 2005 = 1 and divided by population.
Stocks of Foreign Capital (LM)	Foreign claims on domestic capital, from Lane and Milesi-Ferretti (2007, updated 2012). Capital inflows are obtained by first differencing the stock data of LM.
Debt capital (Private and Public)	Private nonguaranteed external debt is an external obligation of a private debtor that is not guaranteed for repayment by a public entity. Public and publicly guaranteed long-term debts are external obligations of a public debtor, including the national government, political subdivision, and autonomous public bodies. Net flows received by the borrower during the year are disbursements minus principal repayments. Long-term external debt is defined as debt has an original or extended maturity of more than one year. Data are taken from WDI, World Bank (2017) and in current U.S. dollars are deflated by US CPI with base year 2005 = 1 and divided by population.
Portfolio Equity	Portfolio equity includes net inflows from equity securities other than those recorded as direct investment and including shares, stocks, depository receipts (American or global), and direct purchases of shares in local stock markets by foreign investors. Data are in current U.S. dollars. Data taken from World Bank.
Private Debt	Net flows on external debt, private nonguaranteed (PNG) (NFL, current US$). Data taken from World Bank.
Current Account Balance to GDP	The current account is based on IFS data from the World Economic Outlook (WEO).

M. Akhtaruzzaman, *International Capital Flows and the Lucas Paradox*,
https://doi.org/10.1007/978-981-13-9069-2

GDP per Capita in 1984 in PPP GDP at PPP from Penn World Tables, Ver. 7.1, Heston et al. (2013), divided by population.

GDP per Capita in Constant GDP from WDI, World Bank (2017), divided by population. Constant dollars (2005).

GDP per Capita Rel. to US Relative income per capital is PPP income per capita relative to the U.S., both in constant 2005 international Dollars. The index has a value of 100 for the U.S. The data are from PWT 8.

Real GDP Gross domestic product represents the sum of value added by all its producers. Local currency series are converted to constant U.S. dollars using an exchange rate in reference year 2005. Data are taken from WDI, World Bank (2017).

GDP per Capita Growth Annual percentage growth rate of GDP per capita based on constant local currency from WDI, World Bank (2017).

Percent Work.-Age Population (WP) is the ratio of dependents—people of ages younger than 15 or older than 65—to the working-age population.

Institutional Quality, ICRG This is a composite index, which is the sum of the yearly rating of the 12 components from International Country Risk Guide, the PRS Group (2016). To ensure consistency of interpretation, each component of the index is rescaled to range from 0 to 10. Thus, the theoretical range of this index is 0 to 120, where a higher score means institutional qualities are better and lower risks. Sub-indexes of ICRG's institutions index are:

Government stability: The government's ability to carry out its declared programs. Average annual rating ranges from 0 to 12 and is converted to 0 to 10 (multiplying by 5/6).

Socio economic condition: Assesses the socioeconomic pressures at work in society that could constrain government action or fuel social dissatisfaction. This risk rating is the sum of three subcomponents: unemployment, consumer confidence, and poverty. It ranges from 0 (very high risk) to 12 (very low risk) and is rescaled from 0 to 10 (multiplying by 5/6).

Investment profile: This is an assessment of factors affecting the risks of investment that are not covered by other political, economic and financial risk components. It is the sum of three subcomponents (contract viability/expropriation risk, payment delays and profit repatriation) each of them scores a maximum of 4 points to a minimum of 0 points. It ranges from a maximum of 12 points to a minimum of 0 points, and rescaled to 0 to 10 (multiplying by 5/6).

Internal conflict: Political violence in the country and its actual or potential impact on governance. Higher score means lower conflict. Average yearly rating from 0 to 12 and converted to 0 to 10 (multiplying by 5/6).

External conflict: Assessment both of the risk of the incumbent government from foreign action, ranging from non-violent external pressure (diplomatic pressures, with-holding of aid, trade restrictions, territorial disputes, sanctions, etc) to violent external pressure (cross-border conflicts to all-out war). The subcomponents are war, cross-border conflict, foreign pressure, each with a maximum score of 4 and a minimum score of 0. Average yearly rating from a minimum of 0 points to a maximum of 12 points is converted to 0 to 10 (multiplying by 5/6).

Corruption: Assesses the corruption within the political system. Such corruption is a big threat to foreign investment and a common form of corruption met by business in the form of demands for special payments, bribes etc. Average yearly rating from 0 to 6 is converted to 0 to 10 (multiplying by 5/3).

Military in politics: Military becomes involved in government and sometimes military force elected government to change policy and cause its replacement by other government more amenable to the military's wishes. Average yearly rating ranges from 0 to 6 and converted to 0 to 10 (multiplying by 5/3).

Religious tensions: Religious tension may stem from the domination of society and government by a single religious group that seeks to replace civil law by religious law and suppress religious freedom. Average yearly rating from 0 to 6 is converted to 0 to 10 (multiplying by 5/3).

Law and order: The law sub-component is an assessment of the strength and impartiality of the legal system; the order sub-component is an assessment of popular observance of the law. Average yearly rating from 0 to 6 is converted to 0 to 10 (multiplying by 5/3).

Ethnic tensions: Assessment of the degree of ethnic tensions within a country attributable to racial, nationality, or language divisions. Average yearly rating from 0 to 6 is converted to 0 to 10 (multiplying by 5/3).

Democratic accountability: Assesses how responsive government is to its people. Average yearly rating from 0 (authoritarian regimes) to 6 (alternating democracies) is converted to 0 to 10 (multiplying by 5/3).

Bureaucratic quality: Institutional strength and quality of the bureaucracy is another shock absorber that tends to minimize revisions of policy when government changes. Average yearly rating from 0 to 4 is converted to 0 to 10 (multiplying by 5/2).

Governance Index, WGI

Governance index is the sum of all yearly rating indicators. The WGI provides consistent ranges of values for each of the six sub-indexes, ranging from −2.5 (worst) to +2.5 (best). The six sub-indexes of WGI are defined as follows: Data period: 1996–2015.

Political stability and absence of violence: measures the perceptions of the likelihood that the government will be destabilized or overthrown by unconstitutional or violent means.

Government effectiveness: measures the perceptions of the quality of public services, the quality of the civil service and the degree of its independence from political pressures, the quality of policy formulation, implementation and the credibility of the government to such policies.

Regulatory quality: captures perceptions of the ability of the government to formulate and implement sound policies and regulations that permit and promote private sector development.

Control of corruption: captures the perceptions of the extent to which public power is exercised for private gain, including both petty and grand forms of corruption, as well the ability of elites and private interests to manipulate policy and laws.

Rule of law: captures the perceptions of the extent to which agents have confidence in and abide by the rules of society, and in particular the quality of contract enforcement, property rights, the police and the courts, as well as the likelihood of crime and violence.

Voice and accountability: captures perceptions of the extent to which a country's citizens are able to participate in selecting their government and freedom of expression, freedom of association, and a free media.

Capital Account Openness

Measures a country's degree of capital account openness based on the IMF's Annual Report on Exchange Arrangements and Exchange Restrictions developed by Chinn and Ito (2008, 2016), where a higher index value indicates greater capital account openness. Values range from 2.6 (most financially open) to −2.6 (least financially open). For restrictions on capital mobility Alfaro et al. (2008) use the mean value of four dummy variables from IMF's Annual Report on Exchange Arrangements and Exchange Restrictions: exchange arrangements; payments restrictions for capital transactions, payments restrictions on payment for capital transactions; and surrender or repatriation requirements for export proceeds.

Schooling Years of schooling of persons of age 25 or above is a measure of stock of human capital (h) at five-year intervals. Linear interpolation is used to fill in the missing date between the 5-yearly observations. Source: Barro and Lee (1996, updated 2010). Data period: 1985–2010.

Financial Development Private credit by deposit money banks and other financial institutions. Domestic credit to the private sector (% of GDP), data are taken from Beck et al. (2000, updated 2013). Beck et al. use raw data from the electronic version of the IMF's IFS.

Trade Sum of exports and imports (% of GDP), data are taken from WDI, World Bank (2017).

Distantness Population weighted distance from the capital city of a country to capital cities of other countries, data are taken from CEPII (2013).

Inflation Inflation as measured by the consumer price index reflects the annual percentage change in the cost to the average consumers of acquiring a basket of goods and services that may be fixed or changed yearly. The Laspeyres formula is generally used. Consumer prices (annual %), data are taken from WDI, World Bank (2017).

Physical Capital Stocks Constructed based on perpetual inventory method (PIM) as in Hall and Jones (1999): $K_t = (1-\delta)K_{t-1} + I_t$, where a depreciation rate (δ) of 6% is assumed. Investments data series are taken from WDI (2013). We calculate initial capital stocks as: $K_0 = \left(\frac{I}{g+\delta}\right)$ where g is predicted growth in investment based on the forward 10 year average and I is also based on 10 year forward trend of the observed investment values. Averages are used to minimize any short-run cyclical factors. For a relatively balanced capital stock dataset, if we find capital stocks data are missing in any country's initial year (1984) or initial year of four-year window, we fill-in these missing years by the available following year's data.

Total Factor Productivity Total factor productivity is constructed following Hall and Jones (1999): $A = \frac{Y}{L}\left(\frac{K}{Y}\right)^{-\frac{\alpha}{1-\alpha}}\frac{1}{h}$ where, A is a labour augmenting measure of productivity and assumes that labour is homogenous within a country and each unit of labour has been trained with s years of schooling (education) in the population over 25 years old and forms human capital, $h = e^{\Phi(S)}$ and s is average years of schooling for the population aged 25 and over, which is observed in the data every five years (source: Barro and Lee 2010) and the function $\Phi(s)$ is piecewise linear with slope 0.13 for the first four years of education, 0.10 for $4 < s \leq 8$, and 0.068 for $8 < s$. The rationale for this functional form is that under perfectly competitive good and factor markets the wage (returns) of a labour with s years of education is proportional to his/her human capital. Since the returns-schooling relationship is thought as linear, so there is a log-linear relationship between h and s. *Y* is output (data are taken from PWT7.1) and *K* is physical capital stocks (as constructed above). Capital share (α) = 1/3.

Logistic Performance Index Logistic performance index is measure based on quality of trade and transport-related infrastructure (e.g., ports, railroads, information technology) and the rating is ranging from 1 (very low) to 5 (very high); however, these data are available only for a maximum of two time points (2007 and 2010). Data are taken form WDI, World Bank (2017).

Stock Market Value Value of listed shares to GDP from Beck et al. (2000, updated 2013) uses Standard and Poor's Emerging Market Database. Data on GDP in US dollars are from the electronic version of the WDI. Data period: 1989–2017.

Paved Roads Paved roads are those surfaced with crushed (macadam) and hydrocarbon binder or bituminized agents, with concrete or with cobblestones, as a percentage of all the country's roads, measured in length. Data are taken from WDI, World Bank (2013a, b). Data period: 1990–2010.

Taxes on Profit Taxes on income, profits and capital gains are levied on the actual or presumptive net income of individuals, on the profits of corporations and enterprises, and on capital gains, whether realized or not, on land, securities, and other assets. Data are taken from WDI, World Bank (2017) and WDI uses International Monetary Fund, Government Finance Statistics Yearbook data files as data sources.

English Language Fraction of the population speaking English as a mother tongue, from Hall and Jones (1999).

Oil Dummy A dummy for the major oil-exporting countries (Algeria, Iran, Nigeria, Saudi Arabia, Ecuador, Gabon, and Oman)

Sahara A dummy for sub-Saharan African countries (Angola, Burkina Faso, Cameroon, Congo, Ivory Coast, Ethiopia, Gambia, Ghana, Guinea, Kenya, Madagascar, Mali, Namibia, Nigeria, Niger, Senegal, Sierra-Leone, South Africa, Uganda, Zambia, and Zimbabwe.

Former British Colony A dummy for former colony countries (Australia, Bangladesh, Canada, Egypt, Ghana, Gambia, Guyana, Hong-Kong, India, Jamaica, Kenya, Malaysia, Nigeria, New Zealand, Pakistan, Singapore, Sierra-Leone, Trinidad and Tobago, Uganda, United States of America, and South Africa.

European Settlers Mortality Historical European settlers' mortality rates from Acemoglu et al. (2001), measured in terms of deaths per annum per 1000.

State Antiquity An index for early history (i.e., antiquity) of a country constructed by Bockstette et al. (2002); a higher value of state antiquity suggests a longer history of greater ethnic homogeneity, dense population.

British Legal Origin Origin of formal legal code in the country: English common law represents the British legal origin. Other available legal origins are: French civil law, German civil law, and Scandinavian civil law, from La Porta et al. (1998, 1999).

Latitude Distance from Equator (absolute value of Latitude), from Hall and Jones (1999)

Summary statistics 1: Benchmark sample of 98 countries from 1984–2017 used in Chap. 4

Variable	Obs.	Mean	Std. dev.	Min	Max
Average capital inflow per capita	98	4.097	9.331	0.040	68.927
Log average capita inflows per capita	98	1.291	1.158	0.040	4.926
Log initial (1984) GDP per capita (PPP)	98	8.416	1.188	5.780	10.269
Average index of institutions (ICRG)	98	77.279	15.893	46.128	111.869
Average governance index (WGI)	98	0.289	5.293	−7.858	11.198
Average capital account openness	98	0.359	1.307	−1.586	2.360
Log average years of schooling	89	2.190	0.576	0.094	2.989
Log average trade	97	4.201	0.464	3.079	5.861
Log distantness	98	8.890	0.261	8.592	9.564
Log average financial development	97	3.588	0.836	1.068	5.171
Log average inflation	97	2.271	1.433	−0.495	6.012
Log initial (1984) capital stock per worker	89	8.586	1.703	4.072	12.346
Log initial (1984) TFP	82	8.897	0.801	6.536	10.412

Summary statistics 2: Four-year panel average 1: benchmark sample of 98 countries (1984–2015) used in Chap. 5

Variable	Obs	Mean	Std. dev.	Min	Max
Capital inflow per capita	576	3.367	7.264	−4.212	76.578
Log capita inflows per capita	576	1.097	1.194	−2.145	5.031
Log initial (1984) GDP per capita (PPP)	686	8.571	1.251	5.619	10.851
Index of institutions (ICRG)	650	76.810	18.186	29.948	114.931
Capital account openness	640	0.346	1.588	−1.864	2.439
Log years of schooling	623	2.125	0.628	−0.419	3.026
Log trade	668	4.172	0.530	2.542	6.043
Log financial development	610	3.397	0.998	0.239	5.586
Log inflation	628	3.781	2.090	−16.651	11.207
Log initial (1984) capital stock per worker	620	8.784	1.635	4.013	12.321
Log initial (1984) TFP	574	8.848	0.802	6.431	10.619

Summary statistics 3 for WGI index: Sample of 83 countries from 1996–2015 used in Chaps. 4 and 6

WGI political index	Obs.	Mean	Std. dev.	Min	Max
Rule of law	83	−0.43	0.64	−1.72	1.25
Political stability	83	−0.45	0.77	−2.32	0.96
Corruption absent	83	−0.44	0.56	−1.48	1.43
Voice and accountability	83	−0.33	0.73	−1.71	1.04
Government effectiveness	83	−0.32	0.62	−1.71	1.19

Summary statistics 4: Sample of 83 countries from 1984–2015 used in Chap. 6

Variable	Obs.	Mean	Std. dev.	Min	Max
log of net FDI inflows per capita	81	4.04	1.66	−4.17	6.68
Log of gross FDI inflows per capita	83	4.32	1.40	1.56	6.87
Log of gross FDI inflows	83	7.10	1.73	2.56	11.38
Log of GNI per capita (PPP, current USD)	82	8.02	1.02	5.80	9.81
Log of GDP per capita (PPP current USD)	82	8.05	1.02	5.88	9.79
Log of GDP (PPP, current)	81	24.88	1.75	21.08	29.26
Log GNI per capita growth	81	1.07	1.04	−1.75	3.09
Log Trade	83	4.16	0.44	3.03	5.23
Log Inflation	83	4.69	0.79	3.51	7.25
Log population	83	16.49	1.48	13.52	20.92
ICRG index					
Investment profile (absence of expropriation risk)	83	5.62	1.01	2.88	7.98
Government stability	83	6.16	0.69	4.64	7.67
Socioeconomic stress absent	83	4.11	1.05	1.06	7.01

(continued)

(continued)

Variable	Obs.	Mean	Std. dev.	Min	Max
Internal conflict absent	83	6.86	1.35	3.20	9.58
External conflict absent	83	7.87	1.05	4.21	9.85
Corruption absent	83	4.29	1.11	1.01	6.66
Military not influence politics	83	5.39	2.41	0.56	10.00
Religious tensions absent	83	7.23	1.98	1.81	10.00
Law and order	83	5.20	1.52	1.65	8.66
Ethnic tension absent	83	6.18	1.96	1.24	10.00
Democratic accountability	83	5.69	1.72	1.71	9.00
Bureaucratic quality	83	4.37	1.81	0.00	8.22

References

Acemoglu D, Johnson S, Robinson JA (2001) The colonial origins of comparative development: an empirical investigation. Am Econ Rev 91(5):1369–1401

Alfaro L, Kalemli-Ozcan S, Volosovych V (2008) Why doesn't capital flow from rich to poor countries? An empirical investigation. Rev Econ Stat 90(2):347–368

Barro RJ, Lee JW (1993) International comparisons of educational attainment. J Monet Econ 32 (3):363–394

Beck T, Demirgüç-Kunt A, Levine R (2000, updated 2013) A new database on financial development and structure. World Bank Econ Rev 14(3):597–605

Bockstette V, Chanda A, Putterman L (2002) States and markets: the advantage of an early start. J Econ Growth 7(4):347–369

CEPII Home. http://www.cepii.fr/CEPII/en/publications/journal_articles.asp

Hall RE, Jones CI (1999) Why do some countries produce so much more output per worker than others? Q J Econ 114(1):83–116

Heston A, Summers R, Aten B (2002) Penn world table version 6.1. Center for International Comparisons at the University of Pennsylvania

La Porta R, Lopez-de-Silanes F, Shleifer A, Vishny R (1999) The quality of government. J Law Econ Org 15(1):222–279

La Porta R, Lopez-de-Silanes F, Shleifer A, Vishny RW (1998) Law and finance. J Political Econ 106(6):1113–1155

Lane PR, Milesi-Ferretti GM (2007) The external wealth of nations mark II: revised and extended estimates of foreign assets and liabilities, 1970–2004. J Int Econ 73(2):223–250

World Bank (2013) Global development horizon: capital for the future: savings and investment in an interdependent World. World Bank, Washington, DC

World Bank (2013) World development indicators, Online data retrieved on March 30, 2013. World Bank, Washington, DC

Appendix C
Histogram Plots and Full Model Estimates

See Figs. C.1, C.2 and C.3.

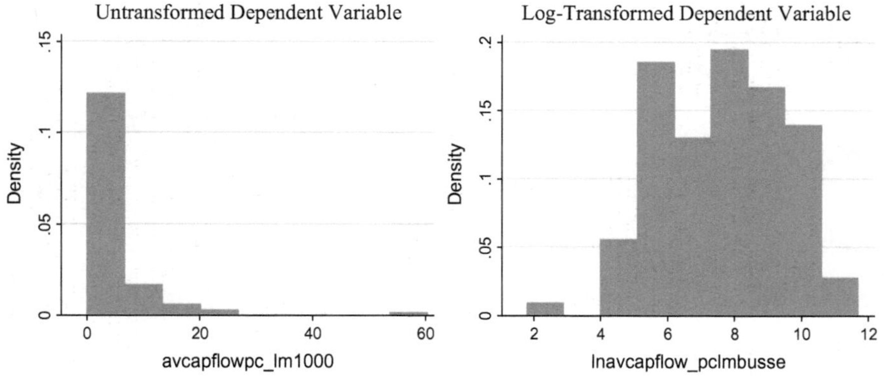

Fig. C.1 Histogram plots for LM data

M. Akhtaruzzaman, *International Capital Flows and the Lucas Paradox*,
https://doi.org/10.1007/978-981-13-9069-2

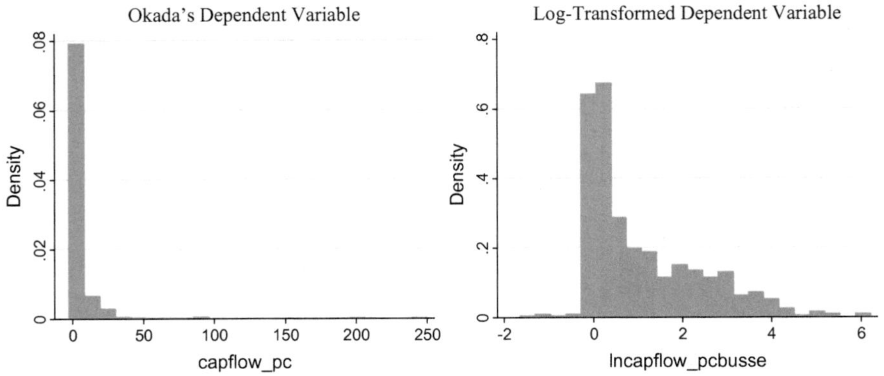

Fig. C.2 Histogram plots for dependent variable in Okada

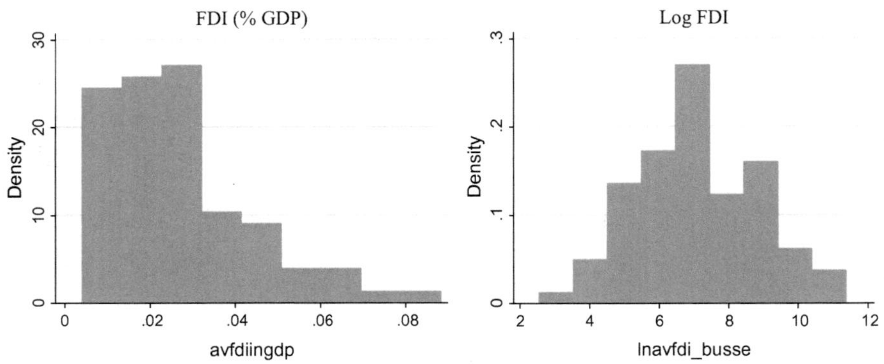

Fig. C.3 Histogram plots for FDI (% of GDP) versus log FDI

Full Model Estimates for Chap. 6

Table 6.2 Appendix: Cross-Section Full Model Estimates of Model D (1984–2015 for ICRG Indexes) and Model E (1996–2015 for WGI Indexes) with t statistics below each estimated coefficient

	ICRG indexes												WGI indexes					
	Expro Abs	Gov Stab	Soci Abs	Inconf Abs	Exco Abs	Corr Abs	Mil Abs	RelTen Abs	Law Order	Eth Abs	Dem Acc	Bur Quality	Rule Law	Pol Stab	Corr Ab	Voice Accy	Gov Eff
Political index	0.09	0.21	0.04	0.04	0.00	0.10	0.00	−0.05	0.08	0.00	0.04	−0.02	0.31*	0.11	0.33*	0.18	0.29
	0.8	1.2	0.3	0.5	0.0	1.3	0.1	−1.1	1.3	0.0	0.7	−0.4	1.9	0.8	2.0	1.4	1.5
Log GNI	0.95***	0.93***	0.97***	0.99***	1.01***	0.97***	1.01***	1.01***	0.96***	1.01***	0.99***	1.04***	0.88***	0.97***	0.87***	0.96***	0.88***
	7.0	8.5	6.8	9.3	9.7	10.1	8.6	10.8	9.2	9.9	10.2	8.0	7.0	8.5	7.1	9.2	6.5
Log trade	0.45*	0.48*	0.53**	0.51**	0.54**	0.55**	0.55**	0.58**	0.52**	0.54**	0.53**	0.56**	0.52**	0.53**	0.57**	0.54**	0.50*
	1.9	2.0	2.1	2.1	2.2	2.1	2.1	2.5	2.0	2.2	2.1	2.3	2.0	2.1	2.2	2.2	1.9
Log inflation	−0.12	−0.12	−0.14	−0.14	−0.15	−0.13	−0.16	−0.17	−0.12	−0.15	−0.15	−0.17	−0.09	−0.14	−0.09	−0.12	−0.08
	−1.1	−1.1	−1.3	−1.3	−1.4	−1.2	−1.4	−1.5	−1.1	−1.3	−1.5	−1.6	−0.9	−1.2	−0.9	−1.2	−0.8
Log pop	−0.04	−0.04	−0.06	−0.07	−0.09	−0.05	−0.10	−0.10	−0.05	−0.09	−0.07	−0.11	0.04	−0.03	0.05	−0.03	0.02
	−0.2	−0.3	−0.4	−0.5	−0.7	−0.3	−0.6	−0.8	−0.4	−0.7	−0.5	−0.7	0.3	−0.2	0.3	−0.2	0.1
Obs.	81	81	81	81	81	81	81	81	81	81	81	81	81	81	81	81	81
R-squared	0.88	0.89	0.88	0.88	0.88	0.89	0.88	0.89	0.89	0.88	0.88	0.88	0.89	0.88	0.89	0.89	0.89

T-statistics are computed using robust standard errors, $^{***}p \leq 0.01$; $^{**}p \leq 0.05$; $^{*}p \leq 0.1$. Model estimates are estimated using our preferred specification, Model D. Missing data for aggregate GNI for Argentina and Syria reduces the sample size to 81 observations. All models include regional dummies of South Asia, East Asia Pacific, Middle-East, Latin America, Sub-Saharan Africa, and Europe and Central Asian Transition Economies. WGI models are estimated using years in which data are available, 1996–2011

Table 6.3 Appendix: Fixed Effects Full Model Estimates of Model D (1984–2015 for ICRG Indexes) and Model E (1996–2015 for WGI Indexes) with t statistics below each estimated coefficient

	ICRG indexes												WGI indexes				
	Expro Abs	Gov Stab	Soci Abs	Inconf Abs	Exco Abs	Corr Abs	Mil Abs	RelTen Abs	Law order	Eth Abs	Dem Acc	Bur quality	Rule Law	Pol Stab	Corr Ab	Voice Accy	Gov Eff
Political index	0.49***	0.35***	0.31**	0.22***	0.09	0.20**	0.16**	0.31***	0.27***	0.22***	0.23***	0.09	0.84*	0.20	1.55***	−0.02	0.49
	5.2	4.1	2.2	2.8	0.9	2.2	2.1	3.3	3.2	2.7	2.7	1.0	1.8	0.4	2.8	0.0	0.9
Log GNI	−0.13	0.89*	0.74	1.07**	1.15**	1.33**	0.90*	1.04**	1.10**	1.10**	0.82	0.99*	1.09	1.14	1.23*	1.10	0.99
	−0.2	1.7	1.5	2.0	2.2	2.4	1.7	2.0	2.1	2.1	1.6	1.9	1.5	1.4	1.7	1.4	1.4
Log trade	1.73**	1.71**	1.88**	1.72**	1.74**	1.76**	1.74**	1.73**	1.85**	1.85**	1.61**	1.69**	1.91*	1.90*	1.73	1.85	1.90*
	2.3	2.2	2.4	2.2	2.2	2.2	2.2	2.2	2.3	2.3	2.1	2.1	1.7	1.8	1.5	1.6	1.7
Log inflation	0.02	−0.02	0.05	0.01	0.03	0.03	0.05	0.04	0.02	0.03	0.02	0.04	−0.48	−0.47	−0.53	−0.42	−0.43
	0.1	−0.1	0.3	0.1	0.2	0.2	0.3	0.3	0.1	0.2	0.1	0.2	−0.7	−0.7	−0.9	−0.7	−0.7
Log pop	4.49***	2.66**	5.52***	3.36**	3.65***	4.04***	4.30***	4.04***	3.49***	3.53***	4.21***	4.26***	3.30*	3.17*	3.69*	3.15	3.51*
	3.5	2.2	3.6	2.5	2.7	3.1	3.3	3.2	2.7	2.7	3.2	3.3	1.8	1.7	1.9	1.6	1.9
Obs.	536	536	536	536	536	536	536	536	536	536	536	536	390	390	390	390	390
R-squared	0.65	0.64	0.63	0.63	0.63	0.63	0.63	0.64	0.64	0.63	0.64	0.63	0.69	0.69	0.69	0.68	0.69
Country FE	Yes	Yes	Yes	Yes	Yes	Yes	Yes	Yes	Yes	Yes	Yes	Yes	Yes	Yes	Yes	Yes	Yes
Year FE	Yes	Yes	Yes	Yes	Yes	Yes	Yes	Yes	Yes	Yes	Yes	Yes	Yes	Yes	Yes	Yes	Yes

T-statistics are computed using robust standard errors, $^{***}p \leq 0.01$; $^{**}p \leq 0.05$; $^{*}p \leq 0.1$. Estimates in this table show our preferred specification using the ICRG indexes, Model D, estimated using data from 1984–2015; and our preferred specification using the WGI indexes, Model E, estimated using data from the years in which WGI data are available, 1996–2015

Table 6.4 Appendix: GMM Full Model Estimates of Model D (1984–2015 for ICRG Indexes) and Model E (1996–2015 for WGI Indexes) with t statistics below each estimated coefficient

	ICRG indexes												WGI indexes				
	Expro Abs	Gov Stab	Soci Abs	Inconf Abs	Exco Abs	Corr Abs	Mil Abs	RelTen Abs	Law order	Eth Abs	Dem Acc	Bur quality	Rule law	Pol Stab	Corr Ab	Voice Accy	Gov Eff
Political index	0.24**	0.18***	0.06	0.28***	0.04	0.11	0.20**	0.24**	0.24***	0.14	0.08	0.11	0.65	−0.27	1.05**	0.12	0.13
	2.5	2.7	0.5	3.7	0.4	1.2	2.4	2.5	2.9	1.6	1.0	1.3	1.1	−0.9	2.1	0.3	0.2
FDI (lagged)	0.39***	0.40***	0.39***	0.38***	0.41***	0.40***	0.41***	0.41***	0.39***	0.40***	0.40***	0.40***	0.51***	0.53***	0.49***	0.51***	0.51***
	5.9	6.0	6.0	5.9	6.0	6.0	6.2	6.2	5.9	6.1	5.9	6.1	5.3	5.5	5.1	5.4	5.3
Log GNI	−0.17	0.23	0.37	0.38	0.38	0.56	0.24	0.51	0.49	0.43	0.32	0.38	0.48	0.43	0.60	0.50	0.48
	−0.4	0.6	1.0	1.0	1.0	1.4	0.6	1.4	1.3	1.2	0.9	1.0	1.2	1.0	1.5	1.2	1.14
Log trade	1.66***	1.71***	1.66***	1.39**	1.66***	1.68***	1.74***	1.50**	1.67***	1.62***	1.64***	1.68***	1.08*	1.05*	1.06*	1.03*	1.04*
	2.7	2.8	2.7	2.3	2.7	2.7	2.8	2.4	2.8	2.6	2.6	2.7	1.8	1.7	1.8	1.7	1.7
Log inflation	0.08	0.05	0.12	0.07	0.09	0.11	0.12	0.09	0.09	0.09	0.09	0.10	−0.22	−0.17	−0.21	−0.20	−0.19
	1.2	0.6	1.6	1.0	1.3	1.6	1.6	1.3	1.2	1.3	1.3	1.4	−1.0	−0.8	−1.1	−1.0	−0.9
Log pop.	2.42***	1.83**	1.87**	1.71**	1.80**	1.59**	1.89**	1.66**	1.50**	1.64**	1.90**	1.77**	0.73	0.64	0.72	0.73	0.75
	3.2	2.5	2.5	2.4	2.4	2.1	2.6	2.3	2.1	2.2	2.6	2.4	1.0	0.9	1.0	1.0	1.0
Obs.	531	531	531	531	531	531	531	531	531	531	531	531	390	390	390	390	390
# of countries	81	81	81	81	81	81	81	81	81	81	81	81	81	81	81	81	81
# of instruments	26	26	26	26	26	26	26	26	26	26	26	26	22	22	22	22	22
Sargan *p*-value	0.12	0.14	0.03	0.08	0.1	0.07	0.05	0.01	0.1	0.09	0.1	0.05	0.00	0.00	0.00	0.00	0.00
AR1 test (*p*-value)	0.01	0.02	0.00	0.01	0.01	0.01	0.01	0.02	0.02	0.01	0.00	0.02	0.06	0.06	0.06	0.06	0.06
AR2 test (*p*-value)	0.51	0.57	0.64	0.69	0.60	0.60	0.62	0.55	0.60	0.56	0.60	0.66	0.70	0.80	0.77	0.77	0.78

T-statistics are computed using robust standard errors, $^{***}p \leq 0.01$; $^{**}p \leq 0.05$; $^{*}p \leq 0.1$. Estimates in this table show our preferred specification using the ICRG indexes, Model D, estimated using data from 1984-2015; and our preferred specification using the WGI indexes, Model E, estimated using data from the years in which WGI data are available, 1996–2015

Appendix D
Country List

Sample of 52 Countries Used for Graphical Analysis of Chap. 4

Poor countries (30) : Algeria (DZA), Burundi (BDI), Bolivia (BOL), Botswana (BWA), Chile (CHL), Colombia (COL), Congo(COG), Costa Rica (CRI), Cote d'Ivore(CIV), Ecuador (ECU), Egypt(EGY), El Salvador (SLV), Jamaica (JAM), Jordan (JOR), Malaysia (MYS), Mauritious (MUS), Marocco(MAR), Mexico (MEX), Panama (PAN), Paraguay (PRY), Peru (PER),Phillipines (PHL), South Africa (ZAF), Singapore (SGP), Srilanka (LKA),Tunisia (TUN), Trinidad and Tobago (TTO), Uruguay (URY), Venzuela (VEN), Zambia (ZMB). **Rich countries (22)**: Australia (AUS), Austria (AUT), Belgium (BEL), Canada (CAN), Denmark (DNK), Finland (FIN), France (FRA), Greece (GRC),Ireland (IRL), Israel (ISR), Italy (ITA), Japan (JAP), Korea (KOR), Netherlands (NLD), New Zealand (NZL), Norway (NOR), Portugal (PRT), Spain (ESP), Sweden (SWE), Switzerland (CHE), United Kingdom (GBR), United States (USA)

Sample of 98 Countries Used for Empirical Analysis of Chaps. 5 and 6

Albania (ALB), Algeria (DZA), Angola (AGO), Argentina (ARG), Armenia (ARM), Australia (AUS), Austria (AUT), Azerbaijan (AZE), Bangladesh (BGD), Belarus (BLR), Bolivia (BOL), Brazil (BRA), Bulgaria (BGR), Burkina Faso (BFA), Canada (CAN), Chile (CHL), Colombia (COL), Congo(COG), Costa Rica (CRI), Cote d'Ivore(CIV), Croatia (HRV), Cyprus (CYP), Czech Rep. (CZE), Denmark (DNK), Dominican Rep. (DOM), Ecuador (ECU), Egypt(EGY), El Salvador (SLV), Estonia (EST), Ethiopia (ETH), Finland (FIN), France (FRA), Gabon (GAB), Gambia (GMB), Germany (DEU), Ghana (GHA), Greece (GRC), Guatemala (GTM), Guinea (GIN), Guyana (GUY), Haiti (HTI), Hondurus (HND), Hungary (HUN), India (IND), Indonesia (IDN), Iran (IRN), Israel (ISR), Italy (ITA), Jamaica (JAM), Japan (JPN), Jordan (JOR), Kazakhstan (KAZ), Kenya (KEN), Korea (KOR), Latvia (LVA), Lithuania (LTU), Madagascar (MDG), Malaysia (MYS), Mali (MLI), Mexico (MEX), Marocco(MAR), Mozamvique (MOZ), Namibia (NAM), Netherlands (NLD), New Zealand (NZL), Nicaragua

M. Akhtaruzzaman, *International Capital Flows and the Lucas Paradox*,
https://doi.org/10.1007/978-981-13-9069-2

(NIC), Niger (NER), Nigeria (NGA), Norway (NOR), Oman (OMN), Pakistan (PAK), Panama (PAN), Papua New Guinea (PNG), Paraguay (PRY), Peru (PER), Phillipines (PHL), Portugal (PRT), Russia (RUS), Saudi Arabia (SAU), Senegal (SEN), Sierra Leone (SLE), Singapore (SGP), Slovenia (SVN), South Africa (ZAF), Spain (ESP), Sweden (SWE), Trinidad and Tobago (TTO), Tunisia (TUN), Turkey (TUR), Uganda (UGA), Ukraine (UKR), United Kingdom (GBR), United States (USA), Uruguay (URY), Vietnam (VNM), Zambia (ZMB), Zimbabwe (ZWE).

Sample of 112 Countries Used for Empirical Analysis of Chap. 6

Argentina (ARG), Armenia (ARM), Australia (AUS), Austria (AUT), Azerbaijan (AZE), Bangladesh (BGD), Bahrain (BH), Belgium (BE), Bolivia (BOL), Botswana (BWA), Brazil (BRA), Bulgaria (BGR), Canada (CAN), Cameroon (CMR), Chile (CHL), China (CHN), Colombia (COL), Congo(COG), Costa Rica (CRI), Cote d'Ivore(CIV), Croatia (HRV), Cyprus (CYP), Czech Rep. (CZE), Denmark (DNK), Dominican Rep. (DOM), Ecuador (ECU), Egypt(EGY), El Salvador (SLV), Estonia (EST), Finland (FIN), France (FRA), Gabon (GAB), Gambia (GMB), Germany (DEU), Ghana (GHA), Greece (GRC), Guatemala (GTM), Guyana (GUY), Haiti (HTI), Hondurus (HND), Hong Kong (HKG), Hungary (HUN), Iceland (ISL), India (IND), Indonesia (IDN), Iran (IRN), Ireland (IRL), Israel (ISR), Italy (ITA), Jamaica (JAM), Japan (JPN), Jordan (JOR), Kazakhstan (KAZ), Kenya (KEN), Korea Rep. (KOR), Kwait (KWT), Latvia (LVA), Liberia (LBR), Libya (LBY), Lithuania (LTU), Malawi (MWI), Malaysia (MYS), Mali (MLI), malta (MLT), Mexico (MEX), Moldova (MDA), Mongolia (MNG), Marocco(MAR), Mozamvique (MOZ), Namibia (NAM), Netherlands (NLD), New Zealand (NZL), Nicaragua (NIC), Niger (NER), Nigeria (NGA), Norway (NOR), Pakistan (PAK), Panama (PAN), Papua New Guinea (PNG), Paraguay (PRY), Peru (PER), Phillipines (PHL), Poland (POL), Portugal (PRT), Romania (ROM), Russia (RUS), Saudi Arabia (SAU), Senegal (SEN), Sierra Leone (SLE), Singapore (SGP), Slovak Rep. (SVK), Slovenia (SVN), South Africa (ZAF), Spain (ESP), Sri Lanka (LKA), Sudan (SDN), Sweden (SWE), Switzerland (CHE), Syria (SYR), Tanzania (TZA), Thailand (THA), Togo (TGO), Trinidad and Tobago (TTO), Tunisia (TUN), Turkey (TUR), Uganda (UGA), Ukraine (UKR), United Kingdom (GBR), United States (USA), Uruguay (URY), Venezuela (VEN), Vietnam (VNM), Yemen (YEM), Zambia (ZMB).

Sample of 83 Countries Used for Empirical Analysis of Chap. 7

Albania (ALB), Algeria(DZA), Angola (AGO), Argentina (ARG), Bangladesh (BGD), Bolivia (BOL), Botswana(BWA), Brazil (BRA), Bulgaria (BGR), Burkina Faso (BFA), Cameroon (CMR), Chile (CHL), China (CHN), Colombia (COL), Congo Democratic Republic (COG), Congo Republic (ZAR), Costa Rica (CRI), Cote d' Ivore (CIV), Czech Republic (CZE), Dominican Republic (DOM), Ecuador (ECU), Egypt (EGY), El Salvador (SLV), Ethiopia (ETH), Gabon (GAB), Gambia (GMB), Ghana (GHA), Guatemala (GTM), Guinea (GIN), Guinea-Bissau (GNB), Guyana (GUY), Haiti (HTI), Honduras (HND), Hungary (HUN), India (IND),

Indonesia (IDN), Iran (IRN), Jamaica (JAM), Jordan (JOR), Kenya (KEN), South Korea (KOR), Lebanon (LBN), Madagascar (MDG), Malawi (MWI), Malaysia (MYS), Mali (MLI), Mexico (MEX), Mongolia (MNG), Morocco (MAR), Namibia (NAM), Nicaragua (NIC), Niger (NER), Nigeria (NGA), Oman (OMN), Pakistan (PAK), Panama (PAN), Papua New Guinea (PNG), Paraguay (PRY), Peru (PER), Philippines (PHL), Poland (POL), Romania (ROM), Russia (RUS), Saudi Arabia (KSA), Senegal (SEN), Sierra Leone (SLE), Slovakia (SLV), South Africa (ZAF), Sri Lanka (LKA), Sudan (SDN), Syrian Arab Republic (SYR), Tanzania (TZA), Thailand (THA), Togo (TGO), Trinidad and Tobago (TTN), Tunisia (TUN), Turkey (TUR), Uganda (UGA), Uruguay (URY), Venezuela (VEN), Vietnam (VNM), Zambia (ZMB), Zimbabwe (ZWE).

Bibliography

Berlemann M, Wesselhöft JE (2012) Estimating aggregate capital stocks using the perpetual inventory method: new empirical evidence for 103 countries. Helmut Schmidt University, discussion paper, no. 125

Brainard SL (1997) An empirical assessment of the proximity-concentration trade-off between multinational sales and trade. Am Econ Rev 87(4):520–544

Denison EF (1962) Sources of economic growth in the United States and the alternatives before us. Committee for Economic Development, New York

Hansen LP, Heaton J, Yaron A (1996) Finite-sample properties of some alternative GMM estimators. J Bus Econ Stat 14(3):262–280

Henry PB (2007) Capital account liberalization: theory, evidence, and speculation. J Econ Lit 45:887–935

International Monetary Fund (2013) International financial statistics. Online data retrieved on March 30, 2013. International Monetary Fund, Washington, DC

Jin K (2012) Industrial structure and capital flows. Am Econ Rev 102(5):2111–2146

Li X, Liu X (2005) Foreign direct investment and economic growth: an increasingly endogenous relationship. World Dev 33(3):393–407

U.S. State Department (2013) 2013 investment climate statement—Venezuela. Washington, DC. Retrieved from http://www.state.gov/e/eb/rls/othr/ics/2013/204759.htm#

M. Akhtaruzzaman, *International Capital Flows and the Lucas Paradox*,
https://doi.org/10.1007/978-981-13-9069-2